# AGAINST
## THE
# FLOW

Tom Fort went to Eton and read English at Oxford before becoming a local newspaper reporter. He joined the BBC and worked as a journalist there for more than twenty years. He is married with five children, and is the author of *Under The Weather* and *Downstream* (published by Century) and *The Grass is Greener* and *The Book of Eels* (published by HarperCollins).

## Praise for Tom Fort

'Elegantly written, filled with fine phrases, wit and provoking thoughts' *Seven Magazine, Sunday Telegraph*

'The pleasure is in the rambling flavour of his travels . . . he writes beautifully' *Daily Telegraph*

'It is difficult not to like Fort, if not simply for his encyclopaedic knowledge of all things fluvial then for his wit and irony too.' *Literary Review*

# AGAINST THE FLOW

## TOM FORT

arrow books

Published in the United Kingdom by Arrow Books in 2011

3 5 7 9 10 8 6 4 2

Copyright © Tom Fort 2010

Tom Fort has asserted his right under the Copyright, Designs and
Patents Act, 1988 to be identified as the author of this work.

First published in the United Kingdom in 2010 by Century

Arrow Books
The Random House Group Limited
20 Vauxhall Bridge Road, London, SW1V 2SA

Addresses for companies within The Random House Group Limited can be found at:
www.randomhouse.co.uk/offices.htm

The Random House Group Limited Reg. No. 954009

www.rbooks.co.uk

A CIP catalogue record for this book
is available from the British Library

ISBN 9780099533429

The Random House Group Limited supports The Forest Stewardship
Council (FSC), the leading international forest certification organisation. All our
titles that are printed on Greenpeace approved FSC certified paper carry the FSC logo.
Our paper procurement policy can be found at www.rbooks.co.uk/environment

**Mixed Sources**
Product group from well-managed
forests and other controlled sources
www.fsc.org Cert no. TF-COC-2139
© 1996 Forest Stewardship Council

Typeset in Spectrum MT by Palimpsest Book Production Limited,
Falkirk, Stirlingshire
Printed and bound in Great Britain by
CPI Bookmarque, Croydon CR0 4TD

To my brothers James, Matthew and Johnny –
and my sister Elizabeth

# Contents

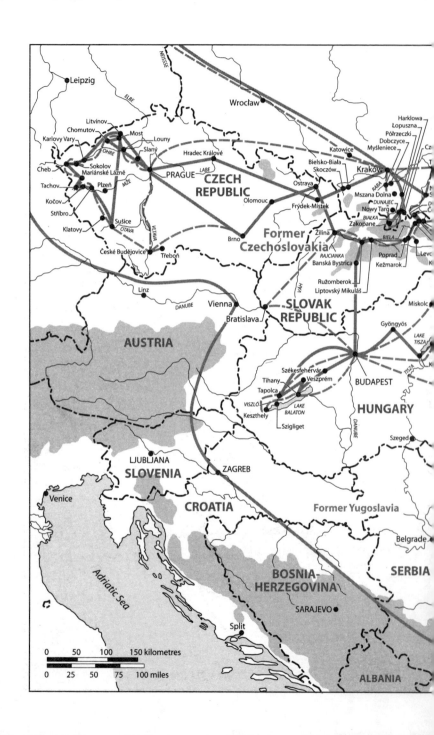

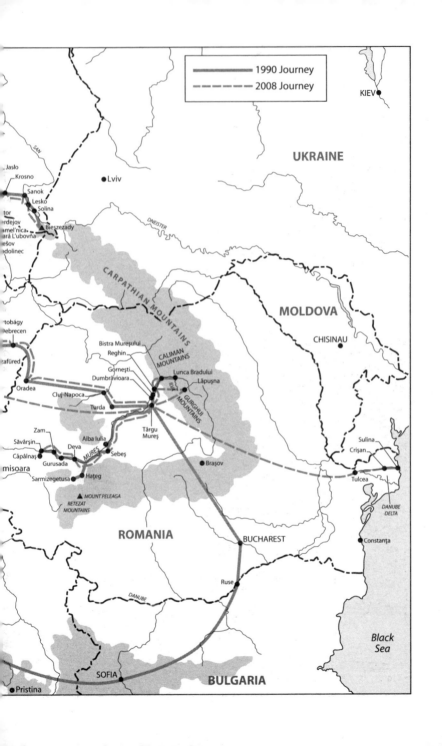

# Chapter 1

## *Leaving*

Eurolines service 194 for Kraków swung out of the dark cavern of Victoria Coach Station at exactly 1.30 on a Monday afternoon, 9 June 2008. London was sunlit, warm, at ease: no bombs, no dark clouds in the sky, no mention of Lehman Brothers, no sign of gathering storm. Sunbeams danced across the brown Thames below Vauxhall Bridge. I looked down, trying to work out which way the tide was flowing. Upstream, Battersea Power Station squatted at the water's edge, brooding on its fate.

The lady ticket inspector made a lengthy announcement in Polish. I waited for the English version, in vain. I felt isolated as well as uninformed, as if I was already in a foreign place where unfamiliar customs prevailed.

Crossing the river, I was thinking of another journey, another time.

May 1990, a gorgeous early summer's day, the sun sparkling on the smooth blue sea as I drove my little red Peugeot on to the ferry at Felixstowe, bound for Hamburg and points east. One great high-pressure system covered northern Europe, giving blue skies and blissful sunshine across the continent. But although we happened to have the same weather, eastern Europe was still a faraway place then, in a way difficult to recall two decades later. Huge upheavals had upset the familiar geopolitical landscape: one earthquake, one landslip, one tidal wave after another. At the same time, Czechoslovakia was still Czechoslovakia – just. We still talked about East Germany and West Germany and the Soviet Union, for a while longer anyway. The Warsaw Pact had not yet been formally dissolved.

Over there, behind the rail from which Churchill's Iron Curtain had hung for so long, people were waking to a new order. They blinked in wonder, torn between hope and fear. And I – what was I doing in my little red car?

At that time I was working as a sub-editor at a BBC news desk in London. From within familiar, unshakeable Broadcasting House I watched and listened to the great events unfolding in Gdańsk, Prague and Berlin, and helped refine them into a form digestible to our Radio Four audience. Like the listeners, I was stirred by the extraordinary spectacle of Europe coming apart at the seams; like them I was ineluctably detached as well. The Polish shipyards exploded. The Berlin Wall was ripped down. The regimes in Prague and Budapest ran for cover. In the Romanian city of Timişoara a priest no one had even heard of before preached revolt, and within a month Nicolae Ceauşescu faced an impromptu firing squad.

I watched and marvelled. We all watched and marvelled. Then we took the train home. I gave the children their breakfast, mowed the lawn, walked the dog.

Distinguished and not-so-distinguished BBC correspondents dashed to the hotspots and, amid the wreckage of the divided continent that we had all grown used to, tried to make sense of it all. They reported what they were told, citing the sources, they analysed as best they could, they speculated as intelligently as the general confusion permitted. They discussed matters with local journalists whose primary – sometimes only – qualification was fluency in English, and with politicians, experts and supposedly informed sources selected on the same grounds. Passers-by were grabbed by eager producers, retained if they could string together a sentence in English, discarded if not.

I used occasionally to wonder, in between bursts of word-churning for news bulletins and summaries, about the story we never heard. Away from the rage and exhilaration foaming through the streets and squares of the cities, there were people – probably quite like us, with children to give breakfast to, dogs to walk, even, conceivably, lawns to mow – looking on. Ordinary people with ordinary lives to organise. They must have been bemused, excited, fearful, uncertain. But who were they?

I had an idea that nagged at me until it drove me into the office of my BBC manager with a request for five months' unpaid leave. The idea was simple. The borders were now open. What if I crossed them? What if I kept away from the cities where the action was concentrated? What if I had a way to reach some of those onlookers and find out what they made of it all and how they were managing? I thought I had a way.

They had rivers, those countries, and where there were rivers there were fish, and where there were fish there would be anglers. I was an angler, and I knew that the passion was essentially the same wherever it was found. It flows between frontiers and differences of culture and language, and creates bridges where politicians and diplomats encounter walls of brick and concrete. If I could find the fishermen and go fishing with them, I would get a different story. That was my idea.

Rather to my surprise (I half-thought I was indispensable), my BBC manager readily agreed to let me go. At the time I was also writing a fishing column for the *Financial Times*, and the wise and far-sighted editor of its Weekend section, Max Wilkinson, commissioned a series of articles about my forthcoming travels and even contrived a useful contribution towards my expenses. The final piece fell into place when a rich friend, with more faith in my abilities than I had, said he would underwrite the enterprise.

So I went. From Hamburg I drove east around Berlin into Poland, then south-east, past a string of grim towns with impossible names

3

such as Strzemieszyce, Zabrze and Krzeszowice, to Kraków; from Poland to Bohemia, Slovakia, Hungary and Romania. I went fishing with a dentist, a doctor, a vet, two factory workers, a traffic policeman turned glass engraver, a company boss, a refrigeration engineer and a painter, among others. In Romania I slept twice in beds that Ceauşescu himself had slept in, and stayed in a village where, the week before, a woman rounding up cattle had been fatally mauled by a bear.

In most of the places I got to I was the first Englishman who'd ever asked for a fishing licence. Apart from letters collected *poste restante* and very occasional telephone conversations from PTT offices on abysmal lines, I was cut off from family and the familiar. I always felt very far from home. There were no laptops then, no email. No one had a mobile phone. It was a very different Europe.

When I returned to the BBC newsroom colleagues peered up at me with short-lived interest and asked if I'd had a good holiday. I wrote a narrative of my journey which ended with my driving across the Danube from Romania to Bulgaria at half-past one on a steamy night, and looking down at the river: 'silent, shrouded in darkness, gleaming quietly like coal, lit here and there by the lights on top of the buoys swaying in the current'. It nearly got published by a reputable publisher, but not quite; which was a great disappointment at the time because I was unsettled by urges to be a writer rather than a BBC word-churner. Much later I realised that whoever had rejected my manuscript had unwittingly done me a favour. There were good things in it, but not enough of them.

I settled back into the old newsroom routine, still troubled by the urges. My first marriage foundered. In time I married again, left the BBC, had more children, wrote some books which were published. A new Europe took shape, which made me think of the old one and of the story I had happened upon there, still untold. I thought I should try again.

\* \* \*

This ancient history came back insistently as I sat in my seat on Eurolines service 194, bound for Kraków. At the same time I began to take more notice of the human geography around me.

The seats immediately in front of me were taken by a woman and a boy, presumably her son, who was clutching a *Charlie and Lola* book. They were seen off at Victoria Coach Station by a man who repeatedly pulled the boy to him in a desperate, longing way, whispering urgently in his ear. The parting between mother and father – assuming that's who they were – was perfunctory. There seemed to be a finality in the air around the three of them, which the boy either did not feel or was unable to acknowledge. The mother was young and pretty in a dark, smouldering fashion. I feared that if I tried to talk to her she would assume that I was trying to pick her up; and that even if I managed to persuade her that this wasn't the case, everyone else on the coach would assume that it was.

Across the aisle from the mother and son was a young woman on her own. I could see only the top of her head, but I knew she spoke English because she was having an urgent conversation on her mobile in which she said she was going back to Wrocław with no money, no clothes, nothing. Her tone was anxious bordering on distraught. I didn't want to intrude. She might also have thought my motives were amorous, even predatory.

Behind me was a dumpy middle-aged Polish woman, and across the aisle from her another, older Polish woman, grey and faded. They quickly struck up an acquaintance, leaning towards one another to exchange chat in low tones. What could they be talking about? Going home? Children, grandchildren, husbands? The English weather? The impenetrable mysteries of England and its customs? I had absolutely no means of knowing.

The coach was less than a third full, and the remaining passengers – one couple, the rest single males, presumably workers returning home – were scattered about the back half of the coach. It was strange, but as the journey went on I felt more and more separated from them, more and more inhibited from getting up, turning to face them, approaching them, asking them anything. Some kind of psychic chasm had opened between us when we took our seats. I made excuses to myself. What would I say to them, anyway? That I was going to Poland to write a book about Polish people going back to Poland? How absurd would that sound?

The truth was that I didn't have the nerve. I had somehow forfeited or mislaid the journalist's impudent assumption of the right to accost anyone and ask anything. Without realising it, I had turned into one of those islanders who, in Emerson's words, 'is an island himself, safe, tranquil, incommunicable'.

A compelling factor in my deciding to take a car to eastern Europe in 1990 was that many people there did not have their own transport. To get to the rivers I would need to drive. Furthermore I took dollars, which in those days still possessed an almost supernatural power to unlock doors in foreign parts. With dollars I would be able to obtain the fuel that was in wretchedly short supply for those with only Polish *złoty*, Czech *korun*, Hungarian *forint* or Romanian *lei* at their disposal.

Eighteen years later none of that applied. Everyone had a car, petrol was as freely available there as anywhere else, and their currencies were in more buoyant shape than the dollar or sterling. The obvious way to get around was by public transport, beginning with the coach. I could, of course, have taken the two-hour flight to southern Poland instead of submitting myself to 26 hours on the road (by air I could have got to New Zealand in the same time). But I was persuaded that the bus was the way to get the story.

The story was, or appeared to be, this. In May 2004 eight countries in eastern Europe – Poland, the Czech Republic, Slovakia, Slovenia, Hungary, Latvia, Lithuania and Estonia – had joined the European Union. Over the next three years somewhere between half a million and one and a half million citizens of the new member states made their way to Britain to live and work, roughly two-thirds of them from Poland. Curiously, no one took the trouble to measure the scale of the influx, which remains a matter of guesswork. The attitude of the British authorities appeared to be that the border was open so what was the point of checking who came in and out so long as they were legal and white (and therefore non-Islamic).

It took a while for the human tide from the east to register in the public consciousness. Then, quite suddenly, it became news. In my local town, Reading, the Poles infiltrated the Oxford Road. Delicatessens appeared where you could buy six kinds of Polish sausage, Polish smoked bacon, Polish bread, ready-made *pierogi*, beer and vodka; whose windows were filled with cards advertising jobs, rooms, travel, church services and social events for Poles. For a time the local newspaper published an edition in Polish. One of the pubs, long on its uppers for want of local patronage, sprang to life as a Polish *gospoda*.

The media woke up. Sections of it responded in the usual sour, mean-spirited, xenophobic way. Thanks to 'the EU' we had been invaded. Our jobs were being taken by an army led by a figure of mythic status, the Polish plumber. With the Polish plumber came his mate and a raggle-taggle horde of bricklayers, plasterers, electricians, bar workers, fruit-and-veg pickers, all accompanied by a train of camp followers intent upon leeching off the proverbially open-handed British welfare system. Polish women were able to obtain the abortions they were denied at home, courtesy of the NHS. Schools were overwhelmed by monoglot Polish children. Councils were besieged by families waving EU rules on emergency housing. Police forces struggled to contain localised crime waves of a sinister Slavic kind, concentrating on drugs and under-age prostitutes, with a distinctly un-English attitude towards casual violence.

Typically, the incomers were depicted either as sabotaging the labour market by their willingness to work incredibly hard at menial jobs, for wages and under conditions no self-respecting British worker would accept (this strand of attack demanding a certain flexibility from commentators more used to berating the British working man for his laziness), or as welfare scroungers. Cultural differences were gleefully seized upon. For a while the angling press was rife with stories of barbarous behaviour by fishermen 'of eastern European origin', who declined to buy licences, poached riotously, used every imaginable illegal means (including submerging a supermarket trolley fitted with a car battery in a lake to electrocute the carp), and were implicated in the unforgivable crime of killing and eating the fish they caught instead of returning them alive.

Local authorities were mocked for putting up road signs in Polish, while an accident involving a Polish driver would automatically be attributed to inability to comprehend traffic instructions in English. Councils that issued leaflets in Polish or trained staff to speak a few words of the language were accused of wasting taxpayers' money. Polish workers who sent money home were charged with depleting the UK economy.

An important element in this narrative was the incomers' mode of arrival. The coaches crossing from the far side of Europe to this little island were the symbolic equivalent of the wagons of the Boer Voortrekkers, the ships of the Pilgrim Fathers, the locomotives thrusting their way through the American West. The budget airlines quickly muscled in on the business but the coach route remained fixed in the public perception as the pathway from the east, with Victoria Coach Station as its portal.

Obscured within this fog of myth-making and journalistic invention was a dry story of economic opportunism. A large number of people – possibly a million or so, the great majority of them young and single – had come to Britain because they were allowed to, and because they could get work easily and earn significantly more than in their countries of origin. The jobs they took were mostly generated by an expanding economy with very low unemployment and were often in sectors affected by existing labour shortages. Some stayed, some travelled home unnoticed, some went back and forth. Comparatively few came with the intention of settling in Britain for good.

The idea was that I would take the bus in order to go back the way they had come. Against the flow . . . hence the title of the book. What I did not know – because hardly anyone had then realised it – was that the flow was no longer a flow but an ebb. The direction had reversed. The Polish plumber, his mate and the rest of them were in fact going home. It is now believed (the absence of precision in these calculations still strikes me as extraordinary) that by May 2008, a month before I boarded the coach for Kraków, around a half of the influx had become an exodus.

There were various reasons for this. Compared with 2004 the pound had lost a quarter of its value against the Polish *zloty*. The vivacious state of the Polish economy had caused a doubling of average wages there, so that emigrant workers in the UK were now earning only two or three times as much as they could at home, where the cost of living was still very much lower. Besides that, the UK economy was contracting, making jobs scarcer, while other EU countries had followed Britain in easing restrictions on workers from the new member states, increasing opportunities elsewhere.

And many – nobody can know how many – left for the very simple reason that they preferred their own familiar country to this strange and often unwelcoming one, and had saved enough money to buy land, build a house, start a business or fulfil other ambitions back home.

While I was away during the summer of 2008 I obtained a perspective on this great movement of people from eastern Europe that was very different from the usual British point of view. To us, this nation of islanders, the human inflow was a major event that had a significant impact on our way of life and materially affected the way we saw ourselves in relation to the rest of our continent. To them, however, it was not a big story. Economic migration from the region has been a recurring historical phenomenon. It has happened throughout the centuries without vitally weakening any country's sense of national identity. Poles are Poles, at least in part, wherever they find themselves, similarly Latvians, Lithuanians, Hungarians and the rest. It's no big deal, my friends said when I asked. You go where the work is. So what?

Thus, in that sense, I was more with the flow than against it, although it took me a while to work that out. I liked the title, though. And as I was to spend good deal of my time working my way up rivers with a fishing rod in my hand, it seemed reasonable to stick with it.

Over the Thames I saw a sign for The Oval, home of Surrey County Cricket Club, and glimpsed the famous gasworks to the northern side of the ground. The coach went up Kennington Lane, past Tesco, along New Kent Road into Old Kent Road. I wondered what the Polish plumber would have made of this. He would probably have recognised Tesco because Tesco had invaded Poland, but would the Polish Tesco help you spend less each day or would it have some equally fatuous and annoying Poland-specific slogan? And what of Sainsbury's, making life taste better? And what of cricket itself? My Polish friend Adam, long resident in England, would watch any sport on TV, including cricket, then telephone me to ask about the terminology. 'What is this No Ball?' he would demand. Then, ten minutes later: 'What is Extras? And what it mean, Declare?'

We passed Julius Ceasar Solicitors, Whistle and Flute Dry Cleaners, Beddy Buyz. More questions suggested themselves. A sign disclosed that Dover was 72 miles away. Leafy Blackheath, with its wide green spaces and old houses in dark chocolate brick, soothed me towards the first of many slumbers.

By the time the A2 delivered us into Dover, the Battle of Borodino was brewing on the road to Moscow. When my journey began I was almost two-thirds of the way through *War and Peace*, a novel which — as anyone will tell you — requires energy and a following wind to get through. I hadn't wanted to leave it behind, fearing that I might never go back to it, or if I did, that I would sink in a confusion of Bolkonskys, Bezukhovs, Rostovs, counts and princes and countesses and princesses, battle lines, retreat lines, supply lines, hussars and cuirassiers, Prussians and Russians. Like Napoleon and Kutuzov, I had to finish what I had started. But I was travelling light and the book was heavy. I had resolved that it must be finished with by the time I reached Kraków.

Cannon were booming and soldiers were dropping like cut corn as we pulled up in the port, between the green sea and the rough, blinding cliffs. An information panel at the quay informed anyone interested that the temperature was 23 degrees Celsius, and that 36,824 passengers, 7,424 cars and more than 4,000 lorries had passed through in the previous 24 hours. We all got off the coach and I asked the pretty young mother of the boy who'd been sitting in front of me if she knew how long we would be waiting. She smiled uncomprehendingly and replied in Polish. I went inside the departure lounge and found a quiet spot. After eight hours of fighting, the French ceased to attack. Napoleon rode away from the battlefield. Kutuzov roused himself from a doze and ate some roast chicken.

Every now and then, like some junior aide-de-campe dispatched by the general to observe and report back, I went outside to make sure that the coach was not embarking without me. Eventually the incoming ferry docked and spewed forth its streams of vehicles. We were waved back on to the coach. At the head of the line next to us, a little man in long shorts tried to coax a very elderly

Winnebago Chieftain into life. Its engine coughed and died. A gang of tough-looking bikers in leathers, scarves, earrings and reflective sunglasses gathered to offer advice. A couple of them partially undressed and poked around underneath the Chieftain's bonnet. Just in time blue smoke plumed from the exhaust and the gallant old wreck heaved itself up the ramp and into the dark belly of the vessel.

It was a very long while since I had travelled anywhere by ferry. After 9/11 I, like everyone else, had got used to tediously intrusive security measures at airports. Their absence at Dover – no baggage screening, no frisking, not even a glance at a passport – was at the same time oddly liberating and more than slightly puzzling. Who, I wondered as I joined the throng clanging their way up the metal stairways from the car decks, had made the calculation that our enemies would refrain from blowing up *Pride of Dover* or *Sea France Berlioz* or any of the other great, gleaming sitting ducks plying the Channel routes?

I stood on deck in the evening sunshine, drinking beer, the breeze coming off the water into my face. The surface churned and boiled at the ferry's stern, as if the kraken or globster or some other leviathan of myth might be about to put in an appearance. England began to edge away. The Kentish cliffs reared above the sea, presenting a formidable physical barrier. Where the green of the downland met the white of the chalk, it looked as though some other monster with mighty incisors had munched its way along the coast, devouring it in a succession of clean downward bites that left tumbles of rock like crumbs where the waves rolled in.

There is no ignoring the separateness of this island. Across much of mainland Europe the dismantling of border controls has blurred the distinctions between countries, so that you have to stay reasonably alert to be sure which one you are in. Northern France merges almost imperceptibly into Belgium, Belgium into Holland, Holland into Germany. But the sea and the sea's boundaries and all that is involved in crossing them constitute an absolute division that no treaty, no political or economic union, no plague of globalisation, can disguise. Visitors from Julius Caesar to the Polish Plumber can have been in no doubt, as England's south coast appeared before them, that they were about to encounter a place very different from anywhere else.

There she goes, I thought. My England. My white cliffs. My Dame Vera.

# Chapter 2

## Bus to Kraków

The light was beginning to fade as our coach slid out of Calais and set off around the northern fringe of a landmass that extended 8,000 miles to the Sea of Japan. And I made a friend of sorts, although I never did find out her name. She was sitting across the aisle from me, a broad, handsome, middle-aged woman in ample blouse and skirt. Beyond her, filling the window seat, was her husband, who was also built on generous lines. He didn't speak much, and not at all to me.

They came from Ironbridge in Shropshire, where she had been brought up by Polish parents. I gathered that her father had made his way to the town during the war and subsequently worked there in a factory. They were on their way to Kraków to stay with her relatives. She said her husband suffered from vertigo and had grommets in his ears, which made flying uncomfortable for him, hence their decision to take the coach. Although she spoke Polish well enough to be able to translate the announcements for me, she had an English reluctance to part with personal information. There was a daughter somewhere, I gathered, and grandchildren in unspecified numbers for whom she liked to cook Polish food. I had visions of gleaming mounds of *pierogi* and *placki* and steaming bowls of *bigos*. 'We all love Polish food,' she said, patting her stomach and gazing fondly in the direction of her husband's. They had a basket of provisions on the floor between them which they dipped into at intervals. Whenever we stopped at a service station they sailed off purposefully to the food counter, where I would spot them with pasties filled with hot cheese and ham; or – once we got to Poland – dishes of steaming cabbage and sausage.

Somewhere in northern France, or possibly Belgium, Prince Andrei Bolkonsky died his lingering death. It was typical of him to have stood on the battlefield of Borodino, pondering eternity and his new-found love of life while staring at a smoking shell until it went off and tore his abdomen apart. I didn't miss him much. I read on, delved into my own stock of food, stared out of the window. At about ten o'clock the lights and the music were switched off and we settled ourselves for sleep. Everyone was swallowed by the darkness except for the driver, his head and shoulders a still upright shape against the orange and yellow lights of his instrument panel.

At 4.20 the next morning we stopped in northern Germany for the lavatory and a coffee break. We stood around in the yellow lamplight, keeping close to our familiar, reassuring vehicle. Most of the younger men smoked, cupping cigarettes in their hands and pulling on them hungrily. No one spoke much. It might have been a chance to open channels of communication, but the restraint on speech seemed to me almost Cistercian. Back on board the psychic barriers came down once more.

Later I watched mist rise from the meadows. We passed a sign: Berlin 215 kilometres. I bit into a cold steak-and-kidney pie, releasing coils of meaty aroma. 'Ooh, that smells good,' groaned the lady from Ironbridge. 'I'm hungry.' She shifted in her seat. 'It's the cheeks of your bum, that's where it gets you.' She was right. We looped around Berlin to the south, heading for the Polish border through pine forests and fields of wheat, rapeseed and potatoes. Wind turbines materialised out of the mist, pale and motionless, as if waiting to be woken up and put to work. A pair of storks, emblematic birds of eastern Europe, trod carefully across the ground, heads down. The rising sun lit the flattened bodies of the host of insects spattered against the windscreen, each individual shape different, like snowflakes.

In Russia, Napoleon and his troops occupied Moscow. Pierre was taken prisoner. Petya Rostov, Natasha's younger brother, was killed. Pierre was rescued. I noticed that we were no longer in Germany but Poland, devouring the miles that had stretched before the retreating French army like an eternal punishment in that appalling winter of 1813. At half-past ten on a radiant summer's morning I bade farewell to Pierre and Natasha after a brief, abortive grapple with Tolstoy's concluding polemic on history, free will and predetermination. (I don't care what anyone says, this has to be the most tedious and ridiculous ending to any great novel. What on earth was his editor thinking of?)

One journey ends, another starts, I reflected with Tolstoyan profundity. The TV screen came alive and we settled down for the morning film. It was some kind of musical celebration of the joys of marriage, in which farcical nuptial episodes were interspersed with rapturous duets and choruses in praise of marital bliss. Our numbers began to thin. The woman who'd left England with nothing got off at Wrocław, the mother and her son at Opole.

On the outskirts of Opole the coach stopped to refuel. The service station nudged my memory. It was just the same as any other, anywhere in Europe: forecourt, shop, café, ranks of pumps,

TF with little red car, 1990

cars, trucks, coaches with nozzles thrust into their sides.

I had come this same way in my Peugeot on 3 May 1990, my head and heart swirling with apprehensions. I'd bowled along an almost empty road from the border with what was then still East Germany (for a few months more), and had suddenly come upon an enormous queue of traffic. For a moment I'd thought there must have been an accident ahead. But the queue was to one side, to let passing vehicles through. The cars – aged Polish-made Fiat 126s, East German Trabants, the odd Czech Škoda, Romanian Dacia or Yugoslav Yugo – were mostly empty. Their owners stood beside or behind them, with hands in pockets or holding a cigarette.

Further on a gap had opened up in the queue. The cars behind it were being pushed forward to fill it. The queue was a mile long at least. At its far end was a petrol station, two antiquated pumps presided over by two attendants in overalls, one to wave the cars forward, one at a time, the other to wield the nozzle. It was a scene I was to witness many times in Poland and Romania. (They seemed to manage better in Czechoslovakia and Hungary; whereas in Bulgaria no one, not even the British Ambassador, had any fuel at all, which was why I had to leave after five days.) Usually there was a sign stating the meagre ration. Sometimes, without warning, the station would be shut and another sign would go up, telling people to try somewhere else. What never changed was the air of resignation hanging over the queue. No one showed anger or impatience. Going short and waiting in line had been part of life for so long. Everyone knew the rules.

Not any more. Polish motorists had become like any other motorists, and their cars were like cars everywhere else. In two months in eastern Europe in the summer of 2008 I didn't see a single Trabant, although I looked hard. A few Fiat 126s and Dacias and ancient Škodas did survive, relics of a departed age, like horses and carts.

The coach sped along a smooth new EU-funded highway that skirted what had previously been known as the Upper Silesian Industrial District, Poland's energy and manufacturing heartland, a swathe of coal mines, blast furnaces, factories, slagheaps, towers and chimneys, overhung by an unmoving blanket of acrid fumes. Now the air smelled the same as it did in Kent and the dark ridges of coal and spoil had been cleared away. On the approach to Kraków the hoardings proclaimed the wonders of mobile phones, power showers, ride-on mowers. Ride-on mowers in the land I remembered for the swish of the scythe! We passed Spar and Ikea, and showrooms with walls of curved glass behind which gleamed burnished ranks of Audis, Mazdas, Suzukis, Grand Vitara people carriers.

As we pulled into the bus station, I tucked my copy of *War and Peace* underneath the window seat in front. I wonder who found it, and if they kept it. Maybe another traveller picked it up and turned the pages. Europe two centuries ago. Austerlitz. *L'Empereur.* Tsar Nicholas. Balls, duels, intrigues, battles . . . It would have made a curious introduction to England in 2008.

# Chapter 3

## Raba

I was met at the bus station in Kraków by a small, bald man with a bristling moustache and brisk, bustling manner. He offered me a quick, strong handshake and introduced himself, speaking English with a strong German accent. His name was Marek Kowalski. He was an atomic physicist, and worked in some kind of research establishment in Kraków. He did not attempt to explain the nature of his work to me, perhaps because he was not allowed to, perhaps because he thought that it would be beyond my understanding, most likely because it had nothing to do with what had brought us together.

Once again, as in 1990, I was entrusting myself to the angling brotherhood, of which Marek was a proud member. Once again I had my rod with me, my waders at the ready, my tackle-bag to hand. Rivers would once more be my pathway, and the company of fishermen my education.

The introduction to Marek had been arranged by a fishing friend from my previous visit, Jurek Kowalski. Jurek said he had not met the other Kowalski in the flesh but had ascertained that he spoke good English and was a keen fly-fisherman. There was no mistake there. Marek's enthusiasm was huge and voluble. He told me his river was called the Raba, which flows north-east out of the Tatras and joins the Wisła – or Vistula in English – east of Kraków.

As we drove out of the city, Marek told me about the revolution that had overtaken fishing in Poland. In the old days it had all been organised by the Fishing Association, a state-appointed bureaucratic apparatus that, through its local branches, exercised total control over every river, stream, lake, reservoir and pond in the country. In the Poland that had emerged during my 18 year absence, familiar monopolies had been challenged everywhere, including the riverbank.

Marek belonged to a club that had secured the rights to the prime section of the Raba by outbidding the Fishing Association. This was a very good thing, according to Marek. Under the old system the river was over-fished, poaching was rife, illegal methods flourished, and every fish caught was killed regardless of size. Now, with the injection of money, commitment and a new business model, everything was incomparably better. Bigger fish were stocked and more of them survived because more fishermen were putting them back alive. Bailiffs had been appointed – he brandished his bailiff's card at me – and the poachers had been sent packing. In fact the locals generally had been elbowed out in favour of well-heeled, enlightened Krakovians such as himself. Such was progress. You embraced it or you were left behind.

The club water was below a big reservoir created by a dam at Dobczyce, about 15 miles south-east of Kraków. The reservoir ensured a supply of cool, clean water suitable for trout and grayling. That and its closeness to the city, Marek explained, gave it a market value way beyond the reach of the peasant fish-slayers who lived in the villages along its valley.

His preparations for fishing were meticulous in the extreme. He took off his driving trousers and folded them precisely on top of socks and shoes before pulling on blue leggings and chest waders. He placed his club permit, licence and bailiff's card in one small plastic bag, his car keys in another, and his mobile phone in a third, putting each bag into a separate pocket of his many-pocketed fishing waistcoat. He took out his rod and reel and assembled them with the care I imagined him devoting to an experiment involving nuclear particles. He clipped a net to his belt and placed a base-ball cap on his hairless head. Throughout this procedure he maintained a fluent commentary on his actions, accompanied by regular rasping clearing of his throat.

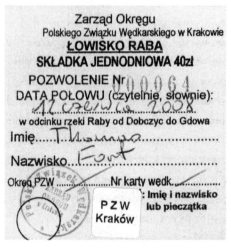

Zarząd Okręgu
Polskiego Związku Wędkarskiego w Krakowie
**ŁOWISKO RABA**
**SKŁADKA JEDNODNIOWA 40zł**
POZWOLENIE Nr 0 0 0 6 4
DATA POŁOWU (czytelnie, słownie):
*11 czerwca 2008*
w odcinku rzeki Raby od Dobczyc do Gdowa
Imię.....*T. Thomas*
Nazwisko...*Fort*
Okrąg PZW ................Nr karty wędk.............
PZW Kraków : Imię i nazwisko lub pieczątka

Fishing permit for the Raba

After a final check of his equipment and possessions, Marek led the way at a sprightly pace upstream, along a path that twisted between willow bushes, giving periodic views of a nice-looking riffly, stony river. We came to his favourite spot, where the water flowed evenly but with good pace and depth past a line of alders. Marek said there had been 'much activity' here the previous Sunday. Several fish had taken his fly although he had not succeeded in landing any of them. He waded out up to his knees and began to cast in a mechanical, metronomic fashion. I executed a few casts downstream from him. There was no activity. 'There is no activity,' Marek observed. 'This is strange. Last Sunday there was much activity.'

After a time he suggested trying somewhere else. As we made our way downstream I spotted two youths casting spinners from the far bank. 'Poachers,' barked Marek, and scuttled off across the water in pursuit. The boys disappeared into the bushes. 'They were poachers,' he confirmed when he returned. 'Before —' referring to the bad old days '— they would not have run away. Now they have respect.' He patted the pocket containing his bailiff's card.

At dusk the river, hitherto wholly lacking in activity, suddenly woke up. Rings appeared across the surface as trout sucked in hatching insects, the circles spreading and drifting down the darkening pool. Marek yelled with excitement. I saw him crouching over the water, rod bent, reaching with his net. 'Forty-two centimetres,' he crowed, holding up the trout for me to admire. 'My biggest this year.'

Not long after, I landed one myself. Marek splashed over to congratulate me. 'It is a very good fish,' he said. 'But not as big as mine.'

Flights of bats chopped through the gathering darkness, too quick and erratic for the eye to follow. It was too dark to see the rises of the trout, but their sips and slurps were audible. Club rules stated that fishing must stop an hour after sundown, Marek said, so we made our way back to his car. He was overflowing with delight. 'Great! Great! That was great. My best fish of the season, and you got a fish too. It was smaller than mine but a good fish. I am happy because I know that you are a true fly-fisherman like me.'

I was happy too.


There is a photograph of the young Józef Jeleński on the front cover of a book he wrote 30 years or so ago about how to catch Polish trout and grayling. It shows him holding a grayling, which is as handsome as all grayling are but eclipsed in good looks by Jeleński himself. (Not always the case with photographs of fish and men.) His dark, soulful eyes are framed by soft brown hair and a fine, full beard, giving an effect simultaneously manly, rugged and sensitive.

Time is not kind, to any of us. Now, at 60 or thereabouts, the hair and the beard are grizzled, the face is weathered and lined, the look from the eyes behind the spectacles is a touch weary.

I didn't meet Józef when I was in Poland in 1990. At that time he was living in Libya, designing and supervising large-scale construction projects on behalf of the Gaddafi regime. But the fishermen all knew him, or of him. His was the first modern account of the Polish way of fishing rivers like the San and the Dunajec. He was in the Polish team at the world championships in England in 1982, with Jurek Kowalski. I was told that he had taken his fly-tying box to Tripoli. His old friends liked to picture him in the north African sands, fingers tweaking nymphs and sedges into shape as his mind dwelled on the racing waters of home.

Józef and his wife Dorothy – whom he called Donia – lived at the southern edge of Myślenice, a town of about 10,000 people on the Raba upstream from the reservoir at Dobczyce. On my first evening there I went with them to the supermarket. 'It will be interesting for you,' Józef said. 'Shopping in Poland has changed since you were here before.'

Dorothy and Józef Jeleński

It was a characteristic understatement. The food stores I remembered were mean, shabby, depressing places staffed by unsmiling women whose attitudes of listlessness and indifference were in perfect harmony with the displays of produce they watched over. Blocks of grimy shelves were occupied by long, low stacks of jars and tins. Pale, flabby gherkins stood upright in cloudy vinegar. Pickled cabbage and beetroot lay in pink clods against the glass. Tins of frankfurters complemented tins of fish in brine. Where there was a bread counter, it was swept clean within minutes of the shop opening. If you were lucky, you might find a trotter or two, or a slab of tripe, in the chilled meat cabinet.

Myślenice's supermarket had been converted from the handsome nineteenth-century brick factory. Now, spread out beneath a high, vaulted roof, there was a scene of abundance, Amalthea's cornucopia accessible to all with the money to pay for it. Nectarines from Spain blushed beside grapes from South Africa. Strawberries and watermelons from the sunny south vied with pyramids of kiwi fruit. Mounds of tomatoes and artichokes rose opposite green hillsides of salad and dark cucumbers. One cabinet was devoted to French and Italian cheeses; another to the coffees and teas of the world. Walls of wines and beers rose head-high. At the fish counter you could buy fresh salmon from Alaska, smoked salmon from Scotland, bloaters and smoked eel, bass, sea bream, conger, tuna, carp, crayfish, oysters. Along one side stretched the fresh meat section, pigs' heads and lamb legs and beef sides and every cut above, below, between and behind; and the delicatessen, a celebration in shades of red and russet of the thousand Polish ways with cured pork.

My jaw dropped, my senses reeled. It was the familiarity of the scene that dumbfounded me. I saw it every week in Waitrose, and thought nothing of it. But that was in Henley-on-Thames, Oxfordshire. This was Myślenice, Poland. In a flash the distance between the two seemed to have shrunk almost to nothing. There was a sardonic edge to Józef's voice. 'You asked me if people here are still growing food on their land. Why should they grow it when they can buy better food here?'

He liked the town, he said, and not only because of its supermarket. It was clean and peaceful and hard-working. There were gypsies and Romanians but they worked and caused no trouble. Everyone in Myślenice had a job if they wanted one.

But despite his professed contentment, an air of slight disappointment hung around Józef like an old jacket. After more than 20 years in Libya and a spell in the United Arab Emirates, he had returned to Poland comparatively flush and sensing opportunities. He had taken up a part-time job teaching civil engineering in Kraków, and there was the promise of lucrative consultancy work as Poland set about rebuilding itself. But Józef's dream was of a river. He wanted to have one, to enhance and develop it, to turn it into a trout fishery to rival the best in Poland. He had studied the modern scientific methods of rearing trout. In the new economic climate there would be fishermen happy to pay good money for the exceptional service Józef would provide, he felt sure.

In the beginning all went well. After a tough battle with the Fishing Association, he secured a long lease on the Raba upstream from the reservoir. He bought a plot of land and built a house and a complex of tanks for hatching trout eggs and growing them to a size suitable for stocking the river. In the first years plenty of anglers came, bought tickets from Józef, and caught plenty of fish. Then . . . disaster. The decision was taken to build a new highway south from Kraków to the main holiday destination in the Tatras, Zakopane, part of it along the upper valley of the Raba.

The watercourse was brutally channelised to keep it out of the way and under control. Weirs were installed to manage surges of floodwater. Bankside tree cover was felled to make way for concrete embankments. The stream lost its natural pattern of pool and riffle, becoming wide, shallow and exposed, which left fewer and fewer places for trout to find cover and depth to stay out of sight. Water abstraction and a succession of dry, hot summers further sapped its spirit. The fishermen who had flocked there in the early days of Józef's management went elsewhere.

His was pretty much a lone voice against the wrecking of the Raba. There was no effective eco lobby, nor anything like our Environment Agency with the muscle to stand against the power of the construction and water engineering industries. The Fishing Association, smarting from their own loss of the water, stayed silent. The multiple ironies of the situation were not lost on Józef, although he did not refer directly to them. He owed his prosperity to the construction industry. It had paid for the land, the comfortable house, the little trout farm, the lease on the water. He had met Dorothy when he was lecturing on civil engineering in Kraków; now she had a well-paid job with a company helping to build a new road network in and around Kraków.

He did not give up. He waged a ceaseless campaign against the authorities and the builders, arguing for a more enlightened approach to environmental protection. No one listened. The new Poland was in too much of a hurry. Money was pouring in from the EU for so-called infrastructure schemes. There was a big pie for greedy fingers to be thrust into. So what if a few streams had to be trashed, a forest or two cut down, an ancient peat bog drained here and there?

Józef's disillusion with the fate of the Raba extended to the other rivers of his youth. They had all been ruined, he said, by dams, road-building, housing, water abstraction or over-fishing; the one exception being the San in the far south-east corner of the country, which he said was too far away for him. In fact, he had largely lost interest in fishing itself. One evening we went down to the Raba together, but Józef only wanted to fish near where he could leave the car and his approach was desultory. I saw enough to see that he was, or had been, a master technician; but also that he had lost the hunger and curiosity about water and fish that drive the true angler on.

Overall he seemed detached from the wider world and its concerns. He expressed contempt for politicians and politics. He watched football on TV (Poland were on their way out of Euro 2008), but without much enthusiasm. He was very friendly towards me, but showed no curiosity about my life or my country. He had been to England several times on business and had fished there quite extensively, but his lasting impression of it seemed to have been formed entirely by two unrelated episodes. The first occurred at the Town Hall in Northampton where the Polish fly-fishing team had attended a civic function to mark the staging of the 1982 world championships, only to find that they were expected to pay for their wine. That was English hospitality. On the second occasion, Józef was taken by a business associate to what was said to be the best restaurant in Knutsford, where he had been served with overcooked lamb with . . . what was it? Something green and bitter. Mint sauce, I said. Ah, yes, mint sauce. That was English cuisine.

Not that he was in the least taciturn. He talked at length about the physics of streams, the geomorphology of valleys and streambeds, and the science of aquaculture – subjects on which he had made himself a considerable authority – deviating every now and them into bitter denunciations of the barbarism and stupidity of the destroyers of his river. He focussed his energy almost obsessively on the trout in the tanks that stretched up from the back of his house towards the dark woods overlooking Myślenice. His day was organised around their feeding patterns. Even when not scattering pellets and minced fish to them, he would watch them for extended periods, tugging gently at his wiry beard, following their ceaseless twisting and darting as if searching for some secret code that might reveal something new about the mysteries of the human condition. He claimed to be checking for signs of disease or stress, but there was more to it than that. I asked him if he ever talked to them when no one was about. Józef laughed and denied it. It was just business, he said.

Dorothy was his second wife, and roughly half his age. I learned in passing that Józef had no children, that his first wife had died, that he had a brother; nothing more about his personal life. His relationship with Dorothy seemed very private, almost fragile. Although she understood some English, she wouldn't speak it at all, so that my exchanges with her tended to be brief — except when Józef could be bothered to translate — and one-sided. She had a square, freckly face with a downturned mouth that made her habitual expression glum and disapproving. Her smile was rare and sweet, and in the four days I stayed with them I heard her laugh only once. It was at something I said; I wish I could remember what.

They got up early and had breakfast together soon after six. They had the radio on in the morning and the TV in the evening, and spoke to each other quietly across the voices of strangers as if afraid that someone might be listening. Each day she left for the motorway site at seven, whereupon he would go out to feed the fish. At some point during the day Józef would devote time to their joint project, which was to install a new path from the front door to the gate. It was edged in small concrete blocks with cobbles between, and progressed down the slope at the rate of two or three feet a day. When Dorothy came home in the evening she would grasp a hammer and go out with Józef to inspect his handiwork. She was never satisfied, and would bend to tap the slabs and cobbles, turning at intervals to lecture him. Then, together, they would bend and tap and scrape and discuss where they were going next.

I liked Józef very much, and Dorothy as far as the language barrier permitted. But I did occasionally feel something of an intruder in their house. His reticence on personal matters did not make for easy conversation. I had expected him to talk about the old days but he didn't, and he did not have a good word to say about the new days. I had the impression that he made little effort to keep up with the fishing friends of his youth. When I mentioned the name of a well-known Polish angler who had written a book about the recent development of Polish methods, Józef launched into a scathing attack on both man and book. 'He sent it to me before the publication to ask for my comments and I told him about all the mistakes. But when the book was published all the mistakes were there. He didn't want to listen.' Józef shrugged his shoulders dismissively.

He still had several hundred copies of his own book, which he had secured at cost-price from the publishers. 'I thought maybe I would sign them and sell and make a profit,' he said. He pointed upwards. 'They are still in the attic.' He laughed.

Jozef said he had made a mistake in taking on the Raba. At the same time he had been offered the chance to buy a house somewhere in the west of Ireland where there were a thousand lakes and rivers to fish. Instead he had chosen to invest in Poland, a new wife, and trout. His friend had bought the house in Connemara, ridden the Irish property boom and sold up for half a million euros.

He smiled and went out to feed the fish.

# Chapter 4

## Leszek

One morning I took the bus from Myślenice into Kraków to see how it had fared in my absence. To say that it had changed would be like describing Margaret Thatcher as combative, or the two George Bushes as unsympathetic to the principles of Karl Marx.

You could never forget Kraków's situation: the old city held in the soft embrace of the Planty gardens, the Wawel and the cathedral raised in splendour above the river, the Wisła, curving its slow, stately way around the southern fringes. The wonder of Kraków would rebuke the darkest barbarism of which we are capable. Even Hitler, ecstatic at the thought of reducing London to rubble, could not bring himself to allow Kraków to be assaulted.

So I knew where I was at once. But beyond the geography almost nothing was familiar. The city looked, smelled, sounded, felt like a different place.

In 1990, it had had an innocence about it, as if it had just woken up to find the witch who had pricked its finger replaced by an eager, virile prince. It was a quiet, shabby, unkempt treasure-house, still blinking in amazement at the events of the previous 12 months, uncertain how a girl should respond to forceful masculine advances. The mansions looking out on to the central square, the Rynek, were dilapidated and grimy, their façades and plasterwork nibbled away by the pollution carried on the air from the notorious Nowa Huta steelworks to the east and the other factories ringing the city. The condition of many of the less grand but equally ancient houses was atrocious: the stucco devoured, the brickwork crumbling, roofs riddled with holes. Quite a number had been abandoned altogether, and were propped upright by towers of wooden scaffolding. Street after street was defaced by unfinished restoration projects, the buildings rotting behind scaffolding and sheets of torn plastic.

The city's commercial life was very restrained. Outside a jewellers in Floriańska Street three matronly ladies were employed as models. Dressed in crisp white blouses and dark skirts, they pirouetted self-consciously with arms outstretched, fingers bright with rings, wrists jangling with bracelets, smiling demurely. A hush prevailed in the covered market in the centre of the Rynek that was hardly disturbed by the traders selling fruit, vegetables, mountain cheeses, leather sandals, clocks, carved walking sticks and sheepskins from the Tatras. There were no bars, except in the international hotels, only tea houses where you were given a cup of barely hot water and a teabag to put in it.

There were tourists about, but they were comparatively thin on the ground and extremely decorous in their behaviour, as if cowed by the silence of the city and the melancholy that seemed to hang over its cobbled streets and squares. To someone accustomed to the grasping commercialism of the Catholic Church in Italy, the Mariacki in Kraków came as a delicious surprise. No racks of postcards and stalls of ecclesiastical tat, no multilingual telephones or coin slots to activate lights in dark chapels, no flashing and snapping of cameras, no squads of yawning foreigners being manoeuvred about and hectored by officious guides jockeying with each other for the best positions; instead, gloom and dusty quiet, the fantastic spectacle of Wit Stwosz's limewood altarpiece, the murmur of prayers and the swish of priestly robes, the constant flow of worshippers crossing themselves, bending their heads, giving thanks and praying for guidance.

Kraków's antique shops and secondhand and antiquarian bookshops seemed to set the trading tone. It was easy to imagine unearthing some extraordinary treasure in them, if you had un-limited time to pick through the mounds of unsorted volumes and rooms stacked with paintings, dust-shrouded furniture, chests of silver and once precious ornaments; less easy to understand how anyone could make any money from these enterprises. Curious literary byways revealed themselves among the sagging shelves of Tauchnitz classics in German and Polish classics in Polish. I came upon a hoard of cowboy books in English – *The Golden Hawk* by Frank Yerby, J. L. Bouma's *The Avenging Gun* – and a run from the *Woman's Weekly Library* bordered in sickly pink with titles like *Love Hath An Island*.

I don't know when Kraków's age of innocence ended but I doubt it lasted long. Strolling around the Rynek once again, I looked in vain for the vestiges of the old, shabby charm. The reliefs and friezes stood out in brilliant white. The colours of the smoothly stuccoed façades – apricot, terracotta, cream, sea-blue, sky-blue, leaf-green – glowed. Where restoration was in progress, the hoard-ings disguising it conveyed urgent consumer messages; the Kamienica Montelupich, on the east side of the square, was hidden behind an immense awning advertising the new Samsung mobile phone with two simcards.

Outside the Mariacki a miniature ensemble was into its musical loop: Bach's *D Minor Toccata and Fugue*, some *Four Seasons*, a dose of Pachelbel's *Canon*, back to the Bach. Inside, the church had got its wares displayed and its act together, and the tour guides were engaged in hot, lucrative competition. A queue of golf buggies was lined up along Mikolajska Street, taking their turn to whisk the infirm and the idle away on the 'Krak Tour', extendable if required to include the old Jewish quarter, the Kazimierz. Blinkered greys, with white plumes and scarlet pompoms oscillating above their ears, clip-clopped over the cobbles pulling white barouches with gilded steps and wheel hubs, piloted by characters in cod mountain shepherd gear, long whip in one hand, reins and mobile phone in the other.

There was not a cabbage or a ewe's cheese to be had in the covered market, just factory-made jewellery, painted boxes, over-priced woollen jerseys, woven bags and the usual souvenir trash. The great space of the square had been gobbled up by tables and chairs and umbrellas spewed forth from the bars, cafés and restaurants. A babel arose on all sides, English predominating, Polish hardly heard except between the gliding waiters.

The volume of human traffic was astonishing to me. It was like the incoming tide meeting the rocks. The stream advanced, paused, advanced again, dividing to swirl around obstacles and flow together on the other side. When one detachment stopped to rest or look at something its place was at once taken, so that sometimes it seemed it must only be a matter of time before every inch of space was filled and all movement ceased. Only when the bars finally closed their doors did the city have a few hours to recover itself, while the rubbish carts came in to clear away the debris.

It was not easy to escape the tourist press. But there was still peace and shade to be had in the Planty, which had somehow managed to remain in the ownership of the city and its residents, and acted as a green sponge, soaking up refugees from the crush. And, almost miraculously, it seemed to me, some of the tradi-tional canteens – known in Kraków as *jadłodajnia* – had survived the relentless advance of Colonel Sanders and the armies of the fast-food empire. You could still find them down passages and alleys and at the back of office buildings, places of extreme func-tionality organised on the sole principle of getting hot, filling, familiar Polish food into mouths fast and cheaply. There, at a Formica-topped table, you can literally rub shoulders with the ordinary Krakovians – students, office workers, street cleaners, low-ranking municipal functionaries – so conspicuously absent from the establishments around the Rynek. There is little opportunity for contemplation or conversation in a *jadłodajnia*. Orders are given and within a few minutes the steaming bowl of *bigos* or *barszcz* or plateful of *pierogi*, *placki* or *gołąbki* is delivered. Custom dictates that you start eating at once. Ten minutes later, stomach reassuringly heavy, you are outside.

Overall, I felt profoundly and uncomfortably ambivalent about the transformation of Kraków. I tried to remind myself that, from the perspective of most of those who lived there, life was surely more enjoyable, more rewarding, less depressing, more comfortable and generally better than it had been under the heavy, hairy fist of the Party; and that that mattered a lot more than the fastidious reservations of an occasional visitor. The city, in the sense of the community of its people, had undoubtedly been reborn, which must be a good thing.

Still, something precious had been lost. When I was there in 1990 it was rundown, dirty, conspicuously lacking in vitality. But it belonged to its people, as it had for a thousand years. They went about the business of being Krakovians while we, the visitors, looked on quietly and marvelled. Now we had taken over and the city had been reorganised to cater for our requirements, the same ones the tourism industry imposes on every place it colonises. In common with other historic and beautiful cities, Kraków had leased itself indefinitely to the tour operators and travel agents representing the massed armies of sightseers. Through this marketing process it seemed to me to have lost much of its particular flavour, its sense, not merely of being Polish, but of being Poland's finest, most beautiful, cultured and treasured possession.

There was also a mystery in Kraków that troubled me, which I tried and failed to solve. Or maybe I was wrong and there was no mystery at all. Maybe it was just that times change and people with them.

Adam Gebel

I have to go back to the Second World War. Adam Gebel, an officer in the Polish army – by then under German control – was ordered to the eastern front to confront the advancing Russians. Recognising a bad move when he saw it coming, he and some others commandeered a truck and went south. Eventually, by devious routes, they found their way to England. I never really grasped what those devious routes were. Budapest was mentioned, and Trieste, and Rome, or possibly Genoa, certainly Paris, where Adam was given artichokes to eat when he was dreaming of meat and champagne.

He ended up in Catterick, in the Polish army-in-exile, where he spent the rest of the war as a motorcycle instructor. In his spare time, Adam learned to speak an idiosyncratic version of English, played the guitar and piano, drank, cooked Polish food, charmed and seduced women, gathered mushrooms, poached game. He did some fishing too; there was an episode in Scotland involving the capture, not by fair angling means, of a pike so enormous that, when lifted to his shoulder, it was said that its tail dragged along the ground.

After the war Adam gravitated to London where he found work in the building trade. One of his employers was an English woman, Pamela Eley, who had a small, classy interior design business. Adam beguiled Pamela, who was several years older than him, and married her, much to the disgust of her family, who were Gloucestershire gentry, and to the dismay of most of her friends.

My father was the exception to the general disfavour. He had known Pamela since childhood. He liked Adam and enjoyed his theatrically Slavic enthusiasm for the pleasures of life. Adam and Pamela used to come and stay with us, and Adam used to make a good deal of noise. My mother was very attached to Pamela and theoretically fond of Adam, although she found extended exposure to his company tiring.

My father was killed in a car crash when I was eight years old. My mother and Pamela remained close, and later Adam and I were drawn together by a shared love of fishing. His approach was both more direct and more underhand than mine. His aim was to catch fish in order to eat them, and he was not too particular about how he did it. If he could get away with putting a maggot on his fly, he would do so. If he could get away with killing more trout than was permitted, he would do so. He regarded the makers of rule-books as adversaries to be outwitted. On one occasion he telephoned me to say that he had been banned from a trout fishery run by someone I regarded as a friend, for taking more than his permitted limit. 'He is Jewish bastard,' Adam said to me. I pointed out that the friend in question was born and bred in Reading. 'Welsh bastard then,' he replied.

Adam seethed with prejudices. He was anti-semitic and racist. Along with Jews and blacks, he disliked the French and the Spanish, and his loathing for the Germans and the Russians was visceral. His attitude to England was complicated. Theoretically he approved the idea of it as a bastion of freedom and tolerance. In practice Adam's own capacity for tolerance was limited, particularly when it came to the liberal tendency. This was the 1970s, the era of industrial conflict, power cuts, unemptied bins in the streets. 'Bloody Scargill,' Adam would growl as we cast our flies. 'Is fucking Communist. You vote for Scargill?' He would glare at me. He had soft, silver hair over a steep, smooth forehead, a falcon's beak of a nose bracketed by jutting cheekbones. I said I had voted Labour. 'Is same. You want bloody Scargill running country? Is same as having fucking Russians.'

Every so often two of my elder brothers and I would be summoned for supper with Pamela and Adam at their house in Holland Park. In the early days we took our wives as well but they tended to find Adam overbearing, and did not take kindly to his habit of embracing them from behind and putting his hands on their breasts, so they dropped out. Pamela would sit at one end of the table, talking quietly of family matters and gardening. At the other end Adam would boom and shout and bark with laughter, delivering tirades of abuse against left-wingers, homosexuals and women's libbers. In between, we brothers would hurl back the obligatory succession of tots of iced vodka and tuck in to slabs of trout and rich stews of Polish sausage, tripe, cabbage and wild mushrooms.

Adam and I often talked of going together to Poland to fish the rivers he had known in his youth. But it was only ever talk. The truth was that he couldn't bear the prospect of being brought close to what had happened to his country. Having extricated his mother and father to England in the early 1950s, he had been back only once and hated everything about it. The events leading to the downfall of the regime in 1989 confused him. When I said that things seemed to be getting better, he would grow angry and assert that it would take more than strikes by trade unionists to roll back the years. He said he was too old. He was right.

Nevertheless he took a close interest in the planning of my Polish adventure, and arranged that when I got to Kraków I would stay with Leszek Trojanowski, who was the son of his oldest Polish friend. I already knew Leszek and his wife, Isa, because they used to come to London each autumn to stay with Pamela and Adam. Adam had a pronounced tyrant's streak and treated Leszek like a poor relation, getting him to run errands and work in the garden, while Isa's role was barely distinguishable from that of a serving girl.

Leszek

I drove into Kraków on 4 May 1990. The weather was as blissful as early May knows how, and the warmth was matched by the welcome I got from the Trojanowskis. They lived in a spacious house just beyond the Planty gardens, which also contained Leszek's dental surgery. I was given a tour, Leszek beaming as he patted the reclining seat and stroked his high-speed drill. In the house I admired the microwave, the washing machine, the dishwasher, the new TV and video. Outside were Leszek's Toyota estate and Isa's Fiat. When I commented on his evident prosperity, Leszek grinned. 'When tooth is hurting it not matter if you are Communist or capitalist, you pay good money to stop the hurting.'

We had lunch at the dining table: grilled pork and potatoes. On one wall of the room was a portrait of Leszek in old-fashioned military uniform, his features and bearing deliberately reminiscent of Napoleon. Isa faced him across the room, bare-shouldered and full-bosomed, every inch an Emperor's wife. Hardly had I cleared my plate than we were off in the Toyota, swooping south past the panting Trabants and Fiats and sooty trucks towards the foothills of the mountains, where they had a weekend house.

A month earlier there had been five feet of snow on the slopes around the village of Półrzeczki. Now the intense green of the meadows was brushed by drifts of buttercups, orchids and poppies. The hilltops were covered in the deeper green of mixed woods, spotted with brown where the conifers had been frosted. The fields were divided into long, narrow strips, all privately owned and worked by hand.

The village was spread across the valleys of two small streams. In the evening I walked with Leszek and Isa up one of the valleys. Horses plodded up and down, dragging wooden ploughs, single furrows snaking out behind. We passed horses and donkeys pulling carts hidden under heaps of grass on which men with walnut-brown faces perched, cigarettes going under straw hats. Outside the single-storey wooden farmhouses yelping dogs flung themselves against the restraints of their chains. Chickens, ducks, geese and turkeys pecked at the dust.

I was taken aback by Leszek and Isa's contempt for what seemed to me a rural idyll. 'They are primitives,' he said. 'Aboriginals. You know, they live in these houses all in one room . . . animals too. In one bed, I think.' The inhabitants were superstitious, depraved, simple-minded, usually drunk, cunning in a low peasant way, apparently. We passed a shack belonging to a forester. He was a good man, Leszek conceded, although primitive and usually drunk.

The spaces between the old wooden houses of Półrzeczki were being rapidly filled. Many of the plots had been sold to Krakovians like Leszek for their weekend houses, usually alpine chalets with steep-hipped roofs, balconies, and strong fences and gates. On the proceeds of these sales, the landowners were building themselves new houses, three or four storeys high, of coarse grey or rusty red blocks, with metal roofs. According to Leszek, though, moving house made no difference to old habits. 'He is still very primitive. Still have animals in house. He is happy with table, chair, bed, TV and vodka. Sometimes no bed. Always vodka.'

The building boom was in full swing along every road and in all the accessible villages of the region. Like some latterday Slavic Mr Toad, Leszek drove at terrific speed through these untidy settlements, blasting his horn and shouting abuse, sending livestock and their owners scuttling for cover. He steered with one arm draped over the wheel, leaving the other free for contemptuous gesticulations at the peasants, while he maintained a commentary on their degenerate character and habits.

That first evening two friends came round after supper. They were having a chalet built a little way up the valley. They talked with Leszek and Isa about city matters: their children's tennis lessons, the opening of private schools, which shops could be relied on to have meat, the petrol shortages and how the Jews must be behind them. They showed no interest at all in the village, its people and life, except for the price of land. To me these steep ribbons etched into the hillsides spoke of a system of husbandry that had served Europe for centuries, and whose survival seemed rather wonderful. To the Trojanowskis and their friends, their only value was as potential building plots, which depended on how easily they could be connected with power and water.

The next day I had an uncomfortable baptism into Polish fly-fishing. We went to the Dunajec, a major tributary of the Wisła, which flowed with foaming urgency out of the mountains. Its water was a milky, steely grey/blue, thickened with snow melt. Leszek cut me a staff of ash to steady myself as I waded. 'Is too early for swimming,' he said with a slightly unnerving grin. A few steps out from the bank I found that my waders were leaking in a number of places. Freezing fingers of water crept down my legs and insinuated themselves into sensitive nooks and crannies. The power of the current dragged at me, and I felt my studded soles sliding across the stones. I cast my flies for a time, and watched them being torn around by the force of the water. I quickly became too cold to continue. Leszek appeared with two little trout that he killed even though they were well below the official size limit.

We gave up fishing and went on an excursion to Mogielnica, a shrine on top of a hill above Półrzeczki. It was a six-hour walk so we drove most of the way in order that Leszek could bring his latest toy, a video camera. On the way we passed an elderly woman riding an ancient horse, with a mangy mongrel trotting behind. She shouted at Leszek, who shouted back. After a stormy exchange she rode off. Leszek said that she had objected to the contamination of the mountain air by the fumes from his car. She was the local doctor, he said, a well-known madwoman and drunkard who preferred to live out here and treat the peasants.

A path led up to the shrine. The wooded crests of the Beskids stretched away to the south. Beyond, 50 miles or so away, the horizon was guarded by the jagged white teeth of the High Tatras. Two sparrowhawks patrolled the woods to our left. A pair of skylarks swung and swooped over the meadows. Leszek's younger son, Wojtek, aged ten, hunted lizards through the grass, whooping with excitement when he grabbed one. Leszek gasped under the weight of the camera. At the top a crudely painted Madonna and Child looked out from beneath a wooden shelter across a clearing scorched by campfires and strewn with rusted cans and empty beer bottles.

\*   \*   \*

The next day more friends came to pay a call: Krszysztof, the owner of a factory and bar, and his pregnant wife Mariola, who owned a smart clothes shop in Kraków. She spoke fluent English and set about educating me in the subject of Poland's glowing future. English was the key, she said, the language of the new Europe. Leszek joined in. 'Give us two years to catch up . . . maybe three. People like us will flourish because we understand the free market, understand capitalism. In fact, we've been practising it for years under the noses of the bastard Communists.' To my subsequent dismay, my own contribution to the conversation – a lamentable string of stale platitudes about the benefits of democracy – was faithfully recorded on the sound-track of his camera.

No one could have been kinder to me than Leszek and Isa were. She fed me and washed my clothes and escorted me around some of the sights of Kraków, and did her best to cheer me up when I was briefly overcome by an acute attack of homesickness. He sorted out all my practical requirements and was touchingly concerned about my welfare, even displaying unmistakable jealousy when I made other Polish friends. When Leszek and Isa pressed me to delay my departure so that I could attend Wojtek's First Communion – a sacred occasion for Polish families – I felt almost one of them, an honorary Trojanowski.

For a while after I returned to England, life resumed its old patterns. Leszek and Isa continued to come for a couple of weeks each September to stay at Pamela and Adam's house in Holland Park – for a few years more anyway. Then Pamela died, aged nearly 90, and Adam slowed down. He wouldn't go fishing any more, and, having always been more than ready to dwell on the pleasures of extra-marital 'dooloo dooloo', as he called it, he now tended to become sentimental about his 'Pamuszka' and their shared bliss and mutual devotion. He was consoled at odd times by the arrival from Poland of unaccompanied female students who would stay in his house while studying and perform various duties in return. He lamented to me that, despite every inducement, 'prick no longer stand up'; adding, with a flicker of the old spirit and the waggling of a finger, that he could still give pleasure. He was then well into his 80s.

Adam died when he was 85. He left more than a million pounds, of which half went to his daughter by a first marriage and her family, and the other half was divided into six equal parts. My brother Matthew, who was Pamela's godson and much loved by both her and Adam, received one share. So did I. I do not remember who got the other four, but I know that Leszek was not one of them. Neither he nor Isa attended the funeral – a dreary crematorium affair somewhere north of Edgware – and contact between us lapsed.

Still, he was the first person I wrote to when I started making arrangements for my return visit. I got no reply. I tried telephoning, but all the numbers in Kraków had been changed. I asked another Polish friend if he could track Leszek down. He emailed me to say that he had spoken to Leszek, who had said that he 'would not have much time to see you'. Then I had an email from Leszek himself, wishing me well for my trip but saying he would not be able to see me at all. There was no explanation.

I found a website for Trojanowski Stomatologic, with an address, and when I was in Kraków I called round. The bell was answered by Wojtek, the boy I remembered catching lizards in his bare hands, now a qualified dentist himself. He said his father would be there later. I came back at one o'clock. This time Leszek opened the door. He was in his smock and trousers, with a dentist's headlamp fastened around his head looking disconcertingly like a third eye.

Time had treated him pretty well. Always thickset, he was now thicker set, fleshier round the face. But he was 62, and 18 years had passed, after all. He had beads of sweat on his face, and his perfunctory handshake was moist. He explained that he and Wojtek divided the working day, with his shift lasting until 8 p.m. His first patient was due in ten minutes and he had preparations to make. It was clear he did not want me to hang around. I asked after Isa. She was in Katowice for treatment to her back, apparently. He told me he had given up fishing two years before. Finally he suggested that we meet that evening at a café on the Rynek. He made it sound like a neutral venue.

He brought Wojtek with him, ostensibly to help out with the conversation, on the grounds that his English was much better than Leszek's. Wojtek, a good-looking, extremely self-assured young man, spoke at some length about his passion for dressing up in US army battle fatigues and crawling around the country-side, pretending to root out units of the Vietcong. He described with great glee appearing one foggy winter's morning with his fellow enthusiasts outside the church at Półrzeczki and terrifying worshippers on their way in to Mass.

Leszek talked affectionately about Adam. He said that he had been to London two or three years before and, for old times' sake, had gone to the house in Holland Park. 'It was just to remember,' he said. 'But is all finished now.' He talked a little about fishing. A dam had been built on the Dunajec, and the stretches near Półrzeczki where he and I had fished together had been submerged or ruined. These days, he said, he preferred gardening. And travel. For the first time he became animated. He and Isa had been to the Bahamas for three weeks in the winter, then Miami, then New York. 'We go to Metropolitan Opera. *La Bohème*. You know how much tickets cost?' I didn't. 'Four hundred and seventy-eight dollars. We go also to *Mamma Mia*. It is musical. And Neil Simon. I like music very much.' In November they would be off to Goa, for three weeks, for the third time. 'Is very nice. Relaxing. The sun, the sea. No waves. Nice girls.'

Not bad for a Polish dentist, eh? I felt I was being challenged. I said I had never been to Goa, or the Bahamas, or the Met. 'You make money from writing books?' Leszek asked. Hardly any, I replied. 'What book you writing now?' I tried to explain. 'Is many changes in Kraków,' Leszek said.

We finished our coffee and walked a little way together before parting. I gave him my address at home and urged him to visit, but I knew he wouldn't. I told him I might be back in Kraków later and would love to see Isa. He said her back was very bad. The implication was that she would have to stay in Katowice indefinitely. I felt that a barrier had been raised between us, though the reason why remained a mystery. He offered no explanation, beyond saying that he had to work very hard to make the money to pay for Goa.

I did manage to solve one minor mystery, however. The address I had for Leszek from long ago was in Ziaji Street. But when I got to Kraków and tried to find it on a street map, it was not listed. According to his website, the practice was located in Jabłonowski Street, just beyond the Planty and the university quarter. When I got there it seemed familiar.

'Is same street. Same house. But different name,' Leszek explained.

It had been Jabłonowski Street in pre-Communist times, named after an illustrious Polish nobleman, soldier and Governor of Kraków, Prince Stanisław Jabłonowski. Under the regime, princes, however illustrious, were out of favour and it was renamed Ziaji Street in honour of Stanisław Ziaji, a hero of the Communist Party killed by the Gestapo in 1944. With the overthrow of Marxist–Leninism, the dice of history rolled again. Prince Jabłonowski, who had fought the Swedes, the Cossacks, the Russians, the Tartars and the Turks, and stood firm for the God-given right of the few to keep the many in their place, was now back; the man who had fought and died for the rights of workers was out.

# Chapter 5

## The Jews

There were posters up all over Kraków – 2008: 18th Annual Festival of Jewish Culture. It occurred to me that the first festival must have taken place the year after my stay with Leszek and Isa.

At that time the hot topic of the moment was the crippling shortage of fuel. Leszek unhesitatingly pointed the finger at 'the Jews'. They had been buying up supplies and hoarding them, waiting for the price to rise, he said. I asked him who these Jews were. He was vague. I asked if the man with the jerrycans in his garage from whom Leszek obtained his fuel was Jewish. He wasn't. I said my understanding was that there were very few Jews in Kraków, or indeed anywhere in Poland. Leszek suggested that strings were being pulled by Jewish fingers from outside the country.

A few days later, without any obvious awareness of incongruity, he urged me to visit the death camp at Auschwitz. No visit to Kraków was complete without seeing it. Did I know, he asked, that many Poles had risked their lives to save Jews from death at the hands of the Nazis?

The unsettling paradox of Polish anti-semitism is that, historically, no country in Europe has been more welcoming to Jews; and in no country did Jews make a bigger cultural and economic contribution. In the fourteenth century, at a time when Jews were the victims of pogroms all over Europe, the Polish king, Kazimierz the Great, signed an edict giving them protection from persecution.

Jewish families flocked into Poland from Spain, Italy and elsewhere. Initially they were concentrated in Kraków, Warsaw and Lublin, but subsequently Jewish communities established themselves in Lithuania, and in most towns and villages in Galicia, which stretched across what is now southern Poland, northern Slovakia and southern Ukraine, as far east as Bukovina.

For six centuries Poland remained the chief refuge and stronghold of European Jewry. Their legal status fluctuated, reaching its highpoint in the mid-sixteenth century when they were granted rights that amounted to a kind of religious and cultural autonomy. Subsequently, as Poland was repeatedly ravaged by foreign invaders, the Jews suffered periodic assaults on their liberties as well as attempts to curtail their economic influence. But they stayed and multiplied and, in the period immediately after the First World War, prospered; so that by 1940 there were 3.3 million Jews in Poland.

Six years later there were 300,000. Of those who survived the Holocaust, the vast majority emigrated soon after the end of the war. Even so, in the late-1950s there were still between 30,000 and 40,000 Jews left. In 1967 the regime led by Władysław Gomułka instituted a purge, accusing them of Zionism and Westernism. By then they were so thoroughly integrated into the general Polish population that some did not even realise they were Jewish. As children they had been passed to Polish families to save them (often with money changing hands) and given Christian names with which they grew up. But the Party, displaying its characteristic thoroughness in such matters, had kept the records. Some 9,000 Jews, spread through the military, the police, the artistic and academic sectors as well as the Party itself, lost their jobs. Between 1968 and 1972, 20,000 Jews left Poland. It is estimated that by 1994 there were no more than 3,500 left in the entire country.

This was the background to the assertion by my friend Leszek and other educated, prosperous members of the emerging entrepreneurial class that 'the Jews' were behind the petrol famine. Small wonder that, to someone from England, the Polish attitude seemed to make no sense at all.

In Kraków itself a population of almost 60,000 Jews in 1939 was reduced to a handful within five years. Thereafter the ghetto, known as Kazimierz, was left to rot, and in 1990 was still in a condition of complete decay. Later, due at least in part to the world-wide success of Spielberg's film *Schindler's List*, the district was brought back to life. Feeding from the curiosity of cineastes and the troubled fascination of the outside world with the fate of the Jews, the city authorities have successfully incorporated Kazimierz into Kraków's tourist menu. Synagogues and some of the fine old merchants' houses have been restored, the covered food market has been resuscitated; bakeries, cafés, bars and kosher restaurants have opened and flourish.

Ten minutes' walk from Oskar Schindler's factory is the Galician Museum, which records the nemesis of the liquidated millions in oral testimony and photographs. The presentation is deliberately dispassionate, the effect crushing. Some of the images – the chimneys, the chambers, the watchtowers, the hollow-chested, hollow-eyed, stick-limbed victims – are familiar. Others make their point through their seeming innocuousness. There is a pond at Auschwitz in which the ash of incinerated Jews was dumped; a furniture store in a provincial town which was once the synagogue; a forest scene near Rzeszów concealing a mass grave; a field near Szczawnica covering a Jewish cemetery; hummocks of grass and copses in place of the Zasław camp near Lesko, where thousands died and thousands more were processed on their way to the extermination centre at Bełżec.

Lesko is a small town in south-east Poland, overlooking the River San. These days its main function is to serve as a gateway to the Bieszczady national park, which extends to the border with Ukraine. In 1939 around 60 per cent of its population was Jewish, and it was a celebrated centre of Chasidism. Jewish politicians served on the town council. There were Jewish schools, Jewish societies, Jewish businesses. The prosperous townsfolk built a fine, handsome synagogue and had inscribed on the façade a quotation from *Genesis*: 'And he was afraid and said: "How dreadful is this place! This is none other but the House of God and this is the gate of Heaven."'

Within three years, four centuries of Lesko's Jewish heritage was erased. Most of its Jewish population died at Bełżec, although a few managed to escape across the San to the east and survived. There are no Jews left there now. The synagogue, carefully restored, houses a gallery displaying the work of local artists and an office of the Polish hiking association.

Down the road from the synagogue is the gate to the cemetery. Two thousand gravestones are spread around a shaded hillside. The oldest of them, dating from 1548, bears an inscription in Hebrew: 'Here rests the God-fearing Eliezer, son of the Rabbi Meszulem, blessed be the memory of the righteous.' Some of the stones stand upright, others lean in attitudes of defeat or exhaustion, or lie prone among the nettles and ground elder. Paths wind beneath the branches of oaks, sycamores and silver birches. Flycatchers dart from trunk to trunk, feet clasping the bark, tiny beaks searching out the insects. But the birdsong hardly dents the silence. There is no one left to tend these graves. Those who would, in the normal course of events, have done so were disposed of.

Inside the gate there is a monument to those who found no resting place of their own. The inscription, in Polish and English, reads: 'Here lie remains of the Jews of Galicia and other lands murdered at Bełżec in 1942, reinterred here in 1995'.

# Chapter 6

## Holy river

I said goodbye to Józef Jeleński at the bus station in Myślenice. The bus to Zakopane took the new highway south, following the valley of his poor, abused Raba. Sunshine washed the meadows and woods along the river. Ahead cloud hugged the Tatras.

The look of the landscape seemed reassuringly familiar: the narrow strip fields wandering in whimsical lines up and down hills and dales. But it dawned on me that there had been a change, a big change. Twenty years before, these fields were jealously defended and diligently cultivated. Periodic attempts by the state to impose collectivisation according to the orthodox Marxist–Leninist model had been stubbornly resisted, and thus these holdings had remained enormously precious, both as sources of food and as symbols of independence.

Now there was almost no ploughed earth, and there were no fields of potatoes, maize or other vegetables. The one crop was grass. Where someone had troubled to cut it, the surface was pale and studded with stooks that, from a distance, looked like green tombstones. But much of it had been left to wave in the wind. I saw one shepherd, in a rough woollen waistcoat and battered felt hat, directing one flock of sheep. Otherwise the countryside was empty.

The situation of Zakopane, Poland's favourite mountain town, has proved over time to be too glorious for its own good. It sits almost in the shadow of the High Tatras, at the head of a plateau that extends north to the junction of the two branches of the

Dunajec in the town of Nowy Targ. Photographs from a century or so ago show two long, straight streets of wooden houses and barns, the mountains rearing behind, green, well-watered meadows all around: a place of fantastic, haunting beauty.

Even then, though, Zakopane's days as an isolated mountain village peopled by simple farmers, wood-carvers and fiddle-players were in the past, and the outsiders were taking over. The occupation was led in the first instance by doctors establishing sanatoriums where their consumptive patients could inhale the healing air of the mountains. They were followed by artists and intellectuals from Kraków, seeking inspiration from the scenery. The incomers swiftly seized upon the architecture, music and quaint customs of the Górale sheep farmers, and proclaimed the discovery of a pure and authentically Polish culture. The word was spread, the road was built, the railway came. Zakopane shed its innocence and soon grew accustomed to a new role.

Today its resident population numbers about 20,000, much the same as 40 years ago. But its capacity for soaking up visitors has reached 100,000 and is still growing. Zakopane calls itself a town but it has no boundaries, no beginning and no end. Like urban bindweed, it has crept along every approach, propagating itself across its environs. Property prices are the same as in central Kraków and Warsaw. Every patch of land is a building plot.

The guidebooks call Zakopane 'bustling'. A stroll along its main thoroughfare, Krupówski Street, reveals the nature of the bustle, and a good deal about what Poles expect when they go on holiday. (It is, overwhelmingly, a Polish resort.) Beer and grilled meat. Amplified pseudo-Górale music. Shops selling folkloric tat, climbing and skiing gear. More grilled meat, more beer, louder music. And everything housed in gross parodies of the mountain-style architecture, wooden temples bristling with turrets, pinnacles, spires, festooned with machine-cut swags and curlicues and floral motifs, waxed and varnished to a honey-coloured burnish.

This school of architecture – flamboyant or grotesque, according to taste – was founded by a painter and art critic from Kraków, Stanisław Witkiewicz. In the 1890s he was commissioned by a wealthy patron to build a house in the mountain style beside what is now Kościeliska Street, which runs south-west from the centre of Zakopane. The Willa Koliba was intended as a model for a new, national style of Polish architecture to be based on the traditions of the highland farmhouses. Of itself, Koliba, with its shingled roofs, recessed eaves, dormer windows and mighty interlocking beams, is a rather wonderful celebration of wood and its possibilities. The wealth of ornamentation and the craftsmanship of the fittings – including door handles, keyholes, furniture and cooking utensils – reveal the phenomenal skill of the carpenters, carvers and metalworkers assembled to create it. But its character is inescapably derivative and backward-looking. Instead of forging a new path, it served to legitimise the so-called 'Zakopane style' whose misbegotten offspring continue to disfigure the town.

One of the rooms in the Willa Koliba contains a collection of the startling portraits churned out in enormous numbers by Witkiewicz's even more celebrated son. This Witkiewicz was also christened Stanisław, but in his lifelong search for his own voice and artistic identity dubbed himself Witkacy. Painter, dramatist, novelist, philosopher, aesthete, sexual athlete, drinker and furious consumer of hallucinogenic drugs, Witkacy's self-appointed mission was to shape his life into an absurdist commentary on the horrors and futilities of his age.

'Why do I exist if I could have been without existence?' he asked, but reached no conclusion. Pressed by an earnest disciple to explain his theories of Pure Form, he would yell '*Après moi, le déluge*', or recite a Russian proverb roughly translated as: 'I would be famous for heroism if it weren't for my haemorrhoids.' In the end the absurdity of the successive invasions of Poland by the Germans and the Russians proved too much even for the absurdist Witkacy.

In September 1939 he took an overdose and slit his wrists. The fame he had longed for arrived posthumously; in 1988 the Polish Culture Ministry arranged for his body to be exhumed from his grave in Ukraine and reburied amid appropriate ceremony in Zakopane. Unfortunately a cursory examination of the remains revealed them to be those of an anonymous Ukrainian woman, and in the end Witkacy's admirers had to settle for a commemorative tablet.

A morning of Zakopane was enough for me. Following the example of the artists, I decided to seek relief and inspiration in mountain scenery, so I took a minibus a few miles out of town to the Dolina Chochołowska, the valley of the Chochołowska stream. According to my *Rough Guide*, it and its neighbour, the Dolina Kościeliska, were acknowledged to be two of the loveliest valleys of the region. They must have been, once; and they might be again, if someone removed the toy train, the coach parks and hotels, the rows of gift shops, the grilled meat and beer kiosks, the gaggle of hawkers peddling rubbish, the turnstiles charging 5 *złoty* to get in, and at least four-fifths of the trippers swarming in all directions.

Do I sound grumpy? I was. The guidebook raised the prospect of 'an immensely rewarding day's hiking' up the valley. I pondered this phrase as I headed up from the turnstiles. The toy train, its little coaches packed, passed me for the first time. Squads of cyclists overtook me, tyres hissing on the smooth tarmac road. To one side a flock of sheep nibbled photogenically. On the other families were getting a taste of the rustic life in a village of rustic chalets. Beyond the chalets, picnic tables and benches were arranged in phalanxes beside the stream.

Having passed or been overtaken by the toy train three or possibly four times, I took a path that led over the ridge separating the Dolina Chochołowska from its rival for the title of most beautiful valley in the Tatras. For an hour and a half or so I exchanged the rattle of train wheels and the tinkle of bicycle bells for the quiet of the woods and some fine views of forested hills stretching away to the border with Slovakia. Descending into the Dolina Kościeliska I surrendered myself once more to the tide of humanity, by now ebbing towards the car parks and coach parks and the road back to Zakopane.

I needed cheering up. Fortunately Marek Kot was waiting for me in a bar, ready to do the trick. Marek was the next link in my chain of Polish anglers. A mad-keen fisherman, he is employed by the Tatra National Park as a geomorphologist and as director of a programme to educate schoolchildren about the Tatras and the ecological threats to them. I felt at once that the mountains could not have recruited a more doughty or delightful champion. Short, broad and barrel-chested, with thick, tufty greying hair and a heavy moustache, Marek quivered with passion and hummed with energy.

He banged his fist on the table then smacked it into his hand as he enumerated the crimes against his mountain rivers. 'Too many problems,' he said furiously. Poachers. Bandits scooping up the stones and gravel with mechanical diggers for building. Abstraction. Pollution. Corrupt government officials. Corrupt angling club officials. He embarked upon a lengthy, fractured account of how he and others had campaigned to expose finagling by the president of the Zakopane Fishing Association.

I asked him about the building of the dam at Czorsztyn on the Dujanec, which had submerged a number of villages and left the stretch of brawling river that I had fished with Leszek lost beneath the flat waters of a reservoir. The fist came down again. '*Katastrof*,' Marek bellowed. The best section on the whole river had been destroyed. And for what? To protect the holiday homes of a few officials and their friends from occasional flooding. He noticed my expression of surprise. 'Is true,' he exclaimed, fist descending. 'Is how Poland works.'

Marek Kot

Sunday was his one day off. He suggested that we fish together on the Białka, which delighted me. Of the Polish streams I had got to know in 1990, it was the Białka that had stamped itself deepest into my memory.

Its source is a small oligotrophic lake called Morskie Oko, the Eye of the Sea, which is held in a bowl overlooked by the High Tatras. Unfortunately for this famously lovely place, the way to it from the direction of Zakopane is smooth and easy. Everyone who comes to Zakopane visits the Dolina Chochołowska and the Dolina Kościeliska, and everyone visits the Eye of the Sea. In the holiday season 20,000 a day squeeze into the car parks and around the shores. Their first question, according to Marek Kot, is: Where is the toilet? Then, Where can I get a beer? Finally, Where is the nature?

The pressure on the lake is extreme, but typical of this area as a whole. The Tatras are shared with Slovakia, but the Polish sector is much the smaller, and much more intensively developed for tourism. Skiing is big business, and hikers swarm along the trails when the snow has melted. Everywhere the fragile ecology is squeezed and compromised.

Somehow the Białka had escaped, like a fugitive on the run. The name means 'white river' and it fits. The stream bed is composed of granite stones and boulders worn and rubbed over the aeons to the pallor of bleached bone. It flows due north from the mountains through a belt of thick coniferous woodland, with no more than the occasional farming village beside it. The valley it has made for itself is wide, and the glacial water wanders hither and thither across it, dividing into braids that flow between islands of willow bushes and unstable bars of stones and gravel, tumbling over shallows into green-tinged pools. If you lift any stone in the pools, you will find it studded with the cases of caddises, like tiny broken twigs, and the nymphs of stoneflies and smaller insects. For a mountain river the feeding is rich, and the Białka teems with trout and grayling. They are mostly small, but make up for it by being eager takers of a fly.

Marek calls it the Holy River; it is where his father taught him to fish. We went first to a stretch downstream of the bridge at a village called Brzegi. This kind of fishing – wading fast water, hopping between boulders, flicking your flies into tiny resting places as you go – takes getting used to if you haven't done it for a while – in my case, a long while. I floundered and struggled and caught nothing, until a great string of kayaks suddenly came through, paddles flying, and Marek suggested moving somewhere else. On the way back to the car we stopped to fish a couple of pools on a sidestream below a ramshackle but still active sawmill. Marek pointed out a well-tended vegetable patch as an item of interest. Otherwise the ground was largely uncultivated. No one bothers with growing anything any more, he said sadly. Tourism pays better. Even the sheep are only there for the tourists.

Four or five miles downstream, the Białka was just as I remembered. It had split into a multiplicity of channels, threading their way through the wide bed created by the floods of a thousand ages. It was easy to tack from one stream to the next, searching out the pools; so that in the course of an afternoon I must have covered two or three miles of water, yet at the end of it I had no more than half a mile to walk back along the path through the woods to get back to where I had started. After a time I lost count of how many fish I'd caught and let go. When I came upon Marek, he'd caught even more. He was grinning from ear to ear, the shaggy moustache tightened at either end, and I was grinning too.

As a finale we went to the Dunajec a little way upstream from the reservoir that had engulfed its junction with the Bialka. It was sad to see it. From studying the map I knew that I had fished here before, but this wasn't the same river. I remembered it as big and sparkling and full of urgency as it pressed its way between high, tree-covered banks down a succession of long, foaming runs and surging pools full of the promise of trout and grayling. Now the water was sluggish, greyish, almost soapy, and carried with it an insistent smell of old socks. It swarmed with little roach and chub and shoals of enormously fat minnows. I wandered upstream for some distance from the bridge, hoping to find a spot that would recapture something of the old Dunajec, and failing.

Back at the bridge Marek had filled a bag with the corpses of minnows and other little fish. They were for his cat, he said. Her name was Pussy. She weighed more than 15 kilos, and would have nothing to do with tinned cat food. She insisted, Marek said with immense pride, on the best fresh fish and meat.

I left him at his house in Zakopane, without – to my regret – making Pussy's acquaintance. He said that the following day he was taking a class of schoolchildren into the mountains. 'It is only by educating the young that we can protect the mountains and the rivers,' he said, crushing my hand in his clasp. I wished him luck. I knew that he would never give up.

# Chapter 7

## Hungarian train

On the distinctly old-fashioned train from Kraków to Budapest, I shared an old-fashioned compartment with bench seats and sliding doors with two employees of Scottish Railways. They were holidaying together, spending a week on the tracks from Warsaw to Istanbul via Kraków, Budapest and Belgrade. For the elder it was the first time, but the younger was a veteran of European train networks. I asked him which was the worst journey he'd had: 16 hours overnight, Thessalonika to Belgrade, arriving nine hours late. He shook his head in horror at the memory.

Their conversation was intermittent and mainly about trains and train-related matters. They took evident enjoyment in analysing the shortcomings of the Polish system and stock, pointing out to each other where sections of worn track had been turned around and connected by dodgy joints, causing a loud, insistent clackety-clack that I rather enjoyed. The condition of the overhead lines was not good, they said, possibly even unsafe. The camber was another cause for concern. To pass from Poland into Slovakia, we followed the valley of the River Poprad where it has cut a north–south pass through a comparatively low-lying section of the Carpathians, the line taking innumerable bends, ascents and descents that often reduced our speed to a strenuous, creaking canter.

Part of the fun for the Scotsmen clearly lay in comparing and contrasting the advanced Caledonian system with the primitive Slavic one. But we all agreed that the more backward model had its plus-points. For instance, the leisurely pace made it possible to appreciate fully the beauty of the passing scenery – not so easy between, say, Carlisle and Edinburgh or Glasgow and Fort William. The river kept us company all the way to the Slovak border, racing along between thick stands of willow and alder which gave way at intervals to steep meadows and fields. Every now and then we slowed to jogging speed to pass by a sleepy village, or through a station with faded ochre buildings and sidings where retired wagons-lits quietly mouldered away.

The occasional polite intrusion of the ticket inspector, in cap and uniform and bearing an old-fashioned ticket machine of the type with a handle at the side, reinforced the impression that we had all retreated into an earlier, more sedate, age of rail. The corridor outside our compartment encouraged an occasional promenade to relieve buttocks tenderised by the unyielding seats, where one could stand by an open window, breathing in the keen fresh air. We liked the old-fashioned restaurant car which we all visited for dinner, though not at the same time (being British, we had to observe limits to our intimacy). It was presided over, not by an on-train catering services team, but by an elderly, immaculately uniformed head-waiter of lugubrious appearance who resembled his fellow countryman Béla

Lugosi, and spoke idiosyncratic English in a suitably theatrical manner. Instead of a damp, microwaved bacon-and-tomato roll in a polystyrene box, we were served spicy *gulyás* with rice on a warmed china plate set upon a table with a laundered white cloth.

I cannot speak for my Scottish friends but I also applauded the train company's policy of discretion regarding announcements. There were no matey greetings from the man in charge of the microwave, no pally commentary from the on-board customer services manager, no annoying exhortations to 'take a few moments of your time' to look at a safety leaflet, also available in braille on request. Generally in eastern Europe, announcements on trains were restricted to identifying the approaching station, or else non-existent. Journeys passed slowly, sometimes very slowly, but peacefully: the peace of authentic train noises, rattling wheels, the whoosh of tunnels, the screech of brakes, an occasional tooting whistle; a peace long ago banished from British railways by personal music systems, mobile phones, laptops and busybody witterings from train staff.

The lavatory on the Kraków–Budapest service was as period as the rest of it, but clean and in sound working order. On the wall was a complex diagram showing how the flushing mechanism worked. It was an indication of the antiquity of the Polish rail system, and its cautious approach to change, that the accompanying text should have been in Polish, Russian, German and French, but not English, now the global language of urination and evacuation as of everything else.

We finally crept into Budapest's Keleti station at ten o'clock on a hot June night, with rain threatening. We were an hour late, but there was no obsequious, meaningless apology for 'the inconvenience we know this will cause you'. By then I was thoroughly soothed and comforted by the rhythm of the journey. In a way I didn't want to leave the train, ever; it was a wrench to wish the Scotsmen well and embark upon the long plod down the platform and out into the city.

# Chapter 8

## A programme

One night at the end of January 2000 an earth and stone dam near the mining town of Baia Mare in north-western Romania collapsed. It had been constructed to contain a lagoon which was used to dump toxic waste from a gold extraction process operated by a joint Romanian–Australian venture called Aurul. In the darkness the contents of the lagoon – including 100 tons of cyanide as well as large quantities of zinc and lead – emptied into the nearest stream. By the time the alarm was raised, the spill was on its way down the River Someş, travelling west. Late in the afternoon of 1 February, 42 hours after the accident, it crossed the border into eastern Hungary, where the Someş becomes the Szamos. Early the next day it reached the Tisza, Hungary's greatest river (if you discount the Danube as belonging to no single nation).

Travelling at four kilometres an hour, it took the 20-kilometre-long contaminated plume 12 days to pass through Hungary. In that time the spillage became an international story. Newspapers and television bulletins carried pictures of dead and dying fish floating on the surface of the river and clogging its margins. The Romanian and Hungarian authorities wrung their hands and avoided saying anything, while journalists, ecologists and environmental campaigners roamed the river talking of catastrophe. The people most directly affected – anglers, fishing guides, birdwatchers, hunters, boat owners, the operators of the many marinas, campsites and holiday resorts – gathered at access points and on the bridges. No one could do anything but watch and wait and weep.

At the time the Tisza was described as finished, destroyed. After decades of reckless pollution from industrial, agricultural and human sources, this was the final, fatal blow. Along the Szamos and the upper Tisza the entire community of planktons, the microscopic organisms at the bottom of the river food chain, was reported to have been eliminated by the cyanide. The insects, molluscs, crustacea and the rest of the host of uncharismatic bottom feeders seemed also to have been wiped out. Altogether, 1,200 tons of fish were killed, and it is likely that two already endangered species – the sturgeon and the Danube salmon – were lost for good.

But even as the corpses were being gathered up, the river's self-healing system was at work. Within three weeks, testing in the upper catchment showed that plankton abundance was already recovering. Floods and warm weather that spring aided the cleansing. Populations of invertebrates returned to normal within two years. Emblematically, the large mayfly unique to the Tisza system – known as the Tisza Flower – was hatching in its usual vast numbers three years later. Although the dynamics of fish populations were certainly changed, there was no evidence of a major impact on overall abundance.

It was a different story for the human population dependent on the river. Tourism, the lifeblood of the Tisza basin since the decline of heavy industry and collapse of intensive agriculture, was beaten to its knees. The journalists who had recorded the death of the river had long since departed. No one paid attention to the biologists and their encouraging findings. Even places untouched by the cyanide – principally Lake Tisza, a reservoir that had been developed as a major holiday destination – were tainted by association. No one wanted to come to a poisoned river. Holiday bookings plummeted, businesses folded, many were forced to seek work elsewhere. Most of those affected by the disaster received no compensation of any kind.

Among those who watched and wept were Gábor and Márta Hegedüs. They had sunk everything they had, and every loan they could raise, into setting up a marina at Tiszafüred, a town on the eastern side of Lake Tisza. To them it seemed that all their hopes and dreams had been washed away and drowned by the slick of poison flowing silently between the endless lines of willows.

When I first met Gábor Hegedüs, in June 1990, he was an employee – albeit a highly disaffected one – of the Hungarian Anglers' Federation. This organisation seemed to have survived the crash of the political system that had created it in surprisingly sprightly shape. Its powers – including direct control of every river, stream, lake, pond, reservoir and canal in Hungary – were intact. It boasted a weighty secretariat based in a spacious suite of offices in downtown Budapest. My first appointment on reaching Hungary was with the secretary himself, Mr Béla Csákó.

My position as fishing correspondent for the *Financial Times* made me, in the eyes of the Hungarian Anglers' Federation, a visitor of some importance. Mr Csákó welcomed me warmly. He had a full head of silver hair, well greased and brushed back, and a suave smile that revealed two rows of dark, crooked teeth glinting with gold repairs. I heard later that Mr Csákó had previously worked in the Party's youth wing and that on becoming assistant-secretary to the Anglers' Federation, he had intrigued and plotted against his boss there whom he had eventually discredited and supplanted. He was said to be savage and tyrannical towards subordinates, but to me he was all genial charm. With a flourish he presented me with a printed itinerary for my stay, which invited me to deploy my 'professional skill' in pursuit of Hungary's fish.

To my dismay I realised, too late, that I had fallen into the stifling embrace of officialdom.

The following day, in accordance with the programme, I returned to the Federation's offices. Mr Csákó was absent on business even more important than me. The Federation's interpreter, a lively, loquacious old bird called Eva Deszenyi, introduced me to his deputy, Mr Attila Hunyadi. Mr Hunyadi was a large, shambling figure with a bright red, memorably ugly face, and spectacles so powerful that, from certain angles, they made his eyeballs appear to be the size of melons. He greeted me with great enthusiasm, pumping my arm up and down and pressing on me copies of the Federation's magazine, consisting largely of articles written by him and illustrated with photographs of him clasping fat carp and hideous catfish to his chest.

He led the way out of Budapest in his aged Wartburg, with Madame Deszenyi and I driving behind. As we passed through the suburbs I learned something of her history. She and her family had fled Hungary after the 1956 uprising, and had ended up in Australia. She was still very bitter towards the Australian immigration authorities: 'We are refugees but because we have passports they think there is something wrong with us, that we are Communist or something. So we come back. I am glad. I never like that country.'

She spoke five or six languages and had been able to make a reasonable living as an interpreter. But now there were so many problems in Hungary. Prices. Jobs. The cost of a flat. Her hands fluttered anxiously. Her daughter was living in Spain, married to a circus acrobat, except that he was too old to manage the high wire any more. She would like her daughter to come back, but where to live? How to work?

I asked her about the Federation. She pointed to the rear of Mr Hunyadi's Wartburg, part obscured by blue fumes. 'That Attila, he is a good man, not like Csákó, but all he thinks about is fish. He has a daughter, very ugly like him. I don't how he did what he must do to make her because he is always fishing! Soon I think he will not have job. The Federation has offices everywhere in Hungary, and camps and pensions and managers. How can we pay for that?'

We reached the Pilis Mountains, which are not mountains at all but a range of low hills north-west of Budapest. Pretty enough once, no doubt, they had been sacrificed to the Hungarian passion for weekend retreats, and were covered in a patchwork of fenced plots, each with its verandah-fronted cabin, vegetable patch and orchard. Near the small town of Pilisvörösvár a stream had been dammed to create a muddy little lake surrounded by potato fields and weekend cottages. At one end was a substantial two-storey building which was the Federation's guest-house.

On arrival, Mr Hunyadi summoned the manager, then addressed me at some length. Madame Deszenyi did not bother to translate. 'He is telling you about the fish. I do not know the names in English. They are fish.' We toured the lake. There were anglers all around, except for the section in front of the guest-house which was reserved for me. It was sizzlingly hot and many of the anglers were asleep on the bank in front of their cars, radios blaring unheard beside them.

Madame Deszenyi informed me that any sizeable fish I caught would be cooked for me by the manager's wife. I said that in England the kind of fish found in a lake like this – bream, roach, carp – were invariably returned alive. This information was relayed to Mr Hunyadi and the manager, who refused to believe it. This was a joke, an example of the famously obscure English sense of humour. I persisted and eventually convinced them. Their incomprehension and scorn were boundless. 'They want to know why English people go fishing if they don't like to eat fish. They want to know what you do with the fish.' I said something about looking at them and enjoying their beauty. There were more gales of hilarity.

I spent two days in this depressing place, with only the manager's silent, expressionless wife, and occasionally the manager himself, for company. I caught no fish, although I cannot say I tried very hard. It was not my kind of fishing at all. From Pilisvörösvár I drove to the next place on my programme, the Federation's guest-house on Lake Velence, a biggish sheet of water about an hour's drive south-west of Budapest. It was full of German and Austrian anglers whose favourite subjects of conversation were the decline of the fishing and the hopeless incompetence of Hungarians in all fields of human endeavour.

One morning a storm broke just as we were all preparing to go out in the boats. A gang of workmen who had been retiling the roof fled, leaving the upper-floor sitting room exposed to the rain. One of the Germans led our party up the stairs to inspect the damage. Water was pouring through the ceiling, spattering on the tables and soaking into the upholstery. Chunks of sodden plaster lay on the bulging cork-tile floor. The manageress appeared with a mop and some buckets. The Germans rocked with laughter. Had it never rained in Hungary before? Had they never heard of plastic sheeting? What a country! What a people! What a system!

Lake Velence – murky, suburban, grossly over-fished and visibly polluted – did nothing to lift my spirits. Balaton – the great lake further to the south-west, commonly referred to in guidebooks as 'the Hungarian Sea' – was even more dispiriting because of the greater scale of the crime against it. Virtually the whole of this amazing natural wonder had been converted into an aquatic holiday park, mainly for the benefit of Germans from the lower socio-economic levels, for whom it represented a cheap and convenient playground where they could have fun and throw their weight about. Most of them seemed to regard Hungary as a *de facto* province of Germany, and the Hungarians as a subject race whose role was to serve and count the *deutschmarks*.

Mr Csákó's programme directed me to the Anglers' Federation complex on the tip of the Tihany peninsular, which thrusts out like a thumb about a third of the way down the northern shore of Lake Balaton. The camp was full of German anglers, intent upon catching and taking home in their camper-van freezers as many of Balaton's carp and famous *fogas* (pike-perch) as they could get their hands on. As a result the staff were generally too busy carrying out their orders to pay much attention to me.

One hot afternoon I scrambled up the bluff behind the camp and spent some time sitting on an outcrop staring across the milky blue expanse of the lake, trying to imagine what it must have been like before the beast of mass tourism was unleashed. Later I wandered into the village of Tihany, which occupies a fabulous position, high above the water. It is an ancient settlement; the bones of the Árpád king, Andrew I, have lain for 950 years in the abbey crypt. Around the abbey are narrow streets of little cottages, built of volcanic tufa, from which the fishermen of Balaton once scanned the waters that sustained them and their families. That past had been comprehensively buried by the lava flow of visitors. The cottages were all souvenir shops now, and the nets draped outside were purely decorative. The stalls clogging the approaches to the abbey all sold the same baskets, the same chess sets and plastic dolls, the same mediocre pottery and embroidery. The stall-holders were united in a single purpose: laying their hands on more of the *deutschmarks* stuffed into the pockets of the Bermuda shorts swaying past.

'We have become . . . I don't know the word . . . people who ask for money in the street.'

'Beggars.'

'That is it.' Susan Péterfi gave me a strained smile. I had the impression that she did not want to say the word. We were in her office in the Academy of Science in Veszprém, a historic town north of Balaton whose unhappy fate had been to find itself in the middle of Hungary's main bauxite mining region. Susan had been drafted in by a friend of hers who was the Anglers' Federation manager for the Veszprém district to explain the next stage in my programme. Instead we were discussing the condition of Hungary. Eleven months before, the barbed-wire fence along the border with Austria had been torn down, allowing a flood of East Germans to pour into the West. Eight months before, the People's Republic of Hungary had reverted to being the Republic. In March 1990 Mikhail Gorbachev had agreed to withdraw Russian forces, and free elections had been held.

But Susan was far from exhilarated by the upheavals. 'It's true, for at least we have got rid of the Russians,' she said. 'But I am afraid what will happen now. You have seen the tourists. So many Germans coming with their *deutschmarks*, and we are here with our hands like this.' She cupped her hand at me. 'It is the same with everything. They say our industry will only live if it has German investment, but what is our future if we can't make it ourselves?'

From Veszprém I crossed a landscape wounded and scarred by mining operations to reach Tapolca where I met Susan's friend, Rajnai Árpád, who had been appointed by the Anglers' Federation to accompany me to Hungary's one and only trout stream. We drove out of town, past an immense bauxite complex encrusted in filth, through rolling grasslands until we came to a gentle, wooded dale where we stopped. I could see no sign of any running water. My companion, who spoke German but almost no English, signalled to me to follow him as he forged his way through a wall of vegetation. I found him standing on the edge of a high bank below which flowed the Viszló, no more than ten feet wide and apparently ten deep, unnervingly clear with thick tresses of coarse green weed.

Rajnai pointed at it and made casting motions. I pointed at the thickets that rose from both banks, almost meeting overhead, and tried to make him understand that fly-fishing would not be possible. He nodded and showed me his rod, which was about four feet long and designed for flicking a spinner under low branches.

He set off on his own into the undergrowth. I spent a very hot and annoying afternoon battling my way downstream in search of open spaces. Every now and then I caught glimpses of the Viszló as it tunnelled its way in the direction of Lake Balaton. In one or two spots I actually managed to land a fly in the water. The weed seethed with shrimp and other invertebrate life, but of trout or any other fish I saw nothing.

The little river was doomed anyway. Susan Péterfi had told me that the water in it came from deep underground and was pumped into it as a by-product of bauxite extraction. The mine was due to close the following year, whereupon the Viszló would cease to flow.

# Chapter 9

## The fishiest river

The tumbling down of the worm-eaten structures of the old system had cleared space in Hungary, as elsewhere, for a breed of eager entrepreneurs to sprout like mustard-and-cress. During the few days I had spent in Budapest immediately after my arrival, I had made contact with one of them, Tamás Hajas. He was dark, bearded, snappily dressed, and smoked a lot of Marlboros, all the time tapping his fingers, brown eyes darting hither and thither, perpetually on the lookout for new business openings. He worked for a German company that sold sporting equipment, and also organised fishing and hunting trips for foreign clients. Through the interpreter he'd brought with him, he launched into a tirade against the Anglers' Federation.

'They are his enemies. They are Stalinists. They are only interested in keeping their power and stopping people like him. He says everything must change. Organisations like the Federation are finished. He says . . . oh, so many things.' The interpreter's voice hardened. 'Mr Hajas has lived in Vienna,' she added sarcastically. 'He knows how they do things in the West.'

I didn't much care for him either. But an invitation to accompany him to his fishing camp on the Tisza, the river of Hungary's Great Plain, was opportune. Mr Csákó's programme had made me heartily sick of Anglers' Federation lodges, bauxite mines, German pothunters, suburbanised countryside and murky lakes. I knew nothing much about the Tisza but the name alone seemed to hold out the promise of something more elemental and less dull. Without telling Mr Csákó, I accepted. After returning to Budapest from Lake Balaton, I rendezvoused with Hajas and followed his car east towards the Great Plain.

His camp was near a riverside settlement called Kisköre, where the Tisza had been dammed to create a lake into which its notoriously destructive winter floods could be diverted. The lake was taking its time to fill, and in the meantime the river flowed past strings of islands that separated it from a network of meres, lagoons and marshes. As a result of some shadowy deal with a malleable official, Hajas had managed to obtain a lease on one of these islands. The arrangement was not sanctioned by the Anglers' Federation, hence the state of war between them.

The camp had an improvised air about it. It consisted of a cluster of canvas tents in a clearing, the biggest of which was the kitchen and, for want of a better word, dining area. Salamis, smoked sausages and cheeses dangled from the overhead frame. A canvas larder, crammed with duck eggs and various leftovers, hung from the main strut. The table supported a battery of bottles of beer and *palinka*, the Hungarian spirit distilled from plums or apricots. Discarded cans and bottles were scattered across the ground outside, along with rat-gnawed loaves of stale bread. A short distance away was a little tent like a telephone box: a Russian-style shit-house, I was informed. One glance into its miasmal interior was enough to immobilise my bowels for the length of my stay.

The kitchen faced the soapy green water of a lagoon. A path led from the camp in the other direction to a wide expanse of yellowish water moving from right to left with massive serenity. This was the Tisza.

The plan was for me to be left at the camp in the care of a grimy, unshaven, dark-skinned fellow called Csaba. He spoke only Hungarian, of which the one word I could pronounce with confidence at that time was *gulyás*, so sparkling conversation was not in prospect. But a party of Germans was expected the next day, and it was confidently predicted that at least one of them would speak English. I couldn't see that this would help much unless they also spoke Hungarian, but I kept my thoughts to myself.

Before returning to the relentless pursuit of business opportunities in Budapest, Hajas had time for a brief excursion. He and I, together with a hunting chum of his called Zoltán who spoke fluent English, headed upstream in the camp boat. Storms in the past few days had raised the river and given it its jaundiced colour. The weather was hot and menacing, the sun a hazy ball in a colourless sky, the air still and heavy. Hajas steered the boat towards what looked like an unbroken bed of reeds, which parted at the last moment to reveal a channel just wider than our craft.

We followed it into open water. Ahead, poised on a branch of a waterlogged tree, was a bird about the size of a chicken with plumage the shade of dead reeds and a sharp, olive beak. It was a bittern, the first I had ever seen. We entered a forest of drowned trees. In the far distance the steeple of a church pricked the sky. Cormorants and herons watched us from the skeletons of the trees. Hajas took us into a wide channel, the water dead still and dark as night.

This was the old Tisza, as it had been before engineering rearranged it to a more convenient place. Beds of water lilies extended from the fringes, ruffled towards the centre where the flowers tilted up, dazzling white, with golden, nectarous stamens into which bees and butterflies dipped hungrily. The water was clear over the black mud. We cast spinners into likely spots while Hajas talked of fishing. On the water he relaxed and seemed more human, less of a caricature of the slick, eager money-man. Once, he said, he caught 90 pike along this channel, in one day. That was in autumn, when the pike fed. Winter was even better; you could fish through the ice or crunch across it to shoot duck and geese.

We caught nothing. We went back to the camp and Hajas and Zoltán left for Budapest. Under the influence of several doses of *palinka*, I went to sleep in my tent for a time. When I woke up, I wandered back to the river. Large pale insects were lifting themselves from the surface into uncertain flight. The numbers increased gradually until the air above the water was pulsing with them. Along the banks objects like little broken twigs surfaced and broke open to reveal segmented bodies and translucent wings struggling to dry. I recognised the insect as the mayfly, known here as the Tisza Flower. At home, on the chalkstreams of Hampshire and Wiltshire, the mayfly's season roused trout into a frenzy of feasting. On the Tisza the feasting was left to the ducks and moorhens, cruising the fringes with their beaks open, and to great squadrons of swallows and wagtails that skimmed and swooped, intercepting insects in mid-air or dipping low to pluck them off the surface, leaving minute rings in the water.

By evening enormous clouds of mayfly had formed above the flag irises and marigolds along the banks and around the branches of the trees. The male of the species rises and falls as it lies in wait for a passing female, and en masse the vertical oscillation is suggestive of some kind of ecstatic ballet. In fact the up-and-down movement is simply more energy-efficient than hovering, and enables the eyes on top of the creature's head to remain focused on its air space and any potential partner ahead. After mating, the males soon perish from exhaustion, while the females rest for a time in the trees and bushes, before the final metamorphosis in which they shed their body coverings, lay their eggs on the water, and die.

Each afternoon I watched this amazing, silent show. I also went fishing with Csaba and caught absolutely nothing, the Hungarian word for which – *semmi* – was added to my vocabulary, together with *nem ehes*, which means 'not hungry'. Csaba would grin and point at the soupy water, indicating that conditions were not favourable. We became so desperate we even tried spearing carp in a reedy bay off the lagoon, but they fled at our approach. The German party did not materialise.

One afternoon, sensing my boredom, Csaba suggested a river trip. The omens were not encouraging as the sky was darkening rapidly in the east and dispatching a steady stream of swollen black clouds in our direction. But I took the view that anything would be better than a further vigil beside my rod pondering aspects of nothingness, so off we went. There was a murmur of thunder as we swung across the current. The clouds came together and filled the sky, threading it with lightning. The thunder became louder. When the rain came, it was as if someone had switched on a power shower. The surface of the river was lashed into a hissing maelstrom. Csaba did some more grinning and steered us into a little inlet where three tents were grouped under a big willow. The campers, two couples and half-a-dozen children, stood around in dripping oilskins.

An awning was stretched between two of the tents, under which a blackened pot was suspended over a fire. A pungent fishy smell came from it. A bowl was produced, filled and handed to me. It contained a dark stew with gobbets of pale flesh, firm and slightly gelatinous. I asked what it was.

Hungarian lad with head of catfish

'*Harcsa*', they said with enthusiasm, pronouncing it 'horcha' with plenty of rolling of the 'r'. One of the boys beckoned me to follow him. He led the way along the bank to a post on which was jammed the head of a fish. Its mouth was almost as wide as its head. Above the mouth protruded two feelers, eight or ten inches long. Four smaller barbels hung from the lower jaw. The eyes, like little black beads, were positioned high on the sloping skull. The mouth was equipped, not with teeth, but with two bars, top and bottom, like hardened sandpaper, for grinding and pulverising. The skin over the head was mottled green, paling beneath the gills to jelly-fish white. Had the body been present, it would have been almost eel-like, tapering from the head to a fleshy, muscular tail, the whole glistening with a thick coat of slime.

I had never seen one in the flesh before, but I knew what this was. In Hungarian, *harcsa*; in German, *wels*; in English catfish; in Latin, *Silurus glanis*; in whatever language unchallengeably the most repellent looking freshwater fish that swims.

I longed to catch one, and began to dream about them. But it wasn't going to happen at Hajas's camp. The Tisza needed to drop, and the weather needed to settle. Fortunately Mr Csákó's programme came to the rescue. It had allocated me a slot about a week later a little way up the Tisza, at Tiszafüred, which was how I first came to meet Gábor Hegedüs and his wife Márta.

Gábor knew Tamás Hajas a little, disliked him thoroughly, and disapproved strongly of his maverick operation. But, although he entirely lacked Hajas's high-octane ambition, he had also, in his own way, been affected by entrepreneurial urges. As well as issuing licences and organising affairs on behalf of the Anglers' Federation, Gábor had set up a small operation catering for visiting German and Austrian anglers. This had received a huge boost the previous season with the capture by an Austrian client of a catfish of 54 kilos, and the subsequent appearance of this whiskery monstrosity on the cover of Germany's leading angling magazine in the arms of its joyful captor.

The publicity had inspired a rush of catfish fanatics whose expectations had put considerable pressure on Gábor. I had never met a man who looked more permanently worried. He had thinning blond hair, a drooping, straw-coloured moustache and blue eyes forever clouded with anxieties. Luckily for him, his wife was both a partner and a pillar. Márta was a strong, solid woman with a handsome, high-cheekboned face, and a serious, almost stern expression which lit easily into a wide, generous smile.

As a teenager, nearly 20 years before, she had spent a month with an English pen-friend and her family at Telford in Shropshire. The experience had left her with an easy command of English and an abiding warmth towards English people, English ways and English culture. The reverse side of her Anglophilia was a fierce Teutophobia. She did the accounts and attended to the office side of Gábor's enterprise, but had as little as possible to do with his clients. I was once sitting under a vine-covered trellis in their garden when a group of German anglers turned up. Gábor was out so I called Márta. She came out on to the verandah, looked with evident distaste at the BMW and Mercedes outside her gate, and greeted the Germans frostily. She could speak German perfectly well but made no effort to engage with them. After the last in a succession of chilly silences they left. She laughed and brought me a cold beer.

'Look at them with their big stomachs and big cars,' she said scornfully. 'They have no good fishing in Germany so they come to poor Hungary to take ours and expect us to be grateful. They pay to come and shout, but I don't have to listen, that is Gábor's job.'

He was too preoccupied with administrative matters to spare time for fishing with me, so he arranged for me to be taken out by his boatman, who was called Zsolt and was younger, and a lot cleaner, than Csaba. I met him at the water's edge soon after dawn. As we set off, the sun rose in a blaze of pink and gold behind the trees, but enough of the night chill remained to cast trails of mist over the dark water, and the seats were wet with dew. We went downstream, past a post recording that we were 415 kilometres away from the Tisza's junction with the Danube. We passed other fishermen, still as herons in their boats. Some had been out all night. None reported any success.

Zsolt tied up to the trailing branch of a willow at a spot that looked to me no different from countless others. A deep chorus of frogs, like a badly out-of-tune wind band, came from the rushes behind us. Zsolt baited the hook with a fat worm and a large burrowing beetle-like creature which he kept in a jar of earth. Having studied tales of the catfish's legendary voraciousness, I had expected something more substantial, like a freshly killed puppy or the whole stomach of a wild boar. I lobbed the cocktail out, propped the rod against the side of the boat, and settled down to wait. Time passed, slowly, then more slowly. The sun ascended. The frogs fell silent. The seat got harder. My longing for some-thing, anything, to happen became steadily more intense, as did the conviction that it never would.

Then it did. Without any warning the rod tip was wrenched down. I did nothing apart from look at it. Zsolt sprang down the boat, grasped the rod and struck. '*Harcsa*,' he cried, grinning, and handed the rod to me. I felt a solid, shuddering resistance, and pictured the wide head shaking in the depths, the muscle-packed tail searching for some root or sunken branch to twist around. But the tackle was strong and I hauled the fish in without much trouble. By catfish standards it was a tiddler, no more than six or seven pounds. Zsolt unhooked it and offered me a slippery hand-shake. I smiled. He smiled. We resumed the vigil.

It grew hotter and hotter. The swirls of feeding fish diminished, then ceased altogether. The silent water kept flowing while everything else seemed to sink into a state of suspension. After several more hours I was put ashore, hungry, thirsty, buttock-sore.

We ate my catfish for lunch the next day, made by Márta into a rich, tasty stew with paprika, onion and garlic. Eased by two bottles of white wine from somewhere near Balaton, Gábor's English suddenly flowered. He insisted on taking me for an excursion. It was still very hot, but a big wind had got up, driving waves up the river, flattening the reedbeds and whirling dust around the picnickers. He took his boat through a channel into the lake. Yellow breakers foamed around the dead trees and dashed against the reeds. Using field glasses I was able to make out the same church steeple that I had seen with Hajas.

Gábor had no time for Hajas's flouting of the regulations. 'He thinks the Federation is stupid. He is right sometimes. But you must stop people doing what is bad for the river and the fishing, like putting in poison and netting too many fish and using . . . I don't know English word . . .' He raised his arm and made stabbing motions. 'I don't think you have this is England.' I refrained from mentioning my spearing expedition with Csaba.

Gábor was worried about his business. 'The Germans, they come and they drink and they drink, and they go fishing and they don't feel so good and they don't fish so good and then they say the fishing is not good.' He tugged his moustache and stared out over the lake. 'I worry because I think maybe they are right. There are too many fishermen, not so many fish.'

In the evening, my last with them, they made a fire in the garden. Márta brought out bread, sliced onions and tomatoes, and slabs of pork fat. Gábor gave me a sharpened stick on which I stuck a piece of fat and held it in the flames until it began to run. I smeared it on the bread, added a layer of onions and tomatoes, and sprinkled paprika over it. Sparks rose into a purple sky as the wind dropped. The flames licked at the hissing fat. I watched Gábor and Márta and their two children, faces half-lit by the fire, chins glistening with grease.

Gábor and Márta Hegedüs, Tiszafüred, 2008

Eighteen years on, Gábor looked more anxious than ever. His hair had mostly gone and what was left was grey. The moustache drooped down over his mouth like a permanent comment on his situation. The clouded blue eyes were dragged down by the sagging skin on his cheekbones.

He met me at the railway station in Tiszafüred. He was driving a beaten-up van – 12 years old, he said, as if concerned I might think he was getting rich. He seemed pleased to see me, but not effusively so. I asked him how the marina business was doing. Not good, he said, puffing out his cheeks. Actually, as I found out later, it was not bad, but Gábor's spirit seemed to have become shackled by chronic pessimism. He had only two moods: gloom, and a slightly fevered excitement that gripped him when he began to float his grand ideas for expanding the business and making some real money.

Márta was waiting at the marina, outside a wooden building with a verandah that served both as a bar for the customers and administrative centre for the business. She was a little wider, a little more solid, her hair – cut short in exactly the same style – now flecked with grey. But the smile was as I had remembered it.

I was surprised by how rusty her English had become. She apologised for this repeatedly, seeming genuinely troubled. She never had a chance to practise it, she said. She used to keep it up by reading children's books in English to her son and daughter – *Swallows and Amazons* was a favourite – and reading novels herself. Now the children were grown up and she had lost the reading habit. One of the pleasures of my return visit was the joy she took in rediscovering the language she loved, like someone tasting good food and wine again after a long period of abstinence.

For some reason that I couldn't fathom, I didn't stay with them and never visited their house. They had arranged rooms for me a couple of streets away from the marina, with a young English-speaking couple who had noisy dogs and no children. The result was that I saw Gábor and Márta only at the marina, where they were both on duty from eight or nine in the morning until sundown seven days a week. It was as if they only existed there; or if they had an alternative life, it was not open to inspection. Each morning I had breakfast at a hotel across the road from the marina, eating my eggs and ham outside in the sun, watching the green Tisza slip by. In the evening I ate with them, very simply, at a table inside the bar/office.

Actually I quite liked the arrangement. Once I had been shown around the wooden self-catering cabins built for holiday lets, and had wandered along the lagoon past the cruisers and fishing boats, there was nothing for me to do at the marina except drink beer and chat with Gábor and Márta when they were not dealing with requests and complaints from customers, which they were most of the time. I kept asking Gábor if there was any chance of my getting out on the river, maybe borrowing some tackle and going after a catfish again. He would nod and rub his cheekbones and pull at his moustache and make vague promises.

I borrowed one of the bicycles they hired out to customers, and set off to follow a paved cycle path that had been laid along the top of the embankment beside the river. It was a pleasant ride, made less exciting than it might have been by the necessity of returning the same way; the alternative being to follow the 80-kilometre circuit of Lake Tisza, which I reckoned was beyond my powers. On one side of the embankment, beyond a strip of trees, fields of maize and sunflowers stretched away to a distant horizon. On the other, confined between its lines of willows, the river rolled south. Occasionally it turned away from the embankment, to leave reed-fringed, lily-carpeted lagoons with dead trees rising from them on which cormorants rested until hunger drove them off to hunt. The far bank was broken at various points to reveal glimpses of the lake.

This flat, tame landscape is man-made, its river subdued by generations of hydraulic engineers. The Tisza has kept its name, but is otherwise severed from its past. But I could not fish a river or cycle along it without needing to know its story.

It rises on the Ukrainian side of the Carpathians, close to the border with Romania. As a mountain stream, it flows through the south-easterly tip of that obscure and neglected corner of Europe known at various times as Carpatho-Ukraine, Carpathian Russia, TransCarpathia, and – most familiarly – Ruthenia. It descends from the forested hills to pass by the city of Khust, entering Hungary at Tiszabecs, the first of scores of towns and villages that take their names from it.

It turns south at Tokaj, beneath the volcanic slopes where for a thousand years grapes have ripened and rotted before being made into sugary wine the colour of topaz. One river settlement follows another — Tiszanagyfalu, Tiszaladány, Tiszalök, Tiszadob, Tiszagyulaháza, Tiszatarján, Tiszadorogma — until Tiszafüred is reached. To the east of Tiszafüred is the Hortobágy, the last remaining significant expanse of the *puszta* (the word means 'bare' or 'bereft' and refers to the vast grassland steppe that once covered the whole of the Great Plain). To the west is the Jászag, where an assortment of unremarkable places with names like Jászfelsöszentgyörgy and Jászalsószentgyörgy recall the arrival in the thirteenth century of the nomadic Jász people from the Caucasus. The Tisza receives the last of its important tributaries, the Maros (Mureş in Romanian), at Szeged. Ten miles or so further on it crosses into Serbia, joining the Danube short of Belgrade.

Until the dismemberment of the Austro-Hungarian Empire effected by the Treaty of Trianon in 1920, the Tisza was entirely Hungarian. Symbolically and spiritually it still is: the liquid spine of the Alföld, the Great Plain, that semi-mythical wellspring of the Magyar imagination. But the self-image moulded by the plain and the river is rooted in the distant past, and has little or no connection with the geographical reality that has obtained for the past century or more.

Geographically, the dominant characteristic of the Tisza is determined by the remarkable flatness of the landscape through which it flows. Its floodplain extends from the Carpathians in the east almost to the Danube in the west. Left to itself, it traversed its plain in a succession of epic meanders in the course of which its flow deviated to all points of the compass. Life beside it, or anywhere near, was a precarious and highly specialised affair.

In early spring the melting of the Carpathian snows would send yellow floods churning down river. The low banks could not contain a rise of more than a foot or so, and in a single day or night thousands of square miles of marsh and low-lying land would be converted into a vast, turbid lake. A journey between Budapest and the important trading city of Debrecen, on the eastern flank of the Great Plain, could be interrupted for weeks until the Tisza ferry crossings reappeared.

To the few travellers who crossed the plain and recorded their impressions, its flatness and emptiness – a 'great nothingness', the novelist Mór Jókai called it – were overwhelming. Landmarks were as rare as objects floating in the ocean: a reed hut, a sheep pen, the long pole of a draw-well. Settlements were scattered far apart and incredibly isolated. Only in dry weather was it possible to travel easily between them along raised mudbanks. The people generally stayed where they were, poling or paddling about on necessary trips in flat-bottomed boats. Winters were savage. In the worst of them, packs of starving, green-eyed wolves came down from the snowbound mountains to range across the ice, harrying humans and livestock alike. Anyone foolhardy or desperate enough to attempt a journey took straw with them, which they burned to keep the wolves at bay.

Even by the standards of those times, the lives of the river people were hard. But the river did provide for them as well as make trouble. The floods spread silt across the fields on which, under the summer sun, crops sprang forth easily. Immense flocks of sheep and long-horned cattle grazed the grasslands. Geese, duck and lesser waterfowl abounded. And then there were the fish.

The Tisza was famous for sturgeon, carp, pike and catfish. Edward Browne, the doctor son of the celebrated Sir Thomas Browne, author of *Religio Medici*, passed through in 1669 and wrote of the 'Tibiscus or Theiss' being 'esteemed the most Fishy river in Europe if not in the world, insomuch they have a common saying that it consisteth of two parts water and one part fish'. Such abundance encouraged tall piscine tales. 'It is said,' recorded the normally sober and sceptical John Paget in the 1840s, 'that after an overflow the fish have been left in such quantities as to be used for feeding the pigs and manuring the ground.'

For the best part of ten centuries after the spread of the Magyars across the Great Plain, the Tisza was left to its wayward self. But in the 1840s a new generation of enlightened aristocratic reformers were making their mark in Budapest, and they determined to address the backwardness, lawlessness and inaccessibility that characterised eastern Hungary. Under the direction of the most celebrated of the reformers, the neurotically self-doubting, manically energetic Count István Széchenyi, the project to tame the Tisza began. It took 35 years to complete, by which time Széchenyi had long since blown out his brains in the asylum near Vienna where he was confined. More than 100 of the Tisza's famously extravagant meanders were cut by new channels. Its length was reduced by more than 350 miles, and as a result many villages found themselves beside loops of ex-river, miles from the new course.

At the time Hungary was struggling to emerge from its centuries of subordination within the Habsburg Empire, and its poets, story-tellers and painters were searching for a source of images of the nation's newly rediscovered soul and identity. Many of them found it in the fabulously unforgiving landscape of the Alföld, and in the elemental lives of its people. Here, beneath a flawless sky confined only by the shimmering horizon, the noble and tragic destiny of the Magyar had been played out.

> My home and my world are there
> In the Alföld, flat as the sea,
> From its prison my soul soars like an eagle
> When the infinity of the plains I see.

These lines were written by Hungary's most famous poet, Sándor Petőfi, whose death in 1849, fighting in Hungary's doomed attempt to achieve independence, contributed appreciably to the mythologising process. They conjured the magnetic pull on the Magyar's soul of the *puszta*, where, across the endless expanse of grass, dust, salt and sand, moustachioed teak-brown shepherds in wide hats and rank sheepskin cloaks, and brown-eyed, booted horsemen, followed their flocks and herds, fought, drank, loved and perished to the strains of the gypsy's lament and the stamping *csárdás*.

As one would expect, Anglo-Saxon observers were sceptical of the myth-making and suspicious of the Magyar's estimation of himself. Andrew Augustus Paton, an indefatigable traveller through eastern Europe in the 1840s, found him 'generous, courageous, sincere', but devoid of any urge 'to labour, to improve, to take pains and persevere'. Most damningly, Paton concluded that 'as to the value of manure they have not the least idea'. John Paget was chiefly struck by the characteristic pride of the Hungarian:

> Which leads him to look down on every other nation by which he is surrounded with sovereign contempt. A Magyar never moves when he can sit still and never walks when he can ride. His step is slow and measured, his countenance pensive, his address imposing and dignified. His character is a singular mixture of habitual passiveness and melancholy mixed up with a great susceptibility to excitement.

Whatever he is, Paget seems to be saying, it is far removed from the English model. (Nevertheless the Englishman fell wholly under the sway of the land and its people, marrying a Hungarian countess and spending the rest of his days managing her estates in Transylvania. He is buried in Koloszvár – Cluj in present-day Romania.)

Inevitably the taming of the Tisza was followed by the taming of the Great Plain. In the course of the twentieth century it was transformed from a wilderness into an agricultural powerhouse. Irrigated from the Tisza, the arid grasslands became orchards, vineyards, vast fields of sunflowers and maize. The low whitewashed *tanyas* where the cowboys used to rest in the shade of the spreading acacias were sold off as weekend houses for the well-to-do of Budapest or turned into guest-houses and riding centres. With large-scale sheep and cattle herding eliminated, the cowboys themselves – the *csikósok* – were recycled as a visitor attraction, employed by the state to pull on their waistcoats and tight breeches, adjust their wide-brimmed hats and perform horseback tricks.

The demystifying of the Alföld is summed up by the fate of the famous nine-arch bridge over the River Hortobágy, and of the equally famous inn beside it. This was once the great meeting-place of the eastern *puszta*. At the cattle markets, the grasslands beside the river's lazy green water were shrouded in dust raised by the herds, watched over by the *csikósok* and their Puli dogs. Buyers, sellers and travellers found sanctuary at the inn, the Nagy Csárda. Outside, every inch of space was taken by conveyances: wagons with teams of oxen, horses, buggies, chaises, drags, coaches, diligences, all gathered into a great camp. Inside, the air was thick with pipe and cigar smoke and alive with the music of tambur, seven-holed pipes, goatskin bagpipes, cymbolons and fiddles.

Petöfi came here and sang of the beauty of the innkeeper's wife. An English woman, Mrs Birkbeck, claimed to have witnessed the single most celebrated incident in the history of the Nagy Csárda: the night the notorious bandit, Rósza Sándor, arrived with the police hot on his heels, staying long enough to perform a wild dance with his axe before fleeing under a hail of gunfire. ('The man was young, of middle stature and muscular frame . . . his grave pale face had a striking expression of sadness, yet his eyes were like burning coals,' wrote Mrs Birkbeck, possibly betraying a weakness for romantic fiction.)

These days the Nagy Csárda plays host to tourists, who queue for their bowls of *gulyás* while a tape of canned pseudo-gypsy music plays. Air-conditioned coaches, BMWs, Mercedes and Opels have replaced the tethered horses. Touts advertise tickets for the riding shows. Where the cattle once stamped and snorted is a sprawl of souvenir shops. A concrete stand has been built to provide a view of the nine-arch bridge.

Since 1990 the economy of the whole region has faltered badly. The collapse of the Communist system led to financial support for factories and farms being cut or withdrawn altogether. Many were forced to close, causing both serious unemployment and an exodus to Budapest or abroad. Tourism, always seen as the benign saviour, took up some of the slack, but was halted in its tracks by the cyanide poisoning. Since then there has been a slow retrenchment, but unemployment in the east of the country remains significantly higher than the national average.

As for the Tisza itself, it came through the pollution calamity but remains in deep trouble. A recent study identified a host of factors ranged against it: heavy metal contamination from the mines of north-west Romania, pollution from paper and cellulose plants in Romania and Ukraine and from chemical factories at Miskolc and Szolnok, long-term nitrate loading from agricultural run-off, grossly inadequate water treatment resulting in sewage dumping on a huge scale. The marvel is that the river still functions at all, and that there are any fish left.

It was hardly surprising therefore that Gábor and Márta should have taken a sombre view of life. They had staked everything on the marina and it had been a struggle all the way. The rent charged by the state for the site kept rising, and Gábor was still embroiled in a long-running legal dispute with the Anglers' Federation over the issuing of permits to anglers. The fishing side of the business had fallen away anyway, although the holiday lets were doing well. At odd moments he would put aside his worries and dwell on his dreams of expansion. He wanted to build a bridge across to a reedy island and develop it with more cabins, extend the moorings for boats. Márta would shake her head. They could not afford to borrow any more, she said.

Márta was keenly curious about my life, which made her quite unusual among the people I met. She wanted to hear what had happened to the children I had told her about in 1990. She frowned when I said I had been divorced, smiled when I said I was married again with two small daughters, and demanded to see their photographs. She was preoccupied equally by the business and by family matters, particularly the impending wedding of her daughter. There was much talk of dresses and guest lists, and several times a day she would engage in long telephone conversations with the bride-to-be about the preparations, after which she would look serious and thoughtful. When I reminded her that a wedding was supposed to be a joyous occasion, Márta shook her head and said she would be glad when it was over.

There were other worries. Márta and her sister were estranged as a result of something that had been said between them. Her son was working for a computer company in Budapest, living on his own and spending all his spare time surfing the internet. This was the modern world and Márta gave me the strong impression that she did not care much for it. She was a regular worshipper at the Calvinist church in Tiszafüred and maintained a gently, humanely Calvinist outlook on life. When she was a student in Budapest, she said, she had smoked and drunk and partied, but it was not easy to imagine.

In general she was less inclined than before to discuss Hungary and its problems, preferring to stick to safer subjects such as family affairs and literature. In part this probably reflected a general tendency as we grow older to steer away from politics and big social issues, as we understand more how little we truly understand. Also 1990 had clearly been a watershed for the countries of eastern Europe, and the future had been the preoccupation of the moment. Now that future had become the recent past. For Márta and Gábor it had brought a measure of fulfilment and independence, but also pain and anxiety. Life had proved to be the usual mixture of confusion, disappointment and pleasure. Clearly no golden age had dawned: unemployment in Tiszafüred was running at 30 per cent, most of the factories had shut, much of the good agricultural land had been annexed by the lake, the river had been poisoned.

Márta felt out of sympathy with the new order that had arisen from the ruins of the old. I did wonder too – it wasn't the kind of question you could ask – if her reticence about the present might have reflected a fear of being suspected of nostalgia for the past. I remembered a conversation with her in 1990 in which she had expressed irritation with the righteous damnation of every aspect of the old days. 'The young people criticise us for allowing Communism,' she had said, chopping onions and tomatoes for a salad. 'They seem to hate us because we did not have the revolution. But it wasn't so bad for ordinary people. It wasn't like Russia. There was work, enough food, there were books and plays and music, and good schools and hospitals, and it was peaceful. Now I am expected to feel guilty because I didn't do anything about the Communists.'

Their daughter, known as Panka, was a lovely, delightful girl, blonde and slender, full of plans for her new life. She said she remembered me from that evening when we had all sat around the fire eating bread and pork fat. On my last evening this time we ate al fresco by the river with various of her and her fiancé's friends. There was a thick venison stew, followed by spicy soup with chunks of sausage, red from the paprika, tomatoes and peppers. No catfish, though. We sat at trestle tables as darkness fell and the mosquitoes marshalled their forces. Bottles of Hungarian Merlot circulated and Gábor became vivacious. I noticed that Márta drank almost no wine.

I told her a ludicrous, hoary fisherman's tale about a man who walks along a river bank and comes upon an angler patiently watching his float. He asks the angler what he is after. 'Bream,' the angler replies. 'Bream, eh? What are they like?' 'Dunno. Never caught one.' She listened intently, with her chin in her hand, as if I was revealing some extraordinary truth. At the punchline she tilted back her head and laughed delightedly; as much, I suspected, from the pleasure of having been able to follow my nonsense as with its humour.

I asked her about Hungarian writers and she wrote me a little list of novelists she liked – Péter Esterházy, Kálmán Mikszáth, Zsigmond Moritz, Frigyes Karinthy. I promised to search for English translations when I got back.

By now the mosquitoes were feasting hard and the conversation was punctuated by the slapping of hands against arms and necks. The river – black against the trees, silvered where it reflected the sky – slid noiselessly by. Márta, I felt, was pretty much indifferent to it. But at the same time I had an image of her chained to it, her fate intertwined with its fate, watching it for years to come.


In the end I did manage to get out on the water. Gábor couldn't take me; he never dared leave the marina for long in case some crisis galloped up in his absence. But he arranged for me to have an outing with one of his regulars, a small, elderly dentist called Attila, who kept a houseboat and a fishing skiff at the marina and came from Budapest most weekends, leaving his wife behind with their cats in their flat on Gellért Hill. He had some words of English, which he extracted from the recesses of his memory with difficulty, rather like teeth, and displayed with pride. He had an impish air, and his movements were quick and precise. Everything in the boat – rods, seats, net, tackle, bait – was arranged with great care to be within reach when the moment came.

It never did. We tried upstream and then downstream. We asked several anglers, some of whom had been at it all night, if they had

had any luck. None of them had. I sat in the bow of Attila's boat, listening to the soughing of the wind in the trees, the rustling of the reeds, the occasional swirl and splash along the margins, and retreated into a familiar meditative daze. It was as if I had merely resumed the vigil begun with Zsolt 18 years before.

'Catfish not feed,' Attila said superfluously. The sun came up over the willows, sucking the last trails of vapour from the surface. He wound in the baits, stowed the rods away, and steered back to the marina. I thanked him and wished him well for his forthcoming trip. I had diagnosed Attila as being in the grip of a severe and probably incurable attack of catfish fever. It had driven him to the Po in Italy and the Ebro in Spain, but the hot catfish destination of the moment was the Ural River in Kazakhstan. Attila shook his head in remembered wonder at the size and abundance of those Kazakh cats. He had already been to the Ural three times and was about to go again.

What about the Danube Delta, I asked? Plenty of catfish there. Attila shook his head vigorously. 'I not like Romanian people,' he said, the words coming at intervals.

The world may be changing, I reflected as I retreated to the Hotel Hableana for some much-needed breakfast, but not everything in it. And one of the things that would never change would be the antipathy between Hungarians and Romanians. Ideologies wax and wane, systems come and go, tyrants fall, democracies totter, but the age-old hostility between these neighbours is as constant as the current of the Tisza itself.

# Chapter 10

## Balaton

Lake Balaton from the castle at Szigliget

The evening light restores some of the lost magic to Balaton.

I was looking down on the lake from the ruins of the medieval castle at Szigliget, a few miles along the northern shore from the western end. The sun was dying to my right, flooding golden light across the water to hide the ugliness of the holiday resorts. The hills and bluffs above Balatongyörök and the slopes of the table-topped Badacsony dropped darkly into the opalescent water. The bay west of Szigliget sparkled like the Field of the Cloth of Gold. The vast lake seemed at peace with itself; the land behind it beautiful and full of pleasing possibilities.

In the 1830s or 40s John Paget made an excursion from Budapest to Balatonfüred, also on the northern shore but well to the east of Szigliget. He bathed in the lake, danced with the local ladies of quality, disparaged the primitive facilities, condescended to one and all, and commented that: 'It is difficult for an Englishman to imagine a fine inland lake of this kind totally useless for the purpose of commerce or pleasure . . . I believe there is not a single trading barge and certainly not one sailing-boat on the whole lake.'

Were he still with us, Paget could hardly complain that the lake was under-exploited now. The beaches seethe with sunbathers. The shallow waters buzz with speedboats and pleasure craft. The southern shore is one unbroken trail of hotels, apartments, marinas, chalets, camps, bars, restaurants and amusement parks; and while the resorts of the northern shore pride themselves on serving a classier clientele, the business they conduct is just the same.

I was in two minds about returning to Balaton. The memories from 1990 were not good. But I did wonder if it could possibly be as grim as I remembered. Re-reading my bleats of dismay at the despoiling of the lake, I was struck by how quick my younger self had been to leap upon the high horse of moral indignation. I was curious, too, about the fate of Hungary's only trout stream, and about Balaton's past, before the concrete mixers moved in.

In the end curiosity won. I hired a car and, on a day of blazing summer heat, went back to the Hungarian Sea.

It took me a while to relocate the Anglers' Federation's camp on the Tihany peninsular where I had stayed before. A navigational error sucked me into the village of Tihany itself, where the abbey rose above a sea of coaches, cars and trippers. Eventually I got on to the lower road, which followed the shore. The beaches were packed, the water churned with bodies. Flesh was everywhere, glistening with sun oil. Uncovered bellies and half-covered breasts and fat arses swung and swayed in all directions.

I passed the Yacht Club and came to the entrance to Club Tihany, a sprawling complex that had managed to grab most of the prime beachfront. I asked a young man on the gate if there was a fishing camp anywhere. He directed me along a track that curved away under a steep ridge studded with the cones of defunct volcanic geysers. It led to the camp, a jumble of modest wooden chalets and a rundown restaurant/bar. There were no German number plates and no sign of any Germans.

A pontoon led from the car park through the reeds out to the lake, where there was a long wooden platform arranged for easy fishing. Three men in swimming trunks were sitting beside their rods towards one end, shaded by umbrellas from the scorching sun. They were part of a group of eight friends, all originally from Budapest but now making money in different parts of the world. They got together for a week each year, to fish for carp, eat carp soup, drink beer and catch up. One of them said it was important to get away together, to unwind, to talk again properly. I asked about wives. They all laughed. No wives.

They had two carp in a net, which they were keeping for supper. The fishing was good, they said, better than a few years back when there were all kinds of problems with pollution and water levels. They all liked it here. The camp was not so smart but it was peaceful, and in the evening deer would come out on to the slopes above to feed. I asked who used the camp these days. Mainly Hungarians, they said. Some Dutch, some Danes. No English, and not so many Germans now. They went to Croatia or Turkey instead.

A motor launch passed by some distance out. One of the men watched it through binoculars, then whistled and burst into a voluble commentary in Hungarian. The glasses were passed to me. A blonde woman, completely naked apart from a pair of sunglasses, was standing in the bow, her body arched against the rail. I gawped for a time before handing back the glasses. A bell tinkled at the end of one of the rods and a carp of about two pounds was hauled in, admired, and released.

The fine municipal museum at Keszthely, the town at the western tip of Balaton, contained a permanent exhibition that revealed something of the lives of the lake people. The lake provided for them and bound them to it. It shaped every important aspect of existence, so that its horizons became their horizons. They stitched nets and wove traps of wicker to lure eels and catfish. They made their homes from reed and willow poles and mud. They shot ducks and geese. They fashioned fishing spears with six- or eight-barbed prongs to impale carp and bream as they spawned and eels as they quested for food. They shaped their canoes from single tree trunks and carved sledges and skates for scooting across the ice.

The museum's old photographs lifted the curtain on another time. Dark, muffled figures gathered around holes in the ice, waiting for the fish to bite. Two brawny fishermen in waistcoats and pork-pie hats, sleeves rolled up for business, one with a long pipe clenched between his teeth, paddled their canoe across a bay towards the reeds. A spear-fisher stood erect in the prow of a boat, his weapon raised to strike.

Another picture showed a group gathered in a clearing near the shore in front of a pair of reed huts, a social function clearly in progress. Bottles and bread were arranged on a rough table. A pot of spicy fish stew hung over a fire. A cone-shaped fish trap lay on the grass in the foreground. The men were all in jackets or waistcoats, most with black moustaches, most smoking, one with glasses and a spreading white beard. You could almost smell fish in the air.

There was no date on it, but the timing must have been about right. Could one of these fellows caught by the camera on Balaton's shore possibly be Michael Varga? Or perhaps his father or uncle?

All I knew of Michael Varga was that he was a Balaton fisherman, active in the years after the Great War, who had known everything a fisherman could about the great carp of the lake.

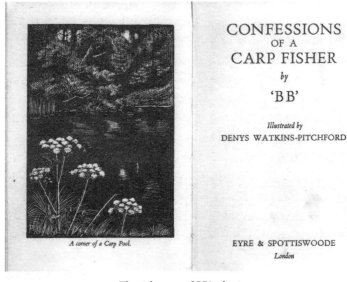

CONFESSIONS
OF A
CARP FISHER
*by*
'BB'

*Illustrated by*
DENYS WATKINS-PITCHFORD

*A corner of a Carp Pool.*

EYRE & SPOTTISWOODE
*London*

The title page of BB's classic

He appears towards the end of a wonderful book called *Confessions of a Carp Fisher*, which was published in 1950, the year before my birth. Loosely modelled on de Quincey's memoir, it is an account of carp and carp waters and the obsessive behaviour they can inspire, and was written – mostly – and illustrated by the writer and artist known as BB, whose real name was Denys Watkins-Pitchford.

The final chapter, entitled 'King of the Carp', was borrowed by BB from a German book called *Horgaszbottal* sent to him by a correspondent. It provides a magical snapshot of Balaton towards the end of its age of innocence. The author, one Wilhelm Kovácsházy, relates how for ten years after the end of the First World War he travelled there each season for the fishing. Initially he was after *fogas*, the pike-perch. But as a result of a chance meeting on the train he is told about the carp, and advised to seek the services of the fisherman Michael Varga.

He comes upon Varga at the boathouse at Balatongyörök, across the bay from Szigliget, and asks him where to go to catch carp. Varga takes him along the reedbeds to a little inlet which he baits up with maize. Over the next few days he comes each morning soon after dawn and catches good carp. One morning, with the mist still on the water, he hooks a monster at least four and a half feet long. After an epic struggle it breaks free, but not before he has noticed five curious gleaming points on its shoulder, shaped like a crown. He tells Varga about this disaster. When he mentions the curious markings, Varga shakes his head. That was the King of the Carp, he explains. 'He is nearly twice as big as the second largest fish of the lake. Perhaps that is the first time in his life that he has felt a hook. So don't feel grieved that you lost him, be grateful that he didn't drag you into the water.'

All the time the spell of Balaton grows on Kovácsházy. One day in June Michael Varga finds him sitting by the water. 'Sir, the carp are spawning,' he cries. Together they make their way across to the mouth of the Tapolca Brook, which enters the lake under the gaze of the castle at Szigliget. At that time, Kovácsházy explains, the flat basin between the lake and the town of Tapolca about five miles to the north was a reedy marsh speckled with ponds into which the carp made their way each year to spawn.

Varga and the angler sit and watch. Families of 20 or 30 carp, tightly packed, glide through the shallow water into the brook and disappear upstream. The volume of arrivals increases, until there are thousands. 'They passed us in hosts and throngs . . . like a living chain', many of 20 pounds, some of 30 and more. The procession goes on and on. 'The scales in their nuptial splendour refracted the sunbeams and dipped the whole wedding procession into a sea of glittering colours of yellow, pink, brown, purple and greenish hue. It seemed as if all jewels and all the colours of the rainbow were being reflected in this mass of fishes.'

Some time in the 1930s the whole of the Tapolca marsh was drained. The various muddy streams that crept through it – including the Tapolca Brook – were regulated, embanked and blocked by hatch-gates, leaving the carp to find somewhere else for their reproductive business. But although the area was regulated to a degree, it remains rough, uncultivated and largely empty of people. The nearer to the lake, the wilder it becomes. Groves of big willows and poplars rise from pools of stagnant water, giving way to a thick belt of reeds, well above head-height, a tawny, rustling jungle cut by dark channels. Enclosed within it, I felt the other Balaton, the brochure Balaton, slip away.

I spent a long, hot afternoon following the paths through this whispering wilderness, looking for the place where the angler and Michael Varga had watched the procession of the carp. In the end I located the Tapolca Brook, which ran from the road towards the lake beside a straight line of poplars, before winding around the edge of the village of Szigliget. I crossed it by a footbridge and came to a cluster of decaying brick buildings, some of which were being used to store reeds cut for thatching. Beyond, the brook widened into a creek. Every yard of bank was claimed by a boat of some kind. I followed the path as far as I could, but it stopped short of the exit to open water. Briefly I contemplated borrowing a boat to paddle out, but they were all firmly chained and padlocked, which would never have been the case in Michael Varga's day.

The next bridge along the road towards Keszthely crossed a dark rivulet making its way furtively towards the lake. The sign beside it identified it as the Viszló, which reminded me of my intention to find out what had happened to Hungary's only trout stream. I still had the map I had acquired on my previous visit, which showed it winding off to the west of Tapolca. I stopped at a couple of places where the road crossed its course, and explored up and down. It was exactly as had been prophesied: the bed was grass, weeds, dry earth and stones. The stream was no more.

Tapolca, on the other hand, was looking refreshed and revived by the death of bauxite mining. It had turned its back on the hideous industrial sprawl left by the Baksony Bauxite Company along its western side, which was decaying fast. It looked busy, prosperous, distinctly spick and span.

It is an old settlement, and interesting both historically and geologically. The centre is built around two small artificial lakes fed by springs that reach deep underground. One lake is higher than the other, and they are connected by a chute installed to drive the wheel of the mill that stands on the spit of land between them. The wheel is still there, turning picturesquely but unprofitably, attached to the side of what is now a rather delightful hotel. The millponds and the old buildings and walls and gardens around them form one of Tapolca's major visitor attractions. The other is a cavern containing a subterranean lagoon which – like the millponds – is fed from the reservoirs beneath the layer of karst on which the whole region sits.

As well as devastating the landscape, bauxite mining played havoc with the region's complex water table. Pumps ran day and night to keep the mine shafts workable. There were incidental beneficiaries – such as the Viszló and its trout – but overall the impact was disastrous. Periodically Tapolca's millponds and caverns ran dry, while at Hévíz – way to the west – Europe's largest thermal lake threatened to disappear. Protests were raised, but the bauxite took precedence over everything else. No more. Now Hévíz is smiling again, the Tapolca cave is full, and the millponds are brimming.

I had my breakfast on the terrace overlooking the upper lake. The surface was glass-smooth, the reflections of the walls and old buildings around its edge unbroken. Then the glass was gently, silently fractured. A silver-haired gent in shorts, with a comfortable stomach, guided a sky-blue boat across the water. It was powered by a small, noiseless electric motor, and attached to the bow was a wide net arranged to trap the clods of algae that had risen to the surface during the previous day, as well as cans, bottles and the like. The boat glided here and there until the silver-haired gent was satisfied that he had gathered up all the unsightly stuff. He took out the litter with a long-handled net, then carefully steered the algae over the outflow, whereupon it dissolved in the foamy water at the bottom.

The operation was conducted without fuss or hurry, in a way very pleasing to the onlooker. What a very useful, worthwhile job, I thought, as I sipped my coffee.

Afterwards I strolled around the water admiring the fish. There were thousands of them, great and small. Shoals of minnows and little roach darkened the gaps between the weedbeds. Goldfish sunned themselves just beneath the surface, some pale, almost white, some a burnished carrot red, a few actually gold.

The top dogs, however, were the carp. They paddled around in slow, dignified style, tilting their snouts down or to the side to take in some choice morsel, casting large, important shadows on the bottom. Some were koi, mottled in outlandish shades of white, gold and black. But there were also common carp and mirror carp, stately grey shapes with wide shoulders and big, questing mouths: descendants, quite possibly, of the fish Michael Varga and the angler watched in the procession up the Tapolca brook long ago.

# Chapter 11

## Saturday in Žilina

A tremendous, crushing heat pressed down from a sky drained of almost all colour. By late morning the thermometer registered 38 degrees. The surface of the lake was ruffled by a wind that felt as if someone had opened the oven door. Sailing boats like little cut-out paper shapes danced over the ripples. To the south, beyond the lake, pavilions and ramparts of cumulo-nimbus were building as the air rose against the hills. The slopes of the Malá Fatra hills to the east were grey-blue humps, so indistinct they looked as if they might disappear at any moment.

I had been invited by my new friend, Peter Bienek, to meet his partner, Petra, and their two children, as well as their respective parents. They all lived in Žilina, a town in north-west Slovakia tucked beneath the westernmost finger of the Carpathians in the valley cut by the River Váh as it bends south towards the Danube. The venue for lunch was Peter's father's weekend holiday home, which sounds a touch Cotswolds or Cornish fishing village but was nothing of the sort, just a basic retreat a couple of miles out of town.

In the days of the regimes these refuges from the grime and smoke of the factory zones, and the cheek-by-jowl communal life of the apartment blocks, were prized beyond price and invested with almost sacred significance. The plots were usually spread across an accessible hillside that the urban planners had deemed surplus to industrial or housing needs. The custom was to grow fruit and vegetables, but also to install a simple dwelling of brick or wood fitted out for basic living. These places provided food and something even more precious: a measure of privacy, freedom from surveillance and state nagging, a place to relax and be normal.

Peter's father's cabin had a single room which acted as kitchen and living quarters, a separate shower, and an outside earth closet. To one side there was a makeshift awning of plastic sheeting attached to wooden beams, under which the families were gathered, dressed for maximum comfort. Peter's father, Pavol, tall, grey-haired, tanned, wore blue shorts below a bronzed torso brushed with drifts of silver hair. Peter's father-in-law, Ivan, was even more minimally dressed, in a pair of brief, electric-blue swimming trunks that fitted snugly beneath a generous swell of stomach. Peter's mother, Tatiana, her hair cut short and dyed a striking white-blonde, glasses poised on a beaky nose in front of quick, eager eyes, wore a shapeless floral dress. His mother-in-law, Janka, wore a bikini and a worried look that never left her face. She looked after Peter and Petra's little daughter, Sára, so that Petra could go to work for a pharmaceuticals company. A few days before there had been a fall in the playground, as a result of which Sára was sporting a starburst of black stitches in the middle of her forehead.

The adult company was completed, for the time being, by Petra's grandmother, who lay back in a chaise longue in the corner, holding her stick and gazing mistily into the middle distance, saying almost nothing. Peter told me she had been like this for a year or so, since her husband's death. They were all very kind and attentive to her, but she was too immersed in her memories and grief to respond.

I was offered a glass of red wine. I was parched after a very hot and sweaty morning's fishing with Peter, and asked if there was any beer. Consternation. A single bottle was all they had. Peter was sent off to the town to get more. His mother and father, and Petra's father, took turns to poke at a stack of chicken wings smoking on the barbecue. I caught glimpses inside the cabin of a slim, pretty woman in denim shorts and striped blue shirt, looking anxious. The little girl tottered around from grandparent to grandparent, hands continually reaching out towards her lest she trip. At one point the grandparents' committee decided she was ready for a sleep, and she was taken inside. Loud cries of protest ensued. She reappeared and the petting and cooing resumed.

Ivan, it turned out, had worked for some time as a hydro-engineer in Nigeria where he had acquired a smattering of English.

Peter Bienek with trout

He now took it upon himself to converse with me. Screwing up his face under his bunch of tight grey curls, he squeezed out some words. Nigerians, very nice people. But working there, very difficult. Weather in Žilina very hot. How was fishing? Very hot, I said. Nigeria very hot, he said.

Peter came back with the beer. He was twenty years younger than me and looked another ten years younger than that. He had a pale, boyish face, fine, sandy hair, glasses, an expression of innocence and slight surprise. He had a naturally quick, restless way; being still and quiet seemed to be a trial to him. He spoke good English and talked a lot to me, mainly about fishing, which was both his obsession and his livelihood. He and a business partner owned four fishing tackle shops, one of them in Žilina, which Peter managed. This meant that he talked fishing, thought fishing, or went fishing much of every day. This suited Peter well enough but was clearly the source of some tension between him and Petra.

The family ambience and the need to attend to parental duties seemed to diminish his usual vivacity. His mother, in contrast, was full of beans. She and Pavol had just returned from a holiday in Tunisia, hence their deep tans. To me, still struggling to adjust to the changed contexts, it seemed extraordinary, almost unreal, that an ordinary retired couple from a provincial town in Slovakia should holiday in North Africa; whereas what was truly extraordinary was that they thought no more of it than a couple from Redditch or Goole would. Tunisia, she said, was very good, very hot. She pressed chicken wings on me, and chunks of grilled pork. I ate one plateful, drank my beer, did my best with another plateful. Across the lake the mountains of cloud darkened.

Peter's sister Andrea arrived with her husband, two children, a little dog and some salad. Husband, children and dog disappeared in the direction of the paddling pool and I did not encounter them again. Andrea sported a bikini that registered a refreshing disregard for the body-beautiful norms promoted by the beauty magazines. There was a good deal of body on show, but she clearly cared not a hoot about such trivial matters as varicose veins, the effect of gravity, cellulite, a roll of flesh here and there. It was the weekend, the sun was shining, it was time to unbutton and let go. She was a nurse and had worked in Italy, so we talked some Italian together, and she was very jolly.

Eventually the little girl did go to sleep for a time, in a pushchair at the bottom of the garden, with her mother on guard beside her. I went and sat with her and we talked in whispers. Petra had lived in London for a year, working as an au pair. I asked how she had liked it. London was good, she said, but she hadn't seen much of the rest of England. The family she worked for were Jewish Orthodox, very strict. The children were very quiet, very polite, very clever. The father read from the Torah every evening and they hardly ever went out.

Her life in Žilina struck me as too full of anxieties for one so young. Her job meant leaving Sára with her mother every day. It was too much to ask, but the job was good and they needed the money. Samuel, their son, was at school but there were problems with his behaviour and it worried her when he played with Sára. Then there was Peter and his fishing. Her face manifested an infinity of exasperation.

I had encountered plenty of cases of extreme fishing mania before, so I knew what she meant. It was particularly acute in his case because he was the mainstay of the national fly-fishing team, and had represented Slovakia in a total of seven world champion-ships in countries as far distant as Australia, Finland, England and – most recently – New Zealand. The New Zealand trip, lasting three weeks, had taken place when Sára was eight months old. Moreover he was away at least one full day nearly every weekend, taking part in regional competitions, and practised like a demon in between.

'Do you know about the house?' she asked. I did because Peter had taken me to see it.

Together, like a nice, normal couple, they had agreed to buy a nice, normal new house on the outskirts of Žilina and move out of their cramped apartment. But one day Peter was passing through a village a few miles out of town on his way to the river when he came upon a plot of land for sale. There was a wrecked dwelling on it, unfit for habitation. Behind, choked by uncut grass, was a neglected orchard of apple and pear trees – and beyond the orchard was a little creek, with trout in it. Peter showed me along it, pointing out a little pool here, a potential spawning gravel there. It's perfect, he said, though I wasn't entirely sure for whom.

I tried to reassure Petra. It's a lovely, peaceful place, I said. The garden will be perfect for the children. And the creek, she answered crossly. And how long will it take? Two years, maybe three. If the money doesn't run out first. She laughed her exasperated laugh. 'He is mad,' she declared. 'This fishing is madness.' I conceded she might have a point.

Sára woke up. I was allowed to retire inside the cabin for a nap. When I woke up I was plied with Spanish brandy by the two fathers. Under its influence Petra's father managed to unlock more of his store of English.

The subject of the gypsies came up, as it usually did in any extended conversation in Slovakia. There were 400,000 of them in the country, the second largest population in Europe (after Romania). The one thing that everyone agreed on was that they represented a massive, intractable social problem. Largely unintegrated, uneducated, impoverished, and unwilling or unable to embrace the standards and aspirations of the rest of the population, they were regarded as a kind of national disfigurement. Their way of life and the frightful conditions in the ghettos and slums where they had been segregated provoked shame and disgust in equal measure.

Under Communist rule the gypsies were shunned, oppressed and victimised in the familiar way – but quietly. Now, with Slovakia in the EU, the problem had to be publicly acknowledged, solutions proposed, measures taken. The collision between the obligation to devise social programmes to help the gypsies and the age-old urge to vilify and demonise them left a nasty taste in everyone's mouth. Most educated Slovakians agreed that it was unacceptable these days to treat anyone as being beyond the pale. But when you saw how they lived! The crime, the prostitution, the squalor, the rampant breeding, the drugs, the idleness – was it any wonder that people were turning to right-wing groups demanding extreme measures including forcible sterilisation and segregation?

At it happened, I'd gained a second-hand insight into 'the gypsy problem' on my way to Slovakia. On the plane I'd found myself sitting next to a police officer from Sheffield. To begin with we'd chatted about fishing, which was one of his passions in life. Then I asked him his line of work. He was attached to a new unit set up to investigate the recruiting and smuggling of young prostitutes within the enlarged EU. He was on his way with two colleagues to Bratislava, to take into custody a Roma man accused of running a vice ring in Sheffield, exploiting under-age gypsy girls from Slovakia. The man was facing trial in Sheffield, where his wife was already serving a lengthy prison sentence. (In the event he got seven years.)

I didn't mention the story the policeman had told me to Peter or Petra or their families. It was a horrible saga of degradation and exploitation that would only have embarrassed them with the thought that this was the one Slovakian export I knew about. They talked about conditions in the gypsy slums. Petra said they were unbelievable. She used the word 'medieval', then explained it to the others. They all nodded. That was right. Medieval. But what could you do? Petra's father said he'd been brought up in a village where there were many gypsies. Some had been his friends, and when he was naughty or went wandering, he would be told that he would have to stay with them. They were not all bad, he said. But different. Just different.

The sky continued to darken. Far away, curtains of rain stretched across the hills. Petra and her children and her mother and the sad grandmother went home, as did Peter's sister and her family. The level in the brandy bottle declined. The two fathers urged me to stay to help finish it and start another. With difficulty I extricated myself. It was time to go fishing.

Slovakians have two endearing habits of speech which help keep their conversations bubbling along. One is the use of 'hey' as a gap-filler, as we might say 'y'know' or 'like' or 'know what I mean'. 'Hey' means nothing, but it gives their speech a lively, positive tone, suggesting that good and interesting things are happening or could happen at any moment. Should they do so, the appropriate exclamation is 'super', pronounced with the syllables stretched: 'SOOPAIR'.

For Peter Bienek, Žilina was 'super' in almost every respect, although to a visitor it may seem a pretty nondescript town. There is a small, pleasant historic centre arranged around a square with the usual arcades, elegant public buildings in pastel shades, fountain and church. The situation, circled by ranges of hills, is picturesque. Otherwise it is sprawling, busy, aesthetically un-appealing, clean, functional, and – at least when I was there, before the crash of autumn 2008 – conspicuously prosperous.

EU development funding, Asian investment, the readiness of the Slovakian government to offer industrial sites at knock-down prices, and the availability of cheap labour, had combined to make Slovakia the biggest car-producer in Europe, and its economy the second fastest-growing (after Poland). Žilina and its Korean-owned Kia car plant led the way. Three thousand people worked directly for Kia, and thousands more in dependent components factories. Many other businesses had been attracted to the town. At that time, Žilina was a place where, if you wanted a job, there was a job to be had. Wages were good by Slovakian standards and people had money to spend.

When I first went to eastern Europe, anglers were aware of who the brand leaders in fishing tackle were, but rather in the way that an agricultural labourer in Elizabethan or Jacobean England might have heard of the silks and spices of the Orient or the strange smoking weed from the New World: as wonders they never expected to see or sample themselves. Brands like Hardy, Farlow, Orvis and Sage were spoken of with a kind of hopeless yearning. A rod made by one of them cost at least six months' wages, and could only be obtained abroad. The fishermen made do with grossly inferior equipment, crudely made glass-fibre rods, tin reels, hopelessly unreliable hooks.

But now Peter Bienek's shop in Žilina stood comparison with anything you could find in the UK or the States. He had the latest Sage and Orvis ranges, cabinets of reels imported from everywhere, shelves of DVDs and fly-tying gear, racks of Gortex and breathable waders. And they were selling. Peter said that when he started out in the tackle trade, Slovakian anglers were interested only in the cheapest. These days the new imported model was like anything else: if you could afford it, you got it; and many did.

So Žilina was super for business. It was super, too, in that both sets of grandparents lived there, freeing Petra to earn good money with the pharmaceuticals firm, and Peter to work and then go fishing whenever he wanted. I told him that at the start of every fishing season I resolved to get to the river at least once a week, but I never quite managed it. He looked at me pityingly. 'I must fish every day,' he said with mock seriousness, 'or I die.' And when he fished, he did so as if his life depended on it. His technical mastery was complete, his concentration intense and unwavering.

When I watched him on the water, I could not help thinking about that look on Petra's face: helpless, resigned, uncomprehending.

His home river — highly super — was the Rajcianka. It flowed out of the hills to the south of Žilina through the western side of town to join the Váh. It was a nice stream, its banks heavily wooded, the water clear but looking dark because of the subfusc colouring of the streambed. The pools and streamy runs and the holes by the roots of the willows and alders were full of grayling, mixed in with some trout.

Slovakian fishing permit

The evening after the lunch with the parents, Peter took me to the town water. In the morning we'd fished a stretch three or four miles upstream, where I caught a few grayling and Peter many. This time, wonder of wonders, he said he needed to go home and put in some family time. He'd be back at nine to pick me up. Before leaving he went into the water with me to show me the best places to try. The sun was almost off the water and rings were beginning to show in the smooth glides beside the trees as the fish fed. He tied on a little nymph for me – I have never seen anyone so swift and sure with knots – and could not resist an exploratory cast or two. He gazed longingly at the river, then turned away.

The Slovakian fly-fishing ethos (the same applies generally in eastern Europe) is very different from ours. In England there is an unspoken understanding that fishing is a quiet, solitary affair. We keep our distance from each other. If we see someone else casting, we circle around them to find another spot, keeping well away. A chance encounter on the bank may lead to a brief exchange of comment about the weather or the quality of sport, but we do not expect to be addressed by a stranger while we are fishing, and would take it very much amiss if one were to barge in next to us because he had seen us catch something or just liked the look of the spot. Such behaviour, however, is entirely the norm on the rivers of the east.

The Žilina town water was thoroughly democratic. Immediately upstream a party was in progress. A radio blared dance music. Meat smoked on a barbecue. Lads in swimming trunks booted a football around, breaking off now and then to dive off a rock into the pool. Children paddled, dogs swam for sticks. I skirted around the merrymaking and found a series of pools hemmed in by trees where I caught some nice grayling as the water darkened and the thunderclouds continued to pile up over the hills. Eventually I went back to wait for Peter. I watched a fisherman play and land a decent fish no more than 15 yards from where three blokes were wallowing up to their waists, hurling sticks and clods of mud at each other.

It would never have done, I reflected, in Hampshire, Berkshire or Wiltshire.

# Chapter 12

## Times change

'We lived with eyes closed. Eyes closed. That's how it was in that time.'

Peter Bienek was 20 in 1989, a student at Brno University (his subject was fish behaviour, which somehow didn't surprise me). He was one of the surging throng on the streets that November, chanting for the end of the regime, by then crumbling from the outside and imploding from within. The students believed that the momentum came from them: their youth, their idealism. It was people power; they called it the Velvet Revolution, change without violence.

Now, older, wiser and more versed in the ways of the world, Peter Bienek believes they were fooled. It wasn't their doing, and it had little or nothing to do with ideals. The levers were pulled from inside the Party. 'For sure. They could see what was coming. They needed to arrange everything so that they would do well, have the power, make the money. For sure.'

The following summer, when it was all over and the system that had controlled everything throughout Peter's life had been swept away, he asked his father a favour. The borders were down and you could go to places you had previously only dreamed of. Peter fixed on Greece as the land of milk and honey. His father worked as an electrical engineer for the state police and had a car that went with the job, a 2.5-litre Russian-made Volga. Peter asked if he could borrow it to go to Greece. His father said no, whereupon Peter said he would hitch. His mother intervened, and in the end he got the car. He and two friends drove the Volga to Greece where they all got jobs packing tomatoes. That was freedom.

Three years before, Peter had been chosen to represent Czechoslovakia in an international fishing competition being staged in Florence. Such events were problematic for the Party. It was necessary for teams to be sent in order to demonstrate socialist sporting prowess. But attendance brought with it the acute danger of competitors being infected by outside influences, even brain-washed into believing that conditions wherever they were going were preferable to those at home. The record of defections on such occasions was extensive and shameful.

Peter had never been abroad. Before leaving for Italy, he was twice summoned before the director of his school in Žilina and lectured at length about the behaviour expected of him. He was forbidden to buy anything, to take photographs, to talk to anyone apart from his fellow team members and their minders, above all to have anything to do with anglers from other countries who might fill his head with dangerous nonsense about rock music and Levi jeans.

'I couldn't believe it when I was in Italy,' he recalled, shaking his head. 'Where were all the poor people they told us about? They said there were people sleeping beside the road, crying because they didn't have food. I was looking for them but I didn't see them. I was so innocent, so stupid.'

What he did see were the shops on the Ponte Vecchio stuffed with fabulous things, and a swarm of people who had money to spend and appeared to be quite happy about it. Peter came home confused. Maybe there was another side to the story. Maybe he hadn't been told everything. He tried to talk to his mother and father about it. They told him to be quiet and get on with his studies. But he couldn't help thinking the unthinkable.

The Eastern Bloc leaders were right to fear the West. In the end it was finding out how others lived that destroyed their system, as much as anything else. Stories of sudden revelation, like Peter's, were common. Sometimes it came very late in the day. Such a case was that of the President of the Polish Fishing Association.

All his adult life he had been a dedicated Communist. The Party had given him everything he had, raising him from the meat-packing factory where he had worked as a furnaceman to a position of status. Its collapse left him bewildered and depressed, but he remained a dedicated Communist. A year later, in September 1990, he accompanied the Polish fly-fishing team to the world championships in Wales, where he was lodged with a local doctor. One day he and another member of the team, who spoke good English, met a couple with a smart new car on the back of which were strapped two mini-motorcycles. The dedicated Communist asked who they were. He was bemused to be told that the woman worked as a cleaner for the doctor with whom he was staying.

Later he was fishing from a boat next to a golf course. The dedicated Communist knew something about golf. It was an English game played by members of the aristocracy on land they had stolen from the poor. They had servants to carry their clubs. He looked more closely. Some of the golfers were elderly, some younger. They all carried their own clubs. They didn't look like aristocrats. They looked like perfectly ordinary people – in fact, rather like him, except that he was a dedicated Communist.

He talked to his team-mate. Perhaps, he suggested, this capitalism wasn't all bad if the doctor's cleaner could afford a new car and motorbikes for her children and people like him were able to play golf. The world that he had known had recently been turned on its head. Perhaps it was time to be an ex-dedicated Communist. He was a good fisherman and tier of flies. Perhaps there might be opportunities here for someone with his skills?

You need to be on your guard when you go back to the special places. You may locate them easily enough on the map, but maps tell only one story. Times change, and places and people change with them. The memory plays curious tricks, and things are often not as you remember, or expect, or hope.

For me, rivers and streams have always been the special places. I carry a portfolio of them in my head: the roots of the horse chestnut washed by the river of my boyhood, with the cavern beneath where the chub and barbel hid; a pool on a burn in the west of Scotland, the sea-trout waiting where the whisky water crashed over the boulders; a wild currant bush on the Eamont in Cumberland, its branches reaching towards a deep, marbled run where the trout watched for the blue-winged olives to hatch; the flawless blue Andean sky, the current etched into the bend on the far side, grasshoppers tumbling on to the water from the waving grass; a mile of broken water on the Zambezi, tiger fish on sentry duty in every pool; these and others, plenty of others.

When I came home from eastern Europe towards the end of that summer of 1990, I brought with me a sheaf of mental images. Four of the sharpest were of little streams – not so much for the fish, although there were fish, but because they had a particular magic about them. Fishermen will know what I mean, even though it cannot be satisfactorily expressed in words. I have warm feelings for all rivers (except those blighted by poison or imprisoned between the concrete embankments favoured by a certain kind of criminal engineer), but I like little rivers the best. They make no big noise and keep themselves to themselves, withholding their delights for those who know them or are lucky enough to stumble upon them.

In Poland there was the Białka, which, when I went back, I found had survived my absence in good fettle. There was one in Romania and one in Bohemia, still to come. And in Slovakia there was the Biela, which means the same in Slovakian as Białka in Polish: 'white river'. They were like a pair of sisters, both tumbling out of the Tatras over worn, pale stones, each sparkling with life.

*　*　*

It was thanks to Pavel Janicek that I found the Biela. Pavel lived and worked in Ostrava, the vast, sulphurous coal and steel city of northern Moravia. But he regarded himself as an honorary citizen of Slovakia because that was where he did his fishing.

At that time Pavel was captain of the Czech fly-fishing team (it was still Czechoslovakia but not for much longer). I met him outside a grey, horrible apartment block in Ostrava. He was a couple of inches shorter than me but twice as wide, with a broad chest and a mighty belly that strained against his blue windcheater. I greeted him in English and he greeted me in German. I explained in English that I couldn't speak German. He explained in German that he couldn't speak English.

We went together to the flat of a friend of his who was head of the English department at one of Ostrava's secondary schools. Like Márta Hegedüs in Hungary, her English was fluent and rooted in a passion for literature. She adored Graham Greene, but he was so sad. For laughter one needed Muriel Spark. And Angus Wilson, she asked, was he still as popular as ever? She greatly admired *Hemlock and After*.

She had visited England once, in 1968, after the Prague Spring, paying her way by picking strawberries in Kent. Oxford was so beautiful, she reminisced, pouring more Twinings. And London. Ah, there was nowhere like London, even if the taxi drivers did speak so strangely. And the English! So friendly, so welcoming. She noticed my sceptical look. Oh, yes, she insisted. The English were the most civilised people in Europe. Look at Chaucer, Shakespeare, Wordsworth, Dickens. So many others. No other language had inspired such genius.

'Now everyone is wanting to learn English,' she said. 'Before, always, it was Russian, Russian, Russian. Now no one learns Russian any more. The young teachers are trying to train to do German, French or English. But the old ones, they are finished. And now everyone at the school is very polite to me.'

She poured more tea, then translated Pavel's arrangements for our excursion to Slovakia. She said it was a great pleasure to meet an Englishman and talk about English writers. One day I must come back to Ostrava and meet some of her pupils. She was only sorry that she was not able to accompany us.

So was I. The linguistic situation looked problematic. But in the course of a long drive around the western flank of the Carpathians and along the southern foothills, vestiges of a long-forgotten, not at all successful, German O-level campaign began to surface like bubbles of marsh gas. At first single words popped off the tip of the tongue – *forelle, fluss, bier* (trout, river, beer); then a smattering of phrases and short sentences: *fliegenfischen, Mann muss trinken bier und schnapps, wir gehen aus Fluss.* It was hard work, demanding all my concentration. Bumping over a level crossing in the town of Ružemberok, I was distracted from trying to make sense of Pavel's flow by the blast of a horn, the ringing of bells and the thunder of wheels as a train roared through, feet from my back bumper.

For much of the way we followed the course of Pavel's favourite river, the Poprad, with the white fangs of the High Tatras gleaming to the south. We went through the town of Poprad, a smoky, shabby, industrial mess, then reached a dusty little place called Podolinec, where we had to stop to collect my fishing licence from the secretary of the local club. As I was the first Englishman in the history of Podolinec to require such a document, the transaction turned into something a ceremony, with handshakes, speeches proclaiming the Brotherhood of the Angle, and many glasses of *slivovice*, the Slovakian answer to Hungarian *palinka*. Finally we sat down beneath the gaze of a gallery of trophy trout and grayling heads collected and preserved by the secretary, and tucked into fried trout and spuds served by his wife.

The final leg of the journey took us from Podolinec towards

the regional capital, Stará L'ubovňa. On one of the bends in the river we came upon a campsite. Tents, wooden hutches and metal cabins were scattered across a wide meadow.

Pavel Janicek (at rear) and friends, Slovakia, 1990

A group of Pavel's friends were waiting for us in the restaurant, which was packed with noisy youths and teenage girls on some kind of field trip. We proceeded to drink a good deal of beer and more *slivovice*, then assembled in one of the metal cabins to tackle a 20-litre container of warm white wine.

In the morning, sore-headed, I rubbed away the condensation on the inside of the window next to my bed and peered out. The grass around the campsite was silver with dew. The sun was showing through the spiky tops of the conifers lining the ridge along the far bank. In between hurried the Poprad, lentil-coloured from the melting of the Tatra snows. We had ham and eggs in the canteen, and toasted the day ahead with glasses of *slivovice*.

The Poprad was too dirty to fish so Pavel had arranged for two local anglers to accompany me to a tributary, the Biela, that ran into the main river a few miles downstream from Podolinec. They were brothers, Stano and Slavo Truska. Stano worked in a factory in Stará L'ubovňa and was markedly more prosperous than his brother, a qualified vet. They met me at the junction, and one of them produced a map that showed the Biela's path from the mountains. It rose just inside the border with Poland and ran east-south-east, so that all that hot, brilliant morning I had the highest peaks of the Tatras in front of me, etched against the blue of the sky as distinctly as if they had been drawn with a newly sharpened pencil.

The water was so clear that, at first, you thought it could hide nothing. But there was concealed life behind the rocks and where the current flowed with any depth over the white stones. A shadow would drift across the bottom as a fish shifted position, or vanish in a stab of movement if it was alarmed.

I went ahead of the brothers and came to a flat concrete bridge supported in the middle by a concrete pillar on a base. The current divided around the base, creating a smooth glide to each side, shaded from the sun. I was about to wade through under the left arch when there was a wink in the shadows. Looking more closely, I saw tiny wings, slate grey against the gleam of the water. They travelled 18 inches or so, then the surface was broken for an instant and the wings disappeared.

Soon after my own fly was following the same route, and in the same spot a nose tilted up. I struck, there was a lunge, the rod arced over and almost immediately straightened as the hook hold gave way. I cursed and shifted across so that I could cast into the right-hand arch. I did better this time and was admiring a plump, vividly spotted trout when Slavo Truska floundered up behind me. He grasped the fish, thumped it over the head and slid it into his pocket. We exchanged a slimy handshake and smiled and laughed and cuffed each other about the shoulders, needing no common words for the common delight we felt.

Slavo Truska on the Biela, 1990

The next afternoon Pavel and his chums had to return to Ostrava – *Mann muss arbeiten* he said, shrugging his big shoulders. The weather had broken overnight and the day was grey, wet and chilly. It was decided that in the time left to us, drinking would be a surer source of amusement than fishing. We sat at a table in the canteen while, outside, buses came to take away the students. We began with beer, progressed to gin, then on to *slivovice*. Pavel was planning my next visit. From Zakopane in Poland he would summon Władysław Trzebunia, the world fly-fishing champion with whom he had made friends at the championships in Finland. The celebrated Slavoj Svoboda would come from Bratislava.

'*Fliegenfischen und trinken*,' Pavel bellowed, banging his big fist on the table.

'*Ja, wunderbar*,' I replied.

His fat forefinger waved indistinctly before my eyes. '*Aber du muss kommen in Oktober wann der ist nicht schneewasser im Poprad. Wann es ist klar und schön und die lipan . . .*' His fingers snapped.

'*Ja, die lipan sind gut.*'

We used the Czech word for grayling as neither of us knew the

120

German. Rain beat down on the tarmac outside. Mist crept across the windows, obscuring the now empty and lifeless camp. At intervals the barman appeared with more beer and *slivovice* and cleared away the empty glasses and overflowing ashtrays. Eventually, after a crescendo and climax of pumping handshakes and declarations of eternal comradeship, Pavel and his friends squeezed themselves into a Škoda and left. I went to my cabin and slept while the rain drummed on the roof. In the evening I returned to the canteen and tried to order an omelette. Omelettes didn't exist, only fried pork, greasy chips and pickled red cabbage. A programme about Solzhenitsyn was being shown on TV, which consisted mostly of heated conversations in Russian or Czech between men wearing shabby jackets who smoked almost as furiously as they talked. But one of the participants was the British peer Lord Bethell – translator of Solzhenitsyn's *Cancer Ward* – whose well-cut grey suit, white shirt and patterned tie, and calm, modulated English tones filled me with acute loneliness and homesickness.

Before leaving, Pavel had procured for me an additional permit to fish the Slovak side of the Dunajec, which formed the border with Poland to the north. The accessible reach was upstream from Červený Kláštor, where a Carthusian monastery has stood beside the river since the fourteenth century. Opposite the monastery on the Polish side, guarding the entrance to the Dunajec Gorge – a favoured destination for kayakers and rafters – was a cluster of jagged crags known as the Three Crowns.

The little road to Červený Kláštor twisted through the Spišská Magura, which means Little Mountains of Spiš. This is the Slovak version of *Zips,* the name given to the region comprising the valleys of the Hornád and the Poprad and the lands around by colonists from Germany who settled there in the thirteenth and fourteenth centuries. The Spišská Magura partially plug the gap made by the Poprad as it breaks north through the Carpathians; and even though they are not very big, they still form a considerable barrier between the valleys of the Poprad and the Dunajec. They are wild and thinly populated, with a sprinkling of hamlets and a very few larger villages.

The march of collectivisation that had claimed all the flatter and more fertile parts of Czechoslovakia had stopped short of these steep slopes. Below the limestone outcrops and woods of beech, fir and spruce, the land was still cultivated in the same narrow strips first cut and dug by hardy German pioneers 700 years before. Most of the work was done by hand, and most of the workers were women, middle-aged or older, stout and strong of leg and body, wearing tough boots, aprons over rough skirts, and headscarves pulled tight around their weathered faces. Legs wide apart, they bent over the wandering furrows, weeding, thinning, sowing or picking. Some worked the soil with hoes, methodically and tirelessly. When I came back down the same road late that evening, the last of them were trudging home with their picks and hoes and buckets, a bundle of grass tucked under one arm for the animals in the farmyards. Upright, they still looked bent, as if bred for closeness to the ground.

It was the grass-cutting season. The air was sweet with the smell and alive with the sweep of scythes and the cries of the cutters, mixed with snatches of song. Narrow frames made from stripped branches of fir were arranged at intervals across the meadows. By evening many were draped with grass, so that from a distance they looked like miniature tailors' dummies covered for the night by pale dustsheets.

The mix of races across this part of Slovakia was as diverse as the landscape itself. A little way to the east was an enormous, disorderly Ruthenian village, Jakubany, spread along several miles of dusty, potholed road, along which modern concrete housing blocks had been thrown up side by side with traditional single-storey houses made from mighty beams edged in yellow, blue or purple mortar, each with its barn, stack of wood, store of grass and hen-infested yard. Near Stará Ľubovňa were several Ukrainian villages, while either side of the border lived the Górale people who spoke a Polish dialect. Elsewhere Slovaks, ethnic Hungarians and the descendants of the original German colonists were indiscriminately jumbled together.

It was late afternoon before I got down to any fishing. I crossed a meadow beside the road and took a path towards the river, disturbing a deer that bounded off through the willow brush. The Dunajec flowed broad and even to a diagonal gravel bar where it broke into two streams, one curving towards Poland, the other washing the Slovak shore. An old woman was driving cattle along the far bank, whacking her stick against their flanks, her shouts of abuse and encouragement carrying across the burble of the water. The sun broke through, lighting the sky and spreading a pinkish glow across the bare summits of the Three Crowns.

I had the river to myself. I waded out a little way then edged downstream, taking no risks with my footing, casting as I went. It was easy work, the line hissing through the rod rings and snaking out over the water, the flies pulling round an inch or two below the surface. I got two or three grayling above the gravel bar, nice fish of three-quarters of a pound or so. Below the bar almost every cast induced a snatch at the flies, but for some reason I could not hook a fish. There was no more than 30 yards or so of fishable water before it dissolved into a fierce-looking rapid. The light was fading, so I reeled in and made my way back to my car. I came upon another deer in the twilight and it leaped away in terror.

I had one more outing with the Truska brothers, to a meagre stream near the border crossing at Mnisek where we caught a few miserably undernourished trout. Afterwards we went back to the canteen in the now deserted and silent campsite on the Poprad. The brothers presented me with two books, one about Czech fly-fishing, the other about Stará Ľubovňa and the Spiš. Slavo had a

Slovak–English dictionary as well as a few words of English; together like a pair of elderly horses yoked to a primitive plough, we managed a slow, wandering furrow of conversation. I wanted to hear about their hopes and fears for the new age. They smiled and shook their heads. Looking around, they saw a country being pulled apart by its interior contradictions, economically crippled, environmentally devastated, demoralised by the decades of heavy-pawed, centralised control. They did not believe the effusions of optimism from the new democrats. They had been conditioned to expect nothing, to hope for nothing, to believe nothing; to take their consolation from sources that would not let them down. Fishing, drinking, the mountains, the streams.

Elections were due in four days. They would solve nothing, the brothers said. Politicians just told you what they thought you wanted to hear. The country was in a mess and would stay in a mess. Thank God for the fishing. We toasted the fishing. Slavo said he would vote Green: 'For our rivers and our children.' Suddenly he grinned at the thought of it, a vote, someone counting it. We shook hands. He said he was glad to have shared the beauty of the Biela with me – 'your beloved Biela', he called it in a letter that reached me in England many months later.

In time I lost touch with the Truskas, and eventually with Pavel Janicek as well. Before going back I tried the address I had for him in Ostrava, and posted messages on Czech and Slovak fishing websites, but with no response. Peter Bienek made some enquiries but no one seemed to remember the big, friendly man who had coached the fly-fishing team. Much later, when I was back in England, I got an email from Pavel via his grandson. He was glad to remember the time we had spent together, he said. Now his health was not so good and he didn't go fishing any more; and anyway, since the so-called Velvet Divorce (legally effected on 1 January 1993) he had no longer felt welcome in Slovakia.

The people faded away, as tends to happen, but I still had my collection of maps, including the one covering the Biela that the Truskas had given me, so retracing my steps was straightforward. I drove over from Žilina on a hot, windy July day, the High Tatras as jagged and toothy as ever, but with hardly a touch of snow on them, as if eighteen years had worn almost all their enamel away.

Peter had spoken to local contacts about the Biela and been told that it was suffering badly from depleted flows and high temperatures, and that a violent flood a winter or two before had swept most of the remaining trout and grayling out into the Poprad. So I was warned. One look over the bridge where I had caught the fat trout and where Slavo Truska and I had shaken hands was enough to shatter the picture I had fondly carried with me for so long. The narrow glides where the fish had fed and sheltered were no more. In their place was an island of gravel covered by weeds and rough grass, strewn with cans and bottles and torn pieces of plastic. A trickle of water crept down each side over brown, slimy stones.

Bridge over the Biela, 2008

I walked downstream, along the edge of a field, towards the junction with the Poprad. I didn't go all the way; it was too dispiriting. The Biela made no sound. There was not enough water for it to chatter over the stones or conjure a miniature cascade. It just slid by, looking ashamed of itself. I spotted a shoal of small chub in one lethargic excuse for a pool, but did not see a single trout or grayling. They need oxygen, cool water against their backs and flanks, life and sparkle. But the lifeblood of the Biela had been drained away. I felt a heavy sadness, as if the fate of this one little stream somehow reflected a whole generation's disappointments.

The Milava campsite where I had caroused with Pavel Janicek and his friends had long since been abandoned. The restaurant where I had poured glass after glass of *slivovice* down my throat was padlocked and rotting away. The malodorous wash-block was falling down. The metal cabins had been removed but the wooden hutches remained, half-submerged in a sea of grass that lapped at the picnic benches and tables near the river. The Poprad itself hurried along on its unchanging business. I remembered Pavel saying that autumn was the best time, when the water would be clear and the beech woods turned gold.

I took the same road through the Spišská Magura towards Červený Kláštor. The way, all meadows and woods, was as lovely as I remembered, but the land was quiet and empty. Apart from an elderly couple rounding up some sheep, I saw no one in the fields. Most of the grass was uncut and the frames made to support it were lying around in untidy heaps.

It seemed that the country folk had all migrated to Červený Kláštor in search of an easier life. Twenty years before, this place had been on the border between two countries which — while proclaiming socialist brotherhood — had rigorously kept their citizens apart and zealously arrested them if they strayed. Now what had been two sleepy riverside settlements, eyeing each other across the swift currents of the Dunajec, had mutated into a single holiday resort united by a footbridge which anybody could saunter across whenever they felt like it, without being asked their business by someone in uniform.

The settlements had seeded themselves along both banks, bringing forth a crop of holiday chalets and flats, pensions, restaurants and campsites. Each building on the Polish side had its satellite dish, like an eyeless eye socket. On the Slovakian shore there was a heavy concentration of Górale restaurants and bars, advertised by a generic billboard displaying a fellow with long hair, a shaggy moustache and foxy grin, wearing a round hat with a feather in it, a short waistcoat and sheepskin leggings. Each restaurant boasted its Górale band, serving medleys of mountain music to go with the grilled meat.

Those insufficiently musical to saw at a fiddle or bellow an air, but still able to supply their own hat and leggings, had found jobs on the rafts, poling the visitors down the boisterous but unthreatening rapids of the Dunajec Gorge. Fishing was only permitted upstream from the main port of disembarkation for the rafts, where the resort petered out. I found a path to the water. There was a fisherman working his way down a promising run close to the near bank. I could see two or three others further upstream, dark shapes against the surface, like upraised fingers.

# Chapter 13

## Ja!

To the east of Stará L'ubovňa, a village called Chmel'nica stands a little way back from the Poprad, against a slope that rises into the hills straddling the border to the north. It's a quiet place, ordinary-looking. There are a few old wooden houses and a lot of modern ones made of cheap building blocks faced with plaster. There is a shop, a bar, a church and a cemetery.

There are two clues to Chmel'nica's unusual past beside the main road. One is a village sign, bidding you welcome in Slovak and in German. Almost opposite is a curious little chapel shaped like an igloo, built in memory of one Johann Nepomuk Helliger, a name with distinctly Teutonic associations.

If you meet one of the elderly souls going about their business and ask them a question in German – *Sprechen Sie Deutsch?* will do fine – the chances are they will answer you in German. The form of the language they speak among themselves is archaic, a Saxon relic centuries old, but they speak it with pride.

In Slovak, Chmel'nica means 'place of hops'. But to the German-speakers – who are still in a majority, though a shrinking one – the name of the village is Hopgarten, which means much the same. It's a while since anyone has grown hops there, but people do not forget.

German emigration and colonisation was one of the great forces that shaped central and eastern Europe in the medieval period. Initially its main thrusts were east along the Baltic, east and south into Silesia, and through Bohemia to Austria. The impetus was strong and sustained. Some stayed, some pushed on: down the Danube to Bratislava (which they called Pressburg) and Buda, across the Carpathians into Slovakia, to Transylvania and Dalmatia.

They came from different parts of the German-speaking world – Bavaria, Saxony, Brandenburg, Swabia, Thuringia, the Tyrol – for the usual reasons: to escape poverty, overcrowding, land shortages, feudal oppression, to seek a better life. What was unusual about this flow of people into the heart of Europe was that it happened mainly, not as a result of aggressive expansionism, but by invitation. In particular, successive Kings of Hungary – whose outlying territories were vulnerable to invaders and plagued by disorder – believed with good reason that German colonists would bring with them measures of German discipline, technology and industry.

These population transfers were highly organised affairs. A kind of promoter, usually a merchant, was hired to recruit colonists and organise the settlement. They came in groups structured according to the feudal model: a noble or two (if persuadable), merchants, priests, craftsmen, artisans, peasants. The lord held the land in fief to the Crown and apportioned manors or estates to vassals, who in turn parcelled them out among the lower orders.

The great advantage of the arrangement was that the German social model was imported in its entirety. It included German law, German class structure, the German system of agriculture, and – where appropriate – specialised technologies, particularly mining. It gave the colonists a sense of security and familiarity, enabling them to get on with their business confident that, however far they might have been from where they or their forbears had started, they were at home. They brought home, in its spiritual sense, with them, creating a corner of Germany wherever they were. Much later the tenacity with which they clung to their sense of national identity was to have appalling consequences.

The settlers of the *Zips* region at the northern fringe of medieval Hungary were granted exceptional privileges, because their settlements were intended as an outer defensive ring against any repetition of the Mongol invasions of the thirteenth century, the havoc and horror of which stayed fresh in the minds of Europe's rulers long after those ferocious men had ridden their horses back to the steppes. The 24 so-called *Zipser* towns were allowed a form of autonomy, run by councils of landowners, merchants and senior members of the craft guilds. They had the right to hold markets, to pay their feudal dues in cash rather than by sending men off to fight, to levy taxes on their citizens and customs dues on travellers, and to exercise trade monopolies.

They did well. A walk around the main square of the town they called Leutschau – now Levoča – gives an idea of how well. In 1321 the town was given the power to require passing traders to spend at least 14 days there, and to offer first refusal on their goods to the locals. As Leutschau stood on the major route for importing Hungarian wine into Poland via the Poprad valley as well as silks and perfumes from the East, the opportunities for milking them were extensive.

During the fifteenth and sixteenth centuries the rich burghers of Leutschau built themselves gabled and portalled mansions around the main square. From the leaded windows beneath the overhanging eaves, they looked out on their splendid arcaded Town Hall, and at the less imposing but equally important Weigh House, where the business of assessing tariffs was done. Closing their heavy studded doors behind them, they would take themselves off across the cobbles to the Church of St James to give thanks for their good fortune. They would heave themselves off their knees into their high-backed seats and fix their eyes on the high altar: 70 feet of limewood chiselled and rubbed into an amazing depiction of the Last Supper, gilded in gold and silver to glint in the dusty light. It took the virtuoso carver known as Master Paul thirty years to complete the work. It and the church and everything else was paid for from the proceeds of trade, and the faces of the saints gathered at the table with Christ are unmistakably German burgher faces. They knew their worth, these fellows, and made sure they received their dues.

In time the *Zipser Sachsen*, as they were known, began to feel their geographical predicament. Cut off from their cultural bedrock and spiritual homeland, they were marooned on the edge of a Europe continually ravaged by plague, wars and power struggles. Increasingly their privileges and wealth stoked jealousy among the natives who surrounded them. In 1876 the Hungarian Diet decided it was time to flex its Magyar muscles. The special status of the *Zips* towns was abolished, German schools were closed, and the pressure to Magyarise – Hungarian names, Hungarian language, Hungarian ways – was intensified. To escape economic hardship and repression, thousands of *Zipser* craftsmen and peasants emigrated, mainly to the United States.

Censuses taken in 1869, 1900 and 1910 show a steadily declining German population in the *Szepes* county, as it had been renamed by the authorities in Budapest. Many of those who remained bent with the breeze, taking Slovak or Hungarian names and gradually letting go of the Teutonic legacy. But many did not. The rump clung with the utmost stubbornness to their German identity and the bond between them and their land, the *Blut und Boden*, Blood and Soil.

After 1918, German political philosophers, reacting to the catastrophe of the war and the loss of overseas colonies, embraced the concept of *Mitteleuropa*, a federation of states across central and eastern Europe brought together by a shared sense of German-ness. It was eagerly seized upon by Nazi ideologues who promoted it into a vision of a Greater Germany, extending from the Saar to the Ukraine, and used it to justify military expansion. The doctrine proved fatally irresistible to the beleaguered fringe populations, particularly the *Sudeten* and *Zipser* Germans within the borders of the hastily and precariously cobbled together state of Czechoslovakia.

In Slovakia, most *Zipser Sachsen* fervently supported the puppet regime of Jozef Tiso, which repudiated ties with Prague and set about deporting Jews with enthusiasm. Their fate was sealed at the end of the conflict by the decision of the Allies to reconstitute Czechoslovakia and allocate it to the Soviet sphere of influence. The Czech president, Edvard Beneš, was given a free hand to organise the mass expulsion of ethnic Germans from Sudeten and Spiš. It was a vicious, cruel, horrible business. Many were murdered in a wave of reprisals. Thousands died of disease and starvation in the internment camps. Only those who were able to prove anti-fascist credentials were allowed to stay. In Slovakia that meant, in practice, that one German village survived. That was Chmel'nica.

The book given to me by Slavo and Stano Truska gave the official version of its history, which was that the inhabitants of Chmel'nica 'proved significant anti-fascist attitude' and were there-fore awarded citizenship by a wise and beneficent state. In fact, on two occasions in 1946 Czech troops surrounded the village with orders to round everyone up and deliver them to the internment camp at Stará L'ubovňa. Each time the villagers were warned by their Slovak and Ukrainian neighbours and slipped away into the forests, where they remained for several weeks. In the end about 100 were expelled, and the rest – 600 of them – were permitted to return to their homes.

Some of this history is hinted at in the cemetery. The graves are distributed across rising ground to the eastern side of the village, a short walk from the church. The space is terraced, so that the gravestones stand or lie in neat lines. None is more than a century or so old, which suggests that there must be another resting place for Hopgarten's departed somewhere else, but I couldn't find it.

A few of the names – Dekker, Schisser, possibly Lompart – were

German, but most were Slovak. The inscriptions told a different story. Most were very simple: *Hier Ruhen* or *Ruhe in Frieden* — Here Lies or Rest in Peace. One, cut into a substantial cross, was more elaborate: *Gekreuzigter Jesus Erbarme Dich Der Armen Seelen Im Pegfeuer* — something about the crucified Jesus being moved to pity poor souls in some kind of fire.

Walking thoughtfully back to my car I met an elderly, upright man making his way slowly along the street. He was dressed in old clothes, with a flat cap above a nut-brown face. I bade him good day: *Guten Tag*. He smiled and responded in kind. Summoning my exiguous German for the first time since saying goodbye to Pavel Janicek nearly twenty years before, I asked him if many people in the village still spoke the language. I understood him to reply that the old people — *Die Alte Leute* — did, but not the young. The village was full of Slovaks. He gestured at one of the new houses. *Alles ist kaput*, he said, turning away.

# Chapter 14

## Brown coal and spotted trout

The destiny of the town of Most, in northern Bohemia, was fixed many millions of years ago when the trees of the great primeval forests fell and decayed. Across a region shaped like the blade of a sickle, stretching across northern Bohemia and south-east Germany into Polish Silesia, an immense stratum of stored energy was deposited. Measured by carbon content, the stuff comes between peat and hard black coal. It is called lignite, or brown coal, and is about the most polluting fuel on earth.

Compared with its black cousin, brown coal has a much lower burning temperature and releases a much higher proportion of its own volume in carbon waste. Its advantage lies in its accessibility.

It lies at the surface or just under. There is no need to sink deep and expensive shafts and dig long and expensive tunnels to get at it. It can just be scooped up and put to use.

The extraction of lignite began at Most four centuries ago, when the town was called Brüx, and Bohemia was part of the Habsburg monarchy. In the second half of the nineteenth century coal production boomed and Brüx with it. Half a million tons were dug in 1860; 18 million in 1913. It was a grimy place, wholly lacking the splendour and elegance of the spa towns of Carlsbad and Marienbad to the west, but in its dusty way it exhibited the same Germanic sense of self-belief. There was a spacious main square lined with hotels, inns, banks and town houses. There was a brewery, a museum, a theatre, a stately town hall and a lavishly endowed guildhall. The old photographs show a typically solid, respectable, unfancy Habsburg town.

The old photographs are pretty much all that is left. Brüx became Most when Czechoslovakia was stitched together by the peacemakers in 1919. In 1938, after the German invasion, it temporarily reverted to being Brüx. In 1945, as Most again, it set about cleansing itself of German infection. Around 50,000 German citizens were rounded up and either booted out or set to work in the mines; those, that is, who were not murdered, did not commit suicide (at least 200 did) and survived the internment camps.

The town went back to its business, digging coal. In time a problem presented itself to the authorities. Surveys showed that the deposits to the east were approaching exhaustion. Plentiful coal remained; the problem was that the town was sitting on it.

These were not men to allow parochial interests or a bourgeois attachment to old buildings to block the march of progress. It was obvious to anyone that the 100 million tons of coal lying beneath the town were more valuable than the town itself. In 1962 the order came from Prague: *Likvidace* or liquidation. Down tumbled the town hall, the guildhall, the fine theatre, the solid, sooty burghers' houses, the rows of miners' hovels. To replace them, a new Most arose to the west, a bristling forest of square towers and cuboids, steel and concrete emblems of the Marxist–Leninist–Stalinist way. 'It is a socialist city from its foundations . . . a representation of our present,' trumpeted local officials.

One building alone was spared, the Church of the Annunciation of the Virgin Mary, which stood on the edge of the mine. This decision was in part a sop to the incurable public attachment to churches. But the Party men also saw an opportunity to demonstrate to the outside world the prowess of socialist technology and an enlightened concern for heritage. The church would be moved in its entirety to a new position, half a mile to the west, where it could continue to overlook the mine.

Trenches were dug, runners were laid, the interior pillars were girdled in steel and concrete belts, and the whole structure was shifted at a speed of two centimetres a minute on a journey lasting 28 days. The church reached its new resting place on 30 September 1975. It was a proud day in the history of the republic and was celebrated in an official film which opens with soothing harp music and a sequence of shots of the old town being smashed down. The Virgin's church then appears, standing over the chasm of the mine. A voice, mincing and precise, asks in English: 'How is a church transferred?' Bulldozers grind, craftsmen chisel, engineers ponder charts, 'heroes in overalls' get the hard work done. Harps twang anew. 'Let praise be given,' the voice exhorts, 'to those who deserve praise' – foremost among these, according to the commentary, the Czech Ministry of Culture.

This nauseating piece of propagandist tosh was released in 1988, the year before the Velvet Revolution. Curiously it was still being shown, entirely unedited, when I visited the church in July 2008. The heroes of the Ministry of Culture who had ordered the *likvidace* of old Most were apparently still heroes. Nor was there any significant reference to the episode in the spacious municipal museum. Having wandered through echoing rooms displaying photos of winter sports, old peasants, wooden churches and the opening of a dam, and inspected the inevitable cabinets of dead birds and desiccated fungi, I demanded to know why the destruction of the old town had been ignored. The museum's deputy director was summoned. He produced a postcard of nineteenth-century Brüx. I asked if that was all they had. He shrugged his shoulders and looked helpless.

On a peach of a summer's day in late May 1990 I took the road that led from Prague towards north Bohemia. I had Smetana in my head, pictures of rolling hills, deep woods filled with birdsong, sweeping fields, market towns of ochre houses with higgledy-piggledy roofs, a gabled tavern with oak benches and tables and flagons of cool, golden beer. I was heading for a place called Litvinov, which was not far from the border with East Germany. Apart from that, I knew nothing about it. I had never heard of the North Bohemian Brown Coal Basin.

Gradually I became aware of a change in the quality of the light, as if someone had stretched a grubby handkerchief across the sky. The blue was infected by a sickly pallor. I stopped whistling *Má Vlast* and looked more closely in front of me. Ahead was a different sky altogether, yellowish-grey, menacing, pressing down on the land.

An airborne warning trembled against my sinus membranes. A few miles further on I was assailed by a dreadful smell of soot, bad eggs, blocked drainpipes and decomposed earthworms, with a sharp tang to it that recalled botched experiments in the chemistry lab at school and an acrid taste that puckered the inside of my mouth.

The road took me along the eastern flank of Litvinov's neighbour, Most. To my right a brown abyss stretched further than I could see, its limits lost in the fog of dust hanging over it. Far below I glimpsed wavering lines of trucks and diggers, like the larvae of caddis flies, crawling across the bottom. Further on, squat cooling towers took shape in the murk, resembling pustules thrust up from an infected limb. A gigantic agglomeration of shapes in steel and concrete began to reveal itself: pipes twisting like snakes in a pit; fat cylinders on their sides, thin cylinders poking up; compressors, turbines, silos webbed with ladders and platforms; storage tanks stained with filth; grimy office blocks. Railway lines threaded their way through this jungle, panting locomotives pulling long lines of rusty red wagons. The whole nightmarish organism smoked and steamed and hissed and clanked and throbbed with an appalling mechanised vitality. I had reached the Czechoslovak–Soviet Friendship Petro-Chemicals Works.

Litvinov was attached to the northern perimeter of the complex and more than 11,000 of its people worked there. They knew their role in the partnership. They were all used to seeing the sun as a furnace in a purulent yellow sky. They were used to keeping their windows shut even on the hottest day. They were used to regarding the wind as their best friend, because on the days without it the toxic gas shield pressed down on them like a cupped hand. On those days – the worst of them in winter – everyone's head ached. Mothers kept small children at home; the older ones went to school wearing breathing masks supplied free by the compassionate Party. Everyone in Litvinov knew that the rates of cancers, viral liver infections, parasitic and respiratory diseases, and allergies were far higher than anywhere else in Czechoslovakia, and that life expectancy was years below.

Another road wound north out of Litvinov towards the border with East Germany. At first, as it climbed, it turned this way and that through luxuriant woods of oak, beech and sycamore, and you could fool yourself that you were getting away from the worst of it. Then the deciduous belt gave way to the coniferous forests that have cloaked these mountains – to the Germans the *Erzgebirge*, to the Czechs the Krušné Hore – through the ages.

A pox was rampant here, devouring and destroying. Whole hill-sides of trees were dead. Pale grey skeletons, trunks mottled with lichen and ivy, stood in lines among their fallen comrades. In some places the tops of the firs and the tips of the branches still showed green, but the leprous grey was advancing. Efforts had been made to clear some of the casualties and plant new species, in particular Canadian spruce said to be resistant to the acid rain and infestations of bark beetle that came with it. A few plantations, protected from the prevailing winds, seemed to have escaped the plague. But overall, silence and death reigned over the sick forest.

The Kroupas – Tomáš, his wife Jarka, and a chubby son, aged two, also called Tomáš – lived in a first-floor flat at 821 Lenin Street, Litvinov. The balcony looked out over the Czechoslovak–Soviet Friendship Petro-Chemicals Works, where Tomáš and Jarka both worked. They had met as chemistry students at university in Prague and had come to Litvinov because their contract with the state required them to do so. Tomáš came from the ancient silver mining town of Kutná Hora, where his parents still lived and to which he longed to return. But there were no jobs or flats in Kutná Hora; and as for Prague, you had to bribe your way on to the housing waiting list, and even then it could take 20 years to be offered anything.

Litvinov guaranteed them work, somewhere to live, schooling, health care, leisure facilities. In return, the Kroupas and thousands like them agreed to put down as a deposit their health and that of their children. They knew well enough that the yellow cloud of dioxides was poisoning them, but what choice did they have? They were not Communists in any ideological sense, but the fact of Communism had been the only reality they knew.

Now, in a matter of weeks, it had all been swept away like the stands of dead trees in the mountains. There were many for whom the revolution brought the hope of a better life. But for the Kroupas it meant bewilderment and fear. Their lives had been a wearying grind but uncomplicated, the system taking care of everything. Now the system was no more. The one improvement they could see in their lives was in the quality of TV: they could watch Havel's banned plays, satires on Husak and the old gang, documentaries exposing the scandals of the past. Yes, they could talk, demonstrate, vote, but to what end? Who was going to save them and their jobs in a manufacturing process that had polluted half of Europe?

Tomáš spoke decent English and was mad about fishing. He had contributed a number of highly technical articles about catching pike to the main Czechoslovak fishing magazine. At his request I had brought with me an English video about pike-fishing, which he watched intently while I tried to convey the gist of the commentary, delivered in a thick Brummie accent. He asked me a number of technical questions, which I struggled to answer to his satisfaction, and sought my opinion of leading figures in the English pike-fishing scene, none of whom I had heard of.

By nine o'clock in the evening he and Jarka were yawning hard. Their shift began at 6.40 a.m., by which time they had deposited young Tomáš at the company crèche. There were two bedrooms in the flat, so I shared one with the boy. The walls were cardboard-thin, making every sound audible; not that there were many, inside or outside, for the whole town was soon asleep. I lay awake for two or three hours, trying to get used to the chemical smell, listening to little Tomáš snoring and snuffling and bouncing around in his cot.

In the morning we left Litvinov to go fishing. It turned out that, because of fatherhood, lack of money and lack of transport, Tomáš had not fished at all for two years. Moreover he knew very little about fly-fishing, which was the purpose of the trip. No matter, he said. He had enlisted the help of an expert, a fellow contributor to the same angling magazine, a man with unrivalled experience of Bohemian trout streams. But first there was the small matter of my licence.

My cheerful, ignorant assumption was that this would be no problem. I was an Englishman and would therefore be welcome – doubly so because I was an Englishman with dollars. Tomáš shook his head gloomily. He had never heard of a Westerner coming to Bohemia to fish. It may well be that none ever had. Therefore there would be no precedent. Officialdom – Czech officialdom – worked according to precedents. Therefore there would be obstacles.

Our first port of call was Karlovy Vary, which was full of Germans calling it Carlsbad. I parked next to a dishwater-grey block of flats. As we walked away I noticed a message in rusting letters ten feet tall stuck to the top of the building:

SOVĚTSKA ŽELEZNIČNÍ DOPRAVA POHODLNE – BEZPEČNE – VŽDY VČAS.

Underneath was an English translation:

SOVIET RAILWAY TRANSPORT COMFORTABLY – QUICKLY – ALWAYS IN TIME.

Tomáš laughed angrily. 'You have ever been in Russian train? No? You must try. Is bloody cold, bloody slow, always bloody late. Maybe it doesn't arrive ever. That is one incredible bloody Russian lie.'

We walked along the Tepla, the small river that snakes through the centre of town, past a monumental and remarkably hideous 1970s thermal sanatorium, with the colonnades, terraces and grand avenues of imperial Carlsbad rising on either side. Tomáš had no interest in the history of this most splendid of spa towns, nor in any of its imposing buildings and monuments. Instead he closely studied the roach and chub finning in the clear shallow stream, clearly believing that anyone who would come here to take the waters rather than fish them must have something seriously wrong with them.

Opposite the Yuri Gagarin Colonnade and next to the exquisite Church of St Mary Magdalene were the offices of the proverbially inefficient and obstructive national tourist authority, Čedok. Tomáš's inquiry about a licence for me prompted a decisive shake of the head from the matron behind the long polished counter. He tried again. Eventually she condescended to inform him that, on that very day, Čedok had assumed the responsibility for issuing fishing licences to foreigners. Unfortunately, in the case of Karlovy Vary – she could not, of course, speak for other outposts of the Čedok empire – the administrative transfer had not been accompanied by the necessary forms.

We proceeded further west, to Sokolov, another sooty centre of brown coal mining, where we picked up the expert on Bohemian trout streams. His name was Standa, an abbreviation of Stanislav. He was a little older than Tomáš, a little younger than me, with a long, drooping body to go with a long, drooping black moustache and long, lank, black hair. Together the three of us went to the Čedok office in Sokolov, where an exchange identical in its essentials to that in Karlovy Vary took place. We were advised to try at Cheb, another 25 miles to the west.

On the way to Cheb I expressed irritation and surprise at the difficulties we were encountering. Surely, I asked, that kind of bureaucratic nonsense must be on its way out? Tomáš and Standa looked at me uncomprehendingly. 'What about the changes?' I asked. Tomáš shook his head. Čedok was Čedok. It was an institution, a feature of the landscape. It would take more than the end of Communism to get rid of Čedok.

I had an idea. I would fish without a licence and plead ignorance if caught. Tomáš was appalled.

'It is against the law,' he said sternly. 'You have laws in England?'

'Yes, but this is fishing.'

'Don't you have laws for fishing in England?'

'Yes, but . . .'

'And don't you obey the laws?'

'Of course. Well, most of the time.'

'In Bohemia fishermen obey the laws. Maybe it is different in Slovakia.'

The forms for issuing fishing licences to foreigners had arrived in Cheb that morning. They were in German, and the completion of one was a lengthy business, beginning with the insertion of multiple carbons to provide copies in triplicate, quadruplicate, or, quite possibly, octuplicate. Each of the many sections had to be translated from German into Czech for the benefit of Tomáš, and by him into English for me. My responses then made the return journey. The process took half an hour. Tomáš then formally advised me of the main terms. I must carry the licence at all times. I must be equipped with various essentials including a net, a pair of scissors, a pair of forceps for removing the hook, and a tape measure to ascertain if a fish was big enough to kill. I must supply a written record of dates, times, locations and catches. The licence allowed me to fish on no more than two days in any one week, only on rivers designated as trout and grayling waters, in just two of the eleven districts into which Bohemia was divided for the purpose of administering fishing. The cost was $68. He must have assumed that, like everyone from the West, I was enormously rich, because he did not blink at this outrageous charge, which was not far off a month's salary for him.

We spent the night at Standa's flat in Sokolov. Two or three times on the way there he opened the window and hailed policemen who were directing traffic. Tomáš explained that, until recently, Standa had been a traffic policeman himself. He was now working as a self-employed engraver. Inside the flat were a number of slabs of marble and slate awaiting inscription. Standa presented me with a glass goblet engraved with a lion rampant, which I suspected of being from unsold stock. There was, I gathered, a Mrs Standa, but she had temporarily moved out to make way for us. For supper we shared a tasty but rather small eel that Standa had caught. He and Tomáš talked incessantly about fishing, their voices mixing with blasts of rock music from the hi-fi. Standa smoked one cigarette after another, but neither of them drank alcohol. There was only tea. I daydreamed of Budvar and Pilsner Urquell.

In the early morning we drove south to Tachov, a small town a few miles from the German border. It was grey, chilly, devoid of life or any prospect of breakfast. We stopped near a bridge next to a truck and bus depot. A brownish stream flowed sluggishly beneath it, the surface broken by several wheels and petrol drums.

'Standa says we fish here,' Tomáš said. 'He says he has caught big grayling here.' Standa stood smoking.

I did not wish to seem unappreciative of my first Bohemian trout stream. 'Here? It doesn't look very . . .' Tomáš and I stood together and stared into the dark, lifeless water.

'I will tell him we don't like to fish here.'

Standa shrugged his shoulders.

Standa and Tomáš, Bohemia, 1990

We drove east out of Tachov, following the course of the stream, the Mže. The sky lightened, grey mutating into pale blue. The countryside was of the rolling variety, enormous undulating hedgeless fields bounded by distant forest, broken by an occasional copse or cluster of long, low concrete barns. We drove into a village of white-washed, red-roofed houses. There was a track to the right that led between walls of maize to a rickety wooden bridge where we stopped.

Tomáš and Standa took their tackle and marched off across a meadow bright with buttercups, marigolds, columbines, and other flowers in shades of blue, violet and yellow. I followed them at a distance. They walked up and down for a time, pausing frequently to consult the map that came with the licences. They examined a sign nailed to a willow, referred to the map, examined the sign again, referred to their rule booklet, discussed the matter and finally pronounced that this was a place we might legitimately fish. They took out pens and began to write in their licences. Tomáš looked up at me.

'You must also write,' he said in his schoolmasterly way. 'The date, time, location, what we fish for.'

'I've left my licence in the car. I'll fill it in later.'

Tomáš was scandalised. 'That is not possible. You must write before fishing. The rules state this.' He waved the booklet at me. I trudged resentfully back to the car.

But it was not possible to be bad-tempered for long on such a day, beside such a stream. It was unrecognisable as the dull, lethargic thing we had seen in Tachov. It weaved its twisting way between willows and alders and clumps of fir trees, racing over pebbly runs, slowing into reflective pools. Where the sun struck the surface, the colour was amber. But there were dark, shaded corners and places where the sunshine was filtered by foliage into a spangle of gold. Butterflies and bees shimmered over the wildflowers.

Standa's reputation as the leading expert on Bohemian trout and grayling streams was significantly enhanced by a delightful morning's fishing. After visiting the nearby town of Stříbro for a wretched lunch of fat pork, cold gravy and cold dumplings – I was sternly forbidden even one little beer because I was driving – we meandered south in accordance with Standa's instructions. In the early evening we reached Sušice, the main centre for the Šumava Mountains, a range of green, thickly wooded hills straddling the border with Austria. At the heart of the town, once we had got through the usual sprawl of factories, depots, dreary stores and drearier apartment blocks, was a fine, spacious square, on which stood the fine, elegant Hotel Fialka, where we booked rooms for one night only.

There was still time for more fishing. Sušice stands on the Otava, a big, strong river that flows north-east out of the hills to join the Vltava north of Písek. Standa said he knew it well. The place to go to was downstream from the town. He had caught many large grayling there. We took a rough track off the main road and crawled along it for what seemed like miles, repeatedly crunching the bottom of my car against the ridge down the middle, until the way was blocked by a fallen lime tree. This was the spot, Standa announced. I got out. There was an insistent rumbling sound in the air, and I noticed that the trees were coated in fine white dust. As we neared the river the rumbling grew louder. A limestone quarry revealed itself beyond the far bank, with a cement factory attached going at full throttle. Standa, oblivious to my scowls of hatred, set off downstream, reappearing later with a tale of a big trout lost at the net. I fished for a time to the accompaniment of limestone being excavated and crushed into powder, but saw no sign of fish life.

The next day we struck gold. We spent the morning driving up and down the Otava valley while Standa alternated between staring intently at the map and blankly at passing landmarks, shrugging his shoulders, uttering expressions of mystification and burning cigarettes. In the end Tomáš and I tired of this, and I drove into a field next to which the Otava flowed swift and clear. It was a delicious day, too good for any more of it to be spent cooped up in the car with Standa and his diminishing store of tobacco. We fished downstream, and in almost every glide and pool we caught trout with golden flanks and big crimson and black spots. The one distraction was the regular passing through of flotillas of kayaks propelled by beefy, talkative Bohemians. I hooked a muscular female paddler on my backcast, prompting a screech of surprise, but she was all smiles when I detached the hook from her lifejacket.

Tents and cabins appeared among the pine trees. Tomáš came over, grinning broadly, his jumble of teeth gleaming. Was this not a beautiful river? Was the fishing not excellent? It turned out that this was the very place Standa had been thinking of all along. It seemed odd to me that he could have forgotten the existence of a campsite strung out along a mile or so of river, but I said nothing. We went to the campsite office and enquired about cabins. Tomáš proposed that we all share one, but the thought of nights next to Standa and his brimming ashtray did not appeal, and I insisted on a billet for myself. The cabins were raised on legs close enough to the water to hear its cadences. Mine was deathly cold and smelled of mildewed sleeping bags.

Setting off in the evening for more fishing, we passed the campsite canteen, where a band was playing a medley of hearty camping songs. Smoke mixed with the scent of pork grilling on a barbecue. It was my thirty-ninth birthday, and I had visions of a birthday dinner: sizzling ribs and fillet, cool beer, the three of us talking over the day and our successes. When we returned a couple of hours later, the bar was shut, the barbecue had been dismantled, and the members of the band were lolling around in a state of drunken hilarity while someone loaded their trumpets, horns and cornets into a van. Very reluctantly the woman in the kitchen produced three plates with a slice of cold ham, a gherkin and a stale bread roll on each. Before we could finish this feast she switched off the lights. It was a quarter past nine. We walked to our frigid quarters under a sky winking with starlight, our feet crunching on the frosted carpet of pine needles.

TF fishing the Otava, 1990

Despite the austere living conditions and provisions, those days beside the Otava were magical. Each night the temperature dropped well below freezing. Each morning revealed a sky of flawless blue above the spiky tops of the pines, the river flashing silver and gold in the sunlight. The fishing was consistently good, its one drawback – from my oh-so-English point of view – being its highly sociable character. Any fish caught within view of another angler, however far away, was regarded as an invitation to splash over and join in the fun. When I shouted 'Oi', which I did a few times, it was interpreted as the universal Bohemian greeting – 'Ahoy' – and met with a wave and a smile.

On our last day I felt a pressing need for space and solitude, so I explored well upstream from the camp, passing through a little village where a church poked its steeple above a screen of beech trees. There was a bridge with a pool below where the trout were very obliging. On my way back to camp I passed an old man in a shapeless black hat, pulling a cart heaped with newly cut grass. His dog raced over to pick an argument with my waders. He called the animal off, then asked me what success I'd had. I held up my hand, raising the fingers one by one. He grinned, evidently pleased that his river had not failed me.

That evening I stood on the wooden footbridge that crossed the Otava in the middle of the camp. A man was fishing a little way below me, but I had had enough. Looking downstream, with the sun setting behind me, I saw a huge cloud approaching above the water. It consisted of millions upon millions of insects – small sedges, maybe, or some kind of evening olive. Its front reached and passed me, but still it extended downstream as far as I could see, from the surface of the water up to the tops of the trees. Where the cloud met the shafts of sunlight, the insects were lit so that they resembled a blizzard of golden snowflakes.

I drove Tomáš back to Litvinov the next day, and retreated from the Brown Coal Basin without much regret. He presented me with a copy of the Czechoslovak–Soviet Friendship Petro-Chemicals Works company brochure in English. When I opened it months later, it still exuded the familiar odours of polyethylene and ethyl-benzene. In the photographs, all the buildings, turbines, silos and sections of pipework were spotlessly, lustrously clean. White-coated technicians were shown leaning over computers in attitudes of fierce and fruitful concentration. Scientists examined the contents of test-tubes. The ice-hockey team raced around the indoor sports arena. ('It is a sport which offsets the one-sided mental and phys-ical stress caused by work,' the text stated.) Solemn couples in formal dress clasped each other on the club dance-floor in front of a fresco of white doves.

Tomáš had drawn a circle around a window in one of the blocks to indicate where he worked. I pictured him in his grey overalls, downy stubble framing his round chin, dreaming of the Mže and the Otava and the flash of a hooked fish.

\*   \*   \*

Neither Czechoslovakia nor the Soviet Union lasted long after 1990, while the 'friendship' between them had never amounted to much more than a fiction promoted by party hacks in Prague and Moscow. The name of the complex at Litvinov was discarded; it is now Chemopetrol, a division of the Polish company PKN Orlen, which doesn't have anything like the same ring to it, although it is doubtless an improvement in other ways. The workforce has shrunk from 11,000 to 3,000 but is still large enough to warrant its own tram station. The chimneys still smoke and the towers steam and the batteries of silos rear from the undergrowth of piping. But the power stations no longer discharge half a million tons of sulphur dioxide a year, and the sky over Litvinov is no longer yellow, and the children no longer wear breathing masks to go to school. The pines of the Ore Mountains have stopped dying and green is creeping back across the grey slopes.

The fuel to feed this beast – not the beast it was, but still hungry enough – no longer comes from the hole on Most's doorstep. The railway that delivered the coal has been abandoned and the buildings beside the tracks have been left to crumble. The wagons stand in frozen lines, wheels rigid with rust, lapped by the encroaching tide of weeds and brambles. The great moonscape of the mine is silent and still. Efforts have been made to disguise it by smoothing down the ridges left by the excavators, sowing grass and planting groves of beeches and oaks. But no cosmetic surgery can conceal the scar tissue of the past, which leads in the centre to a pit, half-filled with grey, dead water, its edges gouged by the tracks of the departed machines.

A spanking new crematorium has been built on reclaimed land near the church. Most itself was much as I remembered: a dismal sprawl of apartment and office blocks deposited along windswept boulevards. There was a new shopping centre, and Tesco had arrived. Most's entry in Wikipedia speaks of a depressing feel to the town, with 'a huge share of people' living in the apartment blocks known as *panelaks*, and unemployment at the highest level anywhere in the Czech Republic.

I found the block of flats in Litvinov where I had stayed with Tomáš and Jarka. Not surprisingly, they did not live there any more and no one I could find remembered them. I managed to talk my way into the personnel office at the petro-chemicals works, where they looked through the records. There had been many Kroupas, but none who fitted my description of Tomáš. I had more luck with Jarka. She had left some years before but a former colleague dug out a mobile number for her. I rang it several times without getting an answer. In the end I left the ruined landscape behind and went south-west in search of the little stream that had given Tomáš and me and the profoundly irritating expert on Bohemian trout-fishing such joy.

Alas for memory! For sure, many, many things had changed for the better for Bohemia and its people in those 18 years . . . but not for the Mže. They had slapped down a motorway a few miles south of the river, bringing its valley within a couple of hours' drive of Prague. The meadows I remembered had been parcelled into plots for cabins, cottages and chalets, with window-boxes, garages and paved parking spaces. Mowers hummed and strimmers snarled in the miniature gardens. I saw an elderly man dead-heading roses. Next door a woman had stacked up her dirty plates and dishes at the water's edge. Every clearing in the woods seemed to have its picnic benches and tables.

I could not find the track we had taken off the road from Tachov, or the dilapidated wooden bridge, or the meadow bright with flowers. But the river was there. The water, which I remembered as clear with a peaty, amber tinge, was now murky and sluggish. I tramped a long way along a well-worn path extending from Kočov, where Tomáš, Standa and I had stopped, downstream to the next village, Pavlovice. My spirits revived briefly as a result of catching two small grayling in the first pool I fished. Thereafter

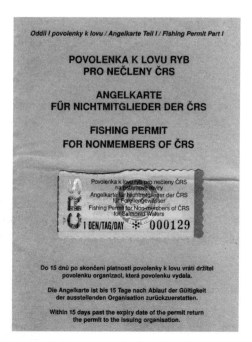

Fishing permit for the Mže, 2008

they sank and kept on sinking. On the bridge back where I had started I met two blokes who pointed at the water and shook their heads. '*Nicht gut — alles essen.*' No good, all eaten.

The Otava near Sušice was no better. Unlike the Milava campsite on the Poprad, the Annin campsite where Tomáš, Standa and I had stayed was still in business, but its haphazard distribution of cabins, tents and caravans now struck me as scruffy rather than picturesque. Its main attraction, the river, had been ruined by someone deciding it would be a good idea to drag a dredger along it and dump the spoil in an unsightly levee along the bank. Dank and dreary weather added to my sense of melancholy. Families shrouded in raincoats wandered around under the dripping branches. Dads played soggy games of football with their sons. Radios tinkled from inside tents and caravans. I didn't see anyone fishing.

I went up through the little village with its church and steeple in search of the bridge and the pool where the trout had obliged. The bridge was gone, washed away by a flood, leaving two jagged ends and chunks of masonry strewn across the riverbed. I stood on the new wooden footbridge that had been strung across the water, looking downstream, trying to work out how my picture fitted. There was a pool, but it was six times bigger than it should have been. There was no beech, no gentle curl of water, but a strong, deep flow the colour of stewed tea. There was no hatch of insects. Not a trout showed itself.

I felt I should go through the motions, so I pulled on my waders and spent half an hour covering the lower half of the pool. I caught nothing, saw nothing, felt nothing. There was none of that sense of latent life that a fisherman draws from a river just by being in it, even when the fish are not feeding. The spirit I had found there before was absent; whether permanently or not, I cannot say.

I finally caught up with Tomáš by phone a few weeks after I got back to England. He and Jarka were living in a village a few miles east of Litvinov. They had both prospered since leaving the petro-chemicals industry. He was working for Ford, testing cars; she had a job in the electricity supply industry. They had built themselves a big house. Tomáš told me at some length about how big their swimming pool was. He still fished occasionally for pike and carp, he said, but had never been back to the Mže and the Otava. He had heard they were no good any more: too many fishermen, too much poaching.

I asked after the expert on Bohemian trout streams. Tomáš said they had lost touch. The last he'd heard, Standa was not well; too much smoking, probably. Tomáš said he came to England once or twice a year, on business. I urged him to give me a call so that we could meet up and have a drink, but I haven't heard from him yet.

## Chapter 15

### *Subtle fish, fool's gold, fallen angels*

One of my favourite monuments anywhere in the world stands on a roundabout on the western side of the town of Třeboň in central Bohemia. It is a bronze cast of four fish entwined around a central pillar garlanded with four roses. Two slender lights rise above the ensemble, which at night bathe it in a lambent glow.

It may not qualify as high art. I suspect that the critics, if they came this way and happened to notice it at all, would probably laugh at it. Never mind them. As an expression of civic pride and a statement of a town's sense of identity, it transcends criticism.

The twin emblems − a fish, a flower − would mean nothing to a casual passer-by. But if he or she stopped long enough for a ramble around the delightful old town of Třeboň, and they observed and enquired intelligently, they would find both pleasingly woven together through the long history of the place.

The flower is a red rose and was the badge of the dynasty that ruled this part of the world in the manner of kings throughout the Middle Ages almost until the onset of the religious wars that tore the region apart in the first half of the seventeenth century. Their family name was Rožmberk, and they styled themselves Lords of the Rose.

The fish, whose representation is splendidly lifelike, should be recognised by anyone who knows anything about the subject. They have wide, powerful, twin-bladed tails, flanks mailed with scales like golden guineas or doubloons, round, slightly protuberant eyes,

Fishy welcome to Třeboň

and great, fat-lipped mouths purpose-built for the sucking in of bloodworms, larvae, and all the other good and nourishing things hidden in the mud at the bottom of ponds and lakes. They are carp, as is confirmed by the legend inscribed into the circular plinth on which they perform their aquatic ballet. It reads: TŘEBOŇSKÝ KAPR, which I roughly translate as TŘEBOŇ CARP TOWN.

But why carp?

'The carp,' Izaak Walton wrote in *The Compleat Angler*, 'is the Queen of Rivers: a stately, good, and a very subtle fish.' Actually, although they are content enough in unhurried flowing water, the carp's natural domain is still water: reed-fringed lakes and meres, monastic ponds, castle moats and the like; where the water is dark but clear, with trees around to keep off the wind, and trailing willow branches to provide refuge, and beds of lilies with waxy leaves in whose shadow the fish may hang motionless, but for the occasional languid wave of a fin and the opening and closing of gills and mouth.

Carp have long had a reputation among anglers for being excep-
tionally cautious and hard to catch. Walton recommends fishing
for them with a bluish marsh or meadow worm, a paste of bean
flour flavoured with honey and the flesh of either cat or rabbit
'cut small', or gentles, otherwise known as maggots. Having caught
your carp (the hard part), Walton suggests stewing it in sweet
marjoram, thyme, parsley, rosemary, savory, onions, mace, orange
and lemon rind, pickled oysters, anchovies, claret, butter, eggs and
salt – 'and so serve it up and much good to you'.

It is usually assumed that carp have been around for ever. In
fact, our carp originated in the eastern part of the Danube,
probably in what is now Slovakia. Scholars argue, as scholars do,
about how they first came to western Europe. One version is that
the Romans sampled carp flesh on their travels and liked it so well
that they arranged for specimens to be transported back to their
*piscinae*. However, the first incontestable references date from much
later, the eleventh century, and are to carp being reared in Bavaria,
Franconia and Swabia – although that simply means they were
definitely being eaten in Germany a thousand years ago, not that
they didn't grace tables in Rome a lot earlier without anyone taking
the trouble to record the fact.

Medieval cooks and their patrons embraced the carp eagerly.
The first recipe for them appeared in a French cookbook in the
late-thirteenth century, by which time carp ponds had been dug
in Picardy, Burgundy, and principalities all the way to the Rhine.
Carp became popular because they grew fast to a considerable size,
were catholic in their eating habits, tolerant of wide variations in
temperature (they like it warm but can survive all but the hardest
frosts), could be kept alive out of water for lengthy periods if
wrapped in damp cloth, and made for good feasting.

England lagged far behind in the emergent technology of fish
farming because sea fish and migratory fish – particularly salmon
– were more readily available. Where ponds were created, they

were more status symbols for the Norman aristocrats than material contributors to a market economy, and were generally used to store favoured species like pike, eels and bream rather than to rear fish. Walton, writing in the mid-seventeenth century, noted that carp 'nor hath been long in England', and attributed their introduction to 'one Mr Mascal, a gentleman that then lived at Plumsted in Sussex, a county that abounds more in this fish than any in the nation'.

The Mascal referred to by Walton is assumed to have been Leonard Mascall, a prolific producer of useful volumes on gardening, growing fruit, managing livestock and kindred subjects, who died in 1589. By then the carp culture of continental Europe had flourished mightily – nowhere more so than in the Kingdom of Bohemia. Outside Prague, power in Bohemia lay not with the king, but with the noble dynasties, of which the two noblest were the Pernštejns and the Rožmberks. Occasional allies, more often rivals, they shared a keen interest in the business of carp and carp ponds.

These, however, were not ponds as we might understand the word. For example, the one Vilem of Pernštejn had excavated below his castle at Hluboká nad Vltavou in the 1490s covered 450 hectares; and the network of waters around his principal stronghold at Pardubice, east of Prague, was fed with water from the Elbe via a canal 20 miles long.

Whatever the Pernštejns did, the Rožmberks liked to do bigger and better. One of their many domains was centred on Třeboň, and included great expanses of wetland and peatbog which were ideal for fish farming. Under the direction of their celebrated superintendent of fisheries, Josef Štěpánek Netolický, a system of ponds great and small was dug to the north and south of Třeboň, fed from the River Lužnice by an artificial channel almost 30 miles long called the Golden Canal, the *Zlatá Stoka*, not on account of its colour, which was muddy brown, but because of the steady stream of income it brought into the Rožmberk coffers.

Two generations later a young man of modest background, Jakub Krčín, was appointed regent of the Rožmberk estates. Krčín seems to have been in the grip of an obscure form of piscine megalomania. It inspired in him the ambition to create an empire of carp ponds that would eclipse the 215 or so surrounding the Perňstejn castle at Pardubice. He began with a big hole just beyond the walls of the Rožmberk castle in Třeboň, which was called *Svet*, meaning World. He extended various of Netolický's ponds and added to them. All the time he was dreaming of a new masterpiece, the pond of ponds, that would surpass anything his predecessors or the Perňstejn lackeys had managed, and would keep his master's name resounding through the ages.

To make room for the 500-hectare Rožmberk Pond, villages to the north of Třeboň were razed, tracts of farmland appropriated, and the dispossessed local peasantry reduced to beggary. A vast army of ditchers and diggers spent five years on the project, the most challenging aspect of which was the construction of a dam a mile long and 30 feet high, held in place by a triple avenue of oaks.

Krčín's master, Vilém Rožmberk, might well have shrugged off the firestorm of protests from his starving tenants, but the cost of his regent's mad scheme was another matter. Upon completion of the pond Krčín was pensioned off and banished. Three years later, in 1592, Vilém himself died, leaving the exchequer so depleted and the estates so burdened by debt that his successor – his younger brother, Petr Vok – was forced into drastic retrenchment. Castles and estates were auctioned off and the family seat was transferred first from Rožmberk nad Vltavou to Český Krumlov, and then from Krumlov to Třeboň. Within a decade the childless Petr Vok was dead too, and the Lords of the Rose were finished.

So much for the waxing and waning of great men. The great sheet of water that bears the Rožmberk name has lasted longer. The Czechs are still very fond of their carp; fried carp with potato salad is eaten in 2 million Czech households each Christmas. Five hundred years after the ponds were dug, they still produce 2,500 tons of carp a year, and the main fish restaurant in Třeboň listed no fewer than 26 ways of preparing them.

Bohemia's rich piscine heritage is celebrated lovingly in a fine museum not far from the Perňstejn pond system at Hluboká nad Vltavou. It occupies the ground floor of a mansion built in the early-eighteenth century for Prince Adam Franz Schwarzenberg, head of the dynasty that succeeded the Rožmberks as top dogs in southern Bohemia. Most tourists who come to Hluboká do so to goggle at the grotesque pastiche castle built on top of the hill for the pleasure of a later Schwarzenberg. Compared with this ludicrous riot of battlements and crenellations, Prince Adam's hunting lodge is a modest affair – though quite big enough to accommodate a few score of the cream of central European nobility in proper style.

The Schwarzenbergs were enormously rich and considered themselves enormously important. For such as they, the killing of animals was pretty much an obligatory hobby (one that cost Prince Adam dearly, as he was fatally wounded on one of his own hunts by the Emperor Charles VI). The upper floor of what is now the Hunting and Fishing Museum testifies to their passion for it. In the central hall, beneath crude frescoes of stags in various attitudes of death and suffering, an immense table constructed mainly of antlers stands on a carpet of fox pelts, surrounded by sofas and chairs covered in deer hide, the whole scene watched over by portraits of generations of Schwarzenberg hunters and their like-minded chums. The corridor outside is lined with the heads of lions, buffaloes, kudu, giraffes, cheetahs and other trophies accumulated on safari in Africa in the 1930s by Count Adam Schwarzenberg and – to judge from the photographs – his equally trigger-happy wife Hilda.

It is a relief to retreat downstairs from these scenes of carnage to the peaceful fishing section of the museum. The lives and works of Jakub Krčín, Josef Štěpánek Netolický and other architects of the Bohemian carp culture are recorded in panels, old prints, scraps of letters and other documents. Proper acknowledgement is made of the seminal contribution of the great Bishop Jan Dubravius of Olomouc, whose book *De Piscinis et Piscibus* – translated into English as *A New Booke of Good Husbandry Concerning the Order and Manner of Making Fish-ponds, with the Breeding, Preserving and Multiplying of the Carpe, Tench, Pike and Troute* – served as the standard textbook for generations of fish-farmers in every part of Europe. Ancient maps show the amazing scale of pond construction (by 1550 there were 26,000 of them in Bohemia, in case you're interested). There is a bronze sculpture of a carp, not as extravagant as the one on the roundabout at Třeboň, but equally full of scaly charm.

Bohemian carp

One old photograph records a visit by notabilities to the Třeboň fishing pavilion, decked out for the occasion with oars and spears and other paraphernalia, and festooned with nets as if it had been trapped in a gigantic spider's web. Another shows a line of 40 or 50 men up to their knees in the water hauling in the catch, while behind them stand wagons filled with barrels ready to take the harvest away.

The carp is the pre-eminent species featured in the museum, but others do get a look in. In one of the rooms there is even a display cabinet dedicated to the European eel, with a map showing its breeding grounds in the Sargasso Sea, as well as an assortment of eel spears and traps and a somewhat wizened specimen of the fish itself. It would have been nice if they had included a Czech translation of my own *The Book of Eels* but one cannot have everything, even in the best of museums.

In the autumn of 1586 two Englishmen arrived in Třeboň with their families, and were made welcome on the orders of Vilém of Rožmberk. They were given comfortable quarters in the castle and a laboratory was established for them in one of the gatehouses, fitted out with all manner of curious equipment. For the best part of three years the activities of the pair gave the people of the town something other than carp to talk about.

Vilém's all-powerful regent, Jakub Krčín, did not take kindly to their presence, denouncing them to his master – with good reason, in the case of one – as spongers, charlatans and scoundrels. But Vilém had more pressing matters on his mind than the outbursts of his temperamental factotum or even the fall-out from his pond-building programme. His difficulty could be summed up thus: three wives, no son. His heir was his younger brother, unmarried and therefore of no dynastic use at all. Vilém was acutely aware that time in which to extend the Rožmberk line was running out. He had his eye on a final throw of the marital dice with Polyxena Pernštejn, daughter of his pond rival to the north, but could not afford another barren match. He needed assurances that the auspices were favourable and help in securing a fruitful outcome, and he believed that the Englishmen might hold the key.

They made an oddly assorted partnership. The senior, by about

30 years, was Doctor John Dee, Elizabeth I's 'noble intelligencer', mathematician, astronomer, geographer, bibliophile, astrologer, philosopher, occultist; at that time just past the zenith of his fame as Europe's leading seeker after obscure truths and explorer of dark mysteries. The reputation of his companion, Edward Kelley, was less exalted. His long curly hair was rumoured to conceal at least one cropped ear, punishment – so it was said – either for forgery or for the more serious offence of entering a graveyard at Walton-le-Dale in Lancashire in order to exhume a corpse and persuade it to 'deliver strange Predictions' of the 'manner and time of death of a Noble young Gentleman as then in Wardship'.

Dee, for all his oddities and failings, was a man of powerful intellect and high principle, whereas Kelley was a conman and cozener. Yet Kelley – like the diabolical Scorpio Murtlock in Anthony Powell's *Hearing Secret Harmonies* – evidently possessed unusual magnetism and other very special gifts. The most precious of these, in the eyes of Doctor Dee and Vilém of Rožmberk, was the easy access he enjoyed to the 'other' world beyond the physical sphere.

It is not easy for twenty-first-century rationalists to understand the deep seriousness with which the invisible spirit forces of the universe were viewed in the pre-scientific age. This was not just the province of cranks and black magicians, although there were plenty of them about. Most educated people believed without question in the existence of the spirits; and, further, that if a discourse with them could be established and maintained, their great powers might be deployed in an earthly setting. To Dee – as to Paracelsus, Tycho Brahe and other great minds of the time – the spirit sphere was as real as the earth beneath their feet. The problem for Dee was gaining access to it. He did not have the skrying skill. Edward Kelley did.

Soon after their first meeting, at Dee's house beside the Thames at Mortlake, Kelley was facilitating extended exchanges with the angels. These were very numerous – 49 of them had names beginning with B, including Blumaza, Blintom and Bmanigal – but one in particular was most keen to talk. She was a little girl in a gown of 'changeable green and red', who skipped in and out between Dee's piles of books and left no reflection when she passed in front of the mirror. She said her name was Madimi. Through Kelley, the Doctor asked her where her home was. She replied that if she told him, she would be beaten. 'You shall not be beaten for telling the truth to them that love the truth,' he replied.

The road from Mortlake to Třeboň was long and circuitous. It took Dee and Kelley and their wives and Dee's children first to Poland with the dangerous and shady Count Olbracht Łaski, who hoped to invoke spirit help to put him on the Polish throne; and from Poland, inevitably, to Prague, where Europe's leading patron of the dark arts, the Holy Roman Emperor Rudolf II, held sway. This erudite, melancholic monarch was – in the opinion of the historian R. J. W. Evans – in the grip of an obsession with the occult that bordered on madness. He had gathered around him a scrum of alchemists, quacks, crooks, soothsayers, Rosicrucian frauds, black magicians, white magicians and the odd genuine man of learning, all offering – at a price – to reveal to him the secrets of the other side.

For a time Dee and Kelley prospered. Kelley had a remarkable flair for self-promotion, and Prague was soon buzzing with the story of how Arthur Dee, the Doctor's eight-year-old son, had been seen playing with gold quoits 'made by projection' in the garret of their lodgings. But in Rudolf's city few stars apart from his own burned brightly for long. Spiteful and envious murmurings against the Englishmen reached the Emperor's ears, and he abruptly banished them. At the same time, though, he acceded to the pleas of his friend Vilém of Rožmberk, who continued to hope that Dee and Kelley could help him in his quest for an heir, and graciously gave permission for them to go to Třeboň.

Edward Kelley could recognise a golden goose when he saw one. Soon after the channel of communication between Třeboň Castle and the angelic host was established, Vilém received assurances – couched in the usual ambiguous terms – that his plan was viewed favourably on high. In January his marriage to Polyxena Perňstejn was celebrated with a four-day feast in the course of which twelve tons of venison, nine tons of sucking pig, two tons of cheese, 20,000 eggs, 1,290 hares and 5,800 carp were consumed.

But Kelley's prime interest soon shifted from skrying to the potentially more lucrative field of alchemy. The lights burned late in the laboratory as he worked on a formula said to have been revealed to him in a document recovered from the crypt at Glastonbury, which involved dissolving silver in Aqua Regia, precipitating it with salt, mixing it with potash and lime, refining the blend, and adding solutions of mercury, depositing black earth, circulating pelican, settling the Red Oil and tincturing it with quicksilver. Another procedure required the rubbing of vinegar rust with sal ammoniac, thickening the resulting oil into stone, adding smears of menstrual fluid and fragments of horse manure, and mixing the pulverised compound with melted silver.

To keep his patron sweet, Kelley was still prepared to consult the angels on such matters as propitious times for Vilém to attempt to impregnate his new wife. But he became increasingly impatient with Dee's endless requests for audiences, which he saw as a tedious and unprofitable waste of time better spent among the tinctures and elixirs. The old man had become a nuisance. Kelley resolved to get rid of him if he could.

One evening during Lent in 1587, Kelley unexpectedly acceded to a request from Dee for him to sit before the seeing stone. He relayed a written message: '*He who commits adultery because of me, let him be blessed for charity and receive the heavenly prize.*' The following day, according to Kelley, the child-like Madimi appeared and opened her cloak to reveal herself naked. Later she went into an orchard and grafted together the branches of a tree. Pressed for an explanation by a dumbfounded Dee, Kelley said the vision amounted to an instruction that he and the Doctor should have sex with each other's wives. Dee was appalled. He clearly suspected that his colleague was up to lustful tricks, but he was also desperate not to lose his route to revelation. In the end he ordered his beloved wife Jane to comply. One night in May the two couples withdrew together to a chamber in the castle. Dee noted in his diary *pactum factum* – pact fulfilled.

Two days later Kelley reported seeing in the globe a Golden Woman who told him that she was '*a harlot for such as ravish me and a virgin with such as know me not*', and promising to '*stand naked before you that your love may be more inflamed towards me*'. That was the final spiritual action that Dee saw fit to record in his diary; quite possibly the final one Kelley performed for him. Forty weeks after the consummation of the 'cross-matching', Jane Dee gave birth to a son christened Theodorus Trebonius. A few months later an old friend of Dee's, Sir Edward Dyer, arrived in Třeboň. Dee's initial pleasure quickly gave way to resentment as it became apparent that Dyer's chief purpose was to try to persuade Kelley to return to England to place his talents at the service of Queen Elizabeth.

In the spring of 1589 the Doctor and his family left Třeboň for home. He never saw his skryer again.

For a time Kelley's reputation as Europe's leading practical alchemist soared. In London Edward Dyer told a dinner party that included the Archbishop of Canterbury how he had seen 'Mr Kelley put of the base metal into the crucible and after it was set a little upon the fire and a very small quantity of medicine put in and stirred with a stick of wood, it came forth in great proportion perfect gold.' Another report, from Prague, described Kelley making gold rings on demand. He was said to have sent a bedpan as a present to Queen Elizabeth, part of which he had transmuted into gold.

The Queen's chief minister, William Cecil, sent a stream of messengers and messages to Bohemia, commanding and then imploring Kelley to return and help England in her time of need. In vain. 'I am not so mad as to run away from my present honour and lands,' he replied. By now he had been created Baron Kelley by a grateful Vilém, who lavished on him estates, nine villages, two mansions in Prague and a castle. Rudolf himself was sufficiently impressed to summon the Baron to Prague to perform his wonders, then had him locked up when he failed to produce the goods. He talked his way out of jail, but after the death of Vilém of Rožmberk (still heirless), was imprisoned again, this time in the formidable fortress standing on a crag overlooking Brüx (as Most was then known).

Fittingly, his eventual fate remains obscure. Doctor Dee recorded in his diary in November 1595: 'Sir E. Kelley slain.' It was reported that, in attempting to escape from his cell window down a rope of knotted sheets, he had fallen and died of his injuries. But some maintained that he had faked his death and escaped. Some years later there was a story that he had been spotted in Moscow, in disguise, still practising alchemy.

With Sir Edward Kelley, Knight of Bohemia and self-styled scion of 'the knightly kin and house of Conaghaku in the Kingdom of Ireland', there were always more questions than answers. One of those questions – not yet addressed by historians, as far as I am aware – is whether he ever took time off from his laboratory in Třeboň to go carp fishing.

I like to think he did. Certainly the fishing was there, on his doorstep. And there is evidence that Kelley was, indeed, a Brother of the Angle, who took delight in what Walton called 'the contemplative man's recreation'. On one occasion, back in Mortlake, Doctor Dee received a party of dignitaries including Count Łaski, who was anxious for news from the other side as to how his bid to become King of Poland might be viewed. Kelley was urgently needed to open the dialogue but was not to be found, and at length the disgruntled party left by boat. When Kelley finally appeared, the Doctor demanded to know where he had been. 'Fishing' was the answer.

I picture the Baron, with his hat pulled down over his mutilated ears, wandering off into the meadows around Třeboň, a long pole of ash in hand, a horsehair line in his pocket, a ball of honey paste in a bag. I see him beside the green water, thinking of carp and gold. I see him catching one and holding it, admiring the glittering scales, like so many sovereigns.

When I visited Třeboň I discovered to my disappointment that I had missed the daily fish market. To make up for this I joined one of the tours of the strikingly sgraffito-ed château built by the last of the Lords of the Rose, Petr Vok. I had a vague hope that it might include a look at Doctor Dee and Edward Kelley's notorious laboratory, or at least their quarters. But it didn't; in fact, it was a severe letdown all round. We shuffled through a succession of gloomy, vaulted chambers while our female guide kept up a relentless commentary about the suits of armour, stacks of halberds and pikes, heavy furniture and mediocre portraits arranged in them. The only exhibits of interest to me were a pair of fantastic late-seventeenth-century maps showing the Třeboň fishpond complex, with houses, churches, woods, fields, embankments and channels individually depicted. As far as I could tell — the guide spoke in Czech only — she said nothing about the ponds, or about the savage Jakub Krčín, or the sinister activities of the English spirit-seekers.

Afterwards I strolled out of the back of the château and up the embankment forming the northern side of Krčín's first major excavation. Its construction required the submerging of one of Třeboň's suburbs, which caused so much trouble with the locals that he initially called it *Nevděk*, meaning Ingratitude. Later Krčín reported proudly to Vilém of Rožmberk that the latest harvest had included 1,224 barrels of carp as well as multitudes of pike – 'such fat carp and bigger pike have we not found in any other pond . . . therefore it would be suitable if your Grace would be pleased for some other ponds still to be added'.

A statue of Krčín stands among the trees near the water's edge. Rough maps of his two epic excavations are carved into the base. Above, the figure of the master pond-builder – bare-headed, bearded, in ruff, doublet, hose, breeches and buckled shoes – stares sternly out over the water. Behind him is the town that he made the Carp Capital of Bohemia.

# Chapter 16

## Town and country in Transylvania

The road from the south-west into the Romanian town of Târgu Mureş is long, straight and uninviting. From far away the prospect is dominated by a smoking, steaming throwback to the Stalinist vision of the factory age: a sprawling confusion of writhing pipework, storage tanks, pylons, chutes, cooling towers, railway tracks and wagons, filthy blocks of brick and concrete, mounds of coal and spoil, from the heart of which pokes a very tall, slender chimney exhaling a crescent-shaped plume of smoke into the sky.

The plant produces fertiliser, and the name of the company – Azomureş – is written in gaunt letters over the main entrance, through which aged trucks coated in grime heave themselves, wheezing under their loads. Beyond the gates to the fertiliser plant loom the first clumps of apartment blocks, inescapable monuments to socialist planning across eastern Europe, which in Romania seemed to achieve a pitch of dinginess and shoddiness unmatched by its neighbours. Looking from the outside at these grey, jerry-built cuboids, it is not easy to picture people making comfortable, even beautiful, homes of their little boxes, or being creative and happy inside them; a failure of the imagination, of course, as many did and were.

Further on, the road reaches the central square of Târgu Mureş, where, aesthetically, matters improve considerably. The square is in fact a long rectangle just wide enough to accommodate a municipal garden of regimented rose beds, paths, benches and trees. Two large and striking public buildings of the pre-1914 vernacular Art Nouveau movement − the City Hall and the Palace of Culture − stand almost side by side at the south-west end. Their mosaics, stained glass windows, spiky towers and turrets, gleaming tiles and soaring majolica-tiled roofs, give them an exotic, almost outlandish flavour. Looming at the other end of the square is the grey, domed bulk of the Orthodox cathedral, deposited there in the 1930s. To one side of it stands the baroque Catholic church of St John the Baptist, a light and airy reminder of the times of Maria Theresa and her repudiated faith.

The flanks of the rectangle and the streets leading away from it are mostly lined with the kind of buildings that give such a pleasant feel to so many Habsburg towns. Their stuccoed fronts, ornamented windows and doors, and pastel colours − daffodil, mustard, peach, sky-blue, strawberry, apricot, cream − combine to give an effect of cheerful good humour. It takes little effort of the imagination to travel back in time and picture their booted, behatted, bewhiskered owners pausing to look back at them, thumbs tucked into waistcoat pockets, watch-chains glinting, with expressions of quiet satisfaction at the state of home, family, the world; then turning away to do some business at the bank, followed perhaps by a game of billiards at the club and half an hour with the newspaper in the smoking room, catching up on the society gossip and news from the Diet in Budapest.

Coming back, I was asked again and again: what did I think of the town? Had I noticed the changes? They knew that I had known it in the old days. It seemed they wanted me to confirm that something almost miraculous had occurred, as if I were in a position to file an independent observer's report approving the new Târgu Mureș.

Both before and after the collapse of Communism, Romania's reputation with its neighbours was dark and unsavoury. Throughout Poland, Czechoslovakia and Hungary, I was repeatedly warned against going there at all. The theme was always the same. Terrorised and brutalised by Ceaușescu, Romania had plumbed depths unknown elsewhere. Even in the bad times, the darkest days, my friends told me, we never let the state take over our lives like that. But that Ceaușescu! An animal, a barbarian. And the people! The implication was that they and the little man with the screwed-up face and the mad ideas had somehow deserved each other; that Romanians were genetically inclined towards brutality and criminality.

Predictions as to my fate varied. I would certainly be robbed, probably beaten, possibly murdered. There would be nothing to eat. There would be no fishing because the rivers had all been poisoned or emptied by poachers. At every turn I would be offered gypsy girls for my pleasure, aged twelve or even younger if I wanted. Or boys. Or both. And all it would cost would be a bottle of lemonade.

After the Great Plain of Hungary, Romania looked very different.

The land rose beyond the border crossing at Oradea into rolling hills cloaked in woods. In the meadows the summer grass cut was in full swing. Beneath the brilliant sun, straw hats and berets were creeping across the pastures like beetles. Scythes flashed, pitchforks stabbed. Mounds like green warts studded the ground where the sward had been cut. Lines of horse-drawn carts rattled and clip-clopped along the road, almost hidden beneath teetering piles of grass on which the cutters sprawled, hats pulled down, cigarettes glued above stubbly chins. The air was hot and still and heavy with the sweet smell. Cries and snatches of song came from the fields.

The villages I passed through were conspicuously poor and shabby. Most of their inhabitants seemed to be outside, waiting for something. At first I assumed it must be for a bus, but when one came hardly anyone got on it. It was as if no one had anything better to do than check that nothing was happening.

The road, compared with those in Hungary, was atrocious. Horse-drawn conveyances decisively outnumbered cars, almost all of which were Romanian Dacias in ruinous condition. The slightest uphill incline was enough to reduce the trucks and buses to little more than trotting speed, their carbon-encrusted rear ends shrouded in blue, black or grey smoke. Petrol stations were very few and far between, each announcing itself well in advance with a mile-long snake of waiting traffic.

I passed by Cluj, ringed by apartment blocks like pale tombstones, and Turda, squatting in a great cloud of dust and fumes from its cement and chemical factories. The road crossed the Mureş, the principal river of Transylvania, then veered north-east towards Târgu Mureş. In the distance I saw the slim chimney of the fertiliser plant issuing forth its trail of mustard-yellow smoke. I drove past one industrial installation after another: the glass factory, the leather factory, the cement factory. The air carried a pungent combination of chemicals.

Grigore Lungu, Romania, 1990

I had an address for a Romanian fly-fisherman, Iuliu Lungu, to whom I had written from England. I hoped very keenly that he was expecting me. I showed the address to a taxi driver who led me into a cluster of dirty white blocks of flats, then stopped and pointed to one. I went in, heart quaking, mounted a dark, evil-smelling staircase, found the door. It was opened by a powerfully built man with short, crinkly grey hair and a pepper-and-salt moustache. 'Ah, you are here. Do you like football?' He gestured towards a German-made television in a comfortably furnished sitting room. 'Romania is playing Ireland. We play good football but I think the Irish will win. They are stronger. I like their manager, Mr Charlton. He is a strong man. You like a beer?' I nodded. 'OK, we watch football, have a beer, then we talk about fishing.' I grasped the glass and sank into a chair, weak with relief.

Eighteen years later I arrived by aeroplane from Budapest. Grigore – no one called him Iuliu – was waiting for me at the airport. He had thickened out a little, but the grizzled hair, the moustache, the wide nose, the searching, friendly, commanding look, were all just as I remembered. He had already told me on the phone that his wife Dana – with whom I had been great friends – had died of cancer six months before. I said how sorry I was and he nodded. On all the occasions he mentioned her, he never showed a sign of grief. Like Jack Charlton, he is a strong man.

We took the same road into Târgu Mureş. The smoke coming from the fertiliser plant chimney was now white rather than purulent yellow. 'Is EU money,' Grigore said. 'They make cleaner. But we don't want this factory. I think it will close soon.' Most of the others – the leather factory, the glass factory, the cement factory – had already gone. Their sites were occupied by new houses, supermarkets, and palaces of glass and steel displaying burnished ranks of Mercedes, Toyotas, Land Cruisers, and Nissan 4x4s like the one Grigore himself was driving.

Most of the cars forming the unbroken streams of traffic were newish, the occasional vintage Dacia standing out like an off-colour joke at a smart dinner party. We crawled into the main square. The smoky glass walls of the Mureş Mall shopping centre rose to our left, watched over with an expression of kindly interest by Colonel Sanders. Opposite was the spanking new headquarters of the Finance Ministry. Next to it was an incongruous relic of the past, the not-at-all Grand Hotel, which looked as if it had recently been shaken by a violent earth tremor and might fall down at any moment. Grigore jerked his head at it disapprovingly. 'Is bad name. I think they will destroy soon.'

The centre of town had been transformed almost beyond recognition. All the dark little food and clothes shops that I remembered had been banished, replaced by a rash of banks, mobile phone shops, bars, restaurants, cafés, even a casino. The grass in the central garden was being strimmed and bedding plants were being put out. The pervasive shabbiness of two decades before had simply been blown away. Girls in sunglasses, swinging smart leather bags, sauntered along with their boyfriends. Men in sharply cut suits hastened between banks, briefcases at the ready, talking urgently into their phones. Groups of friends sipped cappuccino in the open-air cafés or sat on benches licking ice-creams. I could have been anywhere in Europe where people were out enjoying the sunshine.

Three or four years before, Grigore and Dana had moved from their flat to a new house in a street that ran along the side of the Catholic cemetery not far from the castle. It was spacious and extremely comfortable, but a modest affair compared with the balconied, turreted, gated mansions in blue and pink and sunflower yellow that kept it company. Grigore told me that the cost of building land in Târgu Mureş had risen twenty-fold in the past eight years.

So it was easy to give people the answer they wanted. How had the town changed? The answer was that it didn't look, smell or sound like the same place. They were pleased by my astonishment, and tended to take my approval for granted. I think they were aware that, as a foreigner, passing through and not able to speak the language, I was not in any position to seek out other answers.

Back in the 1980s Grigore had made a deal that enabled him to build a wooden holiday house in the country. The *cabana*, as he called it, stood on the edge of the village of Bistra Mureşului, about an hour's drive north-east of Târgu Mureş. Like most Transylvanian villages it was an untidy, attenuated affair, strung out over four miles along a road which ran beside a stream called the Bistra, and began where the stream joined the Mureş, hence its name.

The *cabana* had an orchard in front of it and rolling pastures behind, and I thought it was one of the most magical places I had ever been. The orchard was bright with cherries; you could fill a basket in minutes. Beyond the orchard, plots of maize, vegetables, tomatoes and fruit, stockaded against wild boar and deer, were tucked behind every house. Meadows thick with grass and brushed with drifts of wildflowers rose either side of the village. Ahead, folded against the course of the stream like two rucked green blankets, were the first ridges of the Căliman Mountains, one of the several Romanian subdivisions of the Carpathians. Their lower slopes were cloaked in beech, oak and hazel, broken here and there by grassy banks where speedwell, spiky spotted orchis and yellow and purple pansies grew. Higher up, the deciduous woods gave way to pine and spruce, and the ridges merged into one smoky blue haze.

At dawn each morning the long-horned cattle were driven out

View from Bistra Mureşului

into the fields along a track that ran behind the *cabana*. The cows had big bells around their loose-skinned necks. As the first light stole into the valley, the clanging of the bells mingled with the scraping of hooves against the stones and the sleepy, irritable curses of the boys and girls in charge of the beasts. At dusk or even later, the cattle returned. The bells rang the same tones, but now the accompanying shouts were animated and cheerful at the thought of the day's toil being almost done.

Most of the able-bodied younger people of Bistra Mureşului

either worked for the Forestry or had jobs in the factories in the nearest town, Reghin. When they got home in the evening they were expected to turn out into the fields to help those left behind, who worked all day. At the weekends everyone worked. Toil was the dominant motif of life. People were bent, almost literally, under its weight. But in the context of Ceauşescu's Romania, they were lucky and they knew it. They had land on which to grow food crops, cows to milk, chickens for eggs. The exchange — which required them to give up most of their daylight hours to work — seemed a harsh one to me. But they, looking around at what was happening elsewhere, considered themselves blessed.

Carved door Bistra, Mureşului

The homesteads were generally rectangular, with living quarters set at right angles to the road and screened from it by a high fence with an arched gate, often decorated with carvings of diamond patterns or sunflowers or swags of leaves and bunches of grapes. A few of the houses were built of wood but most of coarse building blocks with a coloured wash. The barns, woodstores and other outbuildings, though, were invariably wooden, with roofs of pine shingles or tin. Everyone kept chickens and geese, and almost every family had at least one cow and one horse. The yards were plastered in dung and strewn with piles of rubbish and rusting machinery, but each had its flower-bed planted with roses, tulips and camellias.

When I was first there, none of the homes had running water. Much of the village's social life was generated by the business of drawing and carrying water and by the washing of clothes, which was done in the stream. Most people had electricity by then, but hardly anyone had a TV. One of those with both was Mr Floria, who had provided the land for Grigore's *cabana* and had made the arrangements.

Mr Floria was the big man in Bistra Mureşului. He managed the timber company, with 200 men beneath him, and was the major landowner. His homestead was oblong and had two dwellings on opposite sides of the yard, one for him and his wife, the other for one of his sons and his family. Along the side facing the gate were a cowshed, a hay-barn, a woodstore and a dark cubicle housing a stinking earth closet into which I ventured once and never again. A track ran down between the shit-house and Mr and Mrs Floria's bungalow to their vegetable plots and fields.

She was a stout, smiling woman, who always wore a cheap print dress, with or without an apron, and stout boots or shoes. She laboured from dawn to dusk about the house or in the fields, often accompanied by her daughter-in-law, who was equally stout. In fact, all the Florias were conspicuously well rounded. They ate enthusiastically, their favourite food being lumps of pork fat with the whiskery skin still attached.

Mr Floria himself was shaped rather like a bale of hay, with massive forearms and a mighty paunch. He always wore a ragged, wide-brimmed straw hat, and emanated a calm, peasant canniness. He was unhurried in his movements, his speech careful and courteous, his authority immediate and impressive. He was a keen-eyed shot and a deadly catcher of trout, and in the way powerful men from different spheres often gravitate together, he and Grigore had become great chums. Dishes of stew and bowls of eggs, milk and fruit were forever being delivered to the *cabana* by Mrs Floria or one or other of her grandchildren. One evening during the 1990 World Cup, England were playing Belgium and I was summoned to sit before the Floria television and plied with pork fat and many glasses of their homemade plum and bilberry *tuică*. The match went to extra time, and it was after midnight when I made an unsteady way back to my bed, under a starry sky, with nightingales singing somewhere.

Two decades had taken their toll on Mr Floria. The occasion for our reunion was another football match – Spain against Russia, Euro 2008 – and this time Grigore was with me. Mrs Floria seemed much the same, down to her print dress. She remembered me and grinned and said something to Grigore. 'He say' – Grigore waged a losing battle with gender in English – 'you look older. But OK.' Mr Floria was laid out on a bed in the middle of the living room, in front of the TV. He looked like one of those whales that, for reasons not understood by naturalists, strand themselves on beaches: vast and helpless. When he turned sideways to shake hands with Grigore, his great stomach spilled across the sheet from his open pyjama jacket. He had had a stroke a couple of years before and his speech was slurred and abrupt. 'She speak not so good,' Grigore said. 'But this' – he tapped his head – 'is still good.'

In the intervening years Grigore's *cabana* had been fitted with a new kitchen, complete with gas cooker, a shower, and a flush lavatory. The next day he had to go off somewhere. I was happy to be left on my own. I wanted to explore the village, to see how the wind of change that had swept through Târgu Mureş was blowing out here.

It had grown, extending its already considerable length by several hundred yards up the valley, and − more hesitantly − spreading into the meadows by the stream. Holiday homes in pseudo-Alpine style, with wooden verandahs and balconies and decorative brickwork, had sprouted wherever a drive could be laid. A drainage pipe was being installed along a trench dug in haphazard fashion down the side of the road. The road itself was gradually being asphalted from the far end, although most of it was still unmade and plentifully pot-holed. As before, the verges were shaded by almond and walnut trees, and every few hundred yards there was a miniature wooden pavilion with seats, for travellers to shelter from sun or rain or old people to sit and exchange the news and watch the world go by.

Cars and motor-scooters had largely replaced horses and carts. The grass in some of the meadows was being cut, but by machine rather than scythe. The vegetable plots, the blocks of maize and potatoes, the vineyards, orchards and little plantations of fir trees, were carefully tended, and there were still plenty of villagers at work in the open. At dusk the cattle came clanking up the road, the animals peeling off to be led into their barns for the night. The yards were as ramshackle as ever, each pecked over by its resident fowls, each with its stack of wood and fodder. Some of the decorated gateways I had photographed before had been replaced by ugly, functional metal ones, but many survived, continuing to offer simple messages of welcome to the passer-by.

Bistra Mureşului remained, unmistakably, a working village: unkempt, wholly unsmart, very much alive. But the sense of its being wholly occupied in a ceaseless struggle for survival had gone. People worked, but they also sat around, sauntered, loitered −

quite a number of them in a place of pleasure quite unimaginable in the old days, the Bar Nirvana. When I ventured an expression of mild regret at the passing of the scythes, the carts and the peace, Grigore's answer echoed Józef Jeleński's in Myślenice: 'Why will people work all day in the fields to grow food when they can buy it in the supermarket?' I realised I didn't have an answer.

## Chapter 17

### Two streams and a castle

The *epoca Ceauşescu*, as Grigore called it, had ended with amazing speed in December 1989. On Christmas Day the blood-streaked bodies of Nicolae and Elena Ceauşescu were shown on television, looking like a pair of old, unwanted dolls. When I arrived in Târgu Mureş a few months later, the journalistic consensus outside Romania was that the country was still reeling from shock and in a perilous state of economic and political instability. Without letting me know it, Grigore was anxious that I shouldn't get the wrong idea about how bad things were, or the direction in which they were going. He himself – again unknown to me – was stretched almost to breaking point by the situation. So he took the precaution of appointing a minder to keep me on track.

Ioan Varlam was older than Grigore, and had recently retired at the end of a long career spent servicing refrigeration equipment on board Romania's fishing fleet. In the course of it he had sailed the oceans of the world and visited almost every port, acquiring reasonably fluent French, German and Italian, passable English, and a mariner's smattering of Russian, Polish, Greek, Bulgarian and Japanese. He was agreeable enough in moderate doses, but combined a slightly servile manner with a deep sense of injury at the hand fate had dealt him. Symbols of affluence – such as Grigore's *cabana* or the sight of a new car – would suddenly set off outbursts of bitterness at his exclusion from this brave new world. Despite his ten languages, it had all come too late for him. While men like Grigore were poised to flourish, all Ioan had were his shabby flat and his measly merchant navy pension.

His main task with me was to counter the false propaganda I had been fed on my travels. His discourse was relentlessly educational. He presented recent Romanian history in a series of simple tableaux. Ceauşescu was a madman and had been got rid of. Tyranny had been replaced by democracy. The Securitate were no more. Those who said that the elections – won by the ex-Communist apparatchik Ion Iliescu – were a fraud were malcontents and troublemakers. Claims that people didn't have enough to eat were false: food and petrol shortages were caused by administrative incompetence. The revolution had brought light in place of darkness. It had shown the world that the real instincts of Romanians were democratic and libertarian (although still requiring a firm hand on the tiller); that Romania was ready to take its rightful place in the community of free nations.

Our first two outings together were evidently intended to show me that there was more to life in Târgu Mureş than mere survival and staying out of trouble. The first was to the zoo, where we admired a panda from China, oryx from Ethiopia, bison from Poland, a tiger from Siberia, monkeys from Cuba, and various other tokens of erstwhile socialist friendship. From there we progressed to a leisure complex with tennis courts and a boating lake surrounded by cheerless blocks of holiday apartments – two of which, Ioan told me proudly, had been allocated to himself and Grigore.

Ioan accompanied us to the *cabana* in Bistra Mureşului and stayed with me when Grigore left for Bucharest, where his business included getting a fishing permit for me. To reinforce the message that no one was starving, Ioan prepared a huge meal of grilled meat on the barbecue, after which he and I set off in my car to explore the valley. We had just got round the corner when

Ioan spotted a man he knew unloading a crate of beer from a van. We stopped and were invited into a garden by the river. Smoke was rising from a barbecue on which was sizzling an array of pork and sausage very similar to the one I had just eaten. Half a dozen men were gathered around, stuffing themselves. Greasy hands were wiped on teeshirts then thrust forward to grasp mine. I was given beer and a plate piled with meaty bones, and amid much hilarity Ioan explained the rumours circulating abroad about Romanians not having enough to eat. A man with a stomach like a sack of grain slammed a thick chop down on my plate in the manner of a court lawyer producing his conclusive piece of evidence.

Beer was followed by *tuică*. Glasses were raised to England and Mrs Thatcher. One bottle was emptied and replaced by another. Dripping with sweat and pork fat, I implored Ioan to tell the company that I was keen to resume our excursion. Eventually, after a final burst of toasts, handshakes and more toasts, we left.

We followed a forest track that kept the stream company until both emerged into the upland above the tree belt. We came to a shack where a ragged, wild-eyed figure sat on a log. Ioan asked him about an alleged waterfall that he had been told about. The man bawled at us that we had taken the wrong fork. Asked about his life up here, he said there were many animals: bears, wolves, lynx. But not many people, I ventured. He yelled with laughter. I gave him a cigarette, an untipped French Gitane which he smoked with luxurious pleasure.

A dog started barking a little way up the hillside, and we watched as a small flock of sheep was driven into a rough pen. The shepherd came down to join us. He wore a little round black hat, a loose woollen shirt, belted leggings and thick socks above his leather boots. I gave him a cigarette as well, then we headed back to the village, leaving the aroma of black tobacco to mingle with the scents of pine and bog myrtle.

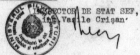

AUTORIZATIE DE PESCUIT
Nr._1_din 27.o6.1990

Domnul TOM FORT din ANGLIA este autorizat să pescuiască, cu undița
timp de 14 zile, în intervalul 28.o6-11.o7.199o , în fondurile de pescuit menționate în anexe din cadrul județelor: Cluj, Hunedoara, Mures
si Suceava.
    Pescuitul este permis în porțiunea dată liberă la pescuit din in-
spectoratele silvice județene menționate mai sus.
    Autorizația dă dreptul la pescuit a 5 buc.păstrăvi sau lipani/zi,
în lungime minimă de: 2o cm - pentru păstrăv și 25 cm - pentru lipan.
    Prezenta este valabilă numai cu achitarea anticipată a taxei de
pescuit, formată din: 168 DM + taxa de însoțire (15 DM x 4 = 60 DM) =
228 DM (140 $), încasată de Departamentul Pădurilor, prin SILVEXIM, cu
chitanța nr. 9541 din 27.o6.1990.

                    INSPECTOR DE STAT SEF,
                    ing.Vasile Crișan

IJ/sd-3 ex.
27.o6.1990

Romanian fishing licence, 1990

Grigore reappeared the next day, triumphantly brandishing my fishing licence. It had taken several hours of patient bargaining at the Forestry Ministry in Bucharest to secure it; the main difficulty, evidently, having been to convince the officials of the existence of an Englishman who wanted to go trout fishing in Romania. The licence ran to six densely printed pages listing more than a hundred rivers in Transylvania that I was now at liberty to fish. A large proportion of these, Grigore explained, were not worth the trouble – not so much because of pollution, which was concentrated in lowland areas, but because of poaching induced by hunger. Most of the accessible reaches of the mountain streams had, he said, been virtually emptied of fish during the *epoca Ceaușescu*. But there were still a few places.

One was the Ilva, which ran into the Mureș 15 miles or so upstream from Bistra Mureșului. Its valley was much steeper and narrower than that of the Bistra, and there was no proper road up it nor dwellings beside it. It was as clear as gin and as pretty as a favourite piece of jewellery. We followed the forestry track high up, where the trees thinned, and began fishing in the late-afternoon when the sun was off the water.

Grigore showed me how to do it, dibbling his flies behind every rock and in every little holding place where the water was more than a few inches deep. Initially I found it impossible to believe that there could be anything worth catching, but after a time I came to a footbridge with a genuine pool below it. The surface was marbled by competing currents and, as I peered more closely at it, I saw it broken by dimples made by feeding fish. From below I cast two small bushy flies up towards the bridge, their hackles nicely visible against the gold reflected from the evening sky. One vanished in a tiny splash, but I was too slow and just felt the fish for a split second. Next time I was quicker and brought a plump grayling to the hand to be unhooked.

It was almost dark by the time we reached the outskirts of the village. There was a bridge that took the track over the Ilva, with a long, slow pool shaped like a boomerang above it. Most of the pool lay in black shadow. But on the far side, below a shelf of rock, was an amber band lit by the last of the sun's light where fish were feeding keenly on a hatch of sedges. I got down opposite. The air was alive with moths and insects. Bats hunting their supper cut sharp, irregular lines through the twilight. I flicked a sedge imitation towards the band of light. Once, twice, fish rushed at it and missed or turned way. Then one took it and I felt the plunge of it.

Ioan heard my cry and came to stand on the bridge. He was joined by two villagers who abandoned their cows to watch the fun. I played the fish in, and at the second attempt got my net under it. I knocked it on the head then struggled up the bank to show it off. It was a trout, perhaps ten ounces in weight, as precious as any I had ever caught. There was an appreciative murmur from the small crowd that had now gathered. An old man in a battered felt hat shook my hand, then turned away to tend to his animals, which were snorting impatiently in the darkness.

'Fishing was better in time of Ceauşescu,' Peter said from the front seat of Grigore's big Nissan. I was sitting in the back with a young man called Calin, the son of Grigore's lawyer friend Vasilie. I had to remind myself that when Ceauşescu was shot, Calin had been less than two years old, the same age I was when Stalin died. The *epoca Ceauşescu* was as remote to him as the era of the purges in Russia to me.

Peter was almost certainly right. Twenty years before, Romania's grinding poverty still acted as a shield to her unspoiled places. Most people simply did not have the leisure or the means to reach them, even had they had the inclination. Now several years of strong economic growth had fed a surge in car owner-ship and building, putting sudden pressure on valleys previously left in peace. Grigore and I had already been to the Ilva, which I hardly recognised as the pristine stream we had fished before. The open patches of ground had been annexed by holiday chalets, the water was murky, and a mechanical digger was helping itself, quite illegally but without hindrance, to gravel from the streambed.

Now we were on our way to try the Gurghui, a bigger stream that runs westward out of the bear-infested Gurghui Mountains (another Carpathian offshoot) to join the Mureş at Reghin. The road alongside it was abysmal even by Romanian standards, which – despite the economic improvement and the availability of EU investment – are the lowest anywhere in supposedly civilised Europe. It was extravagantly pot-holed, jarringly uneven, and inclined to relapse in each of the villages into undulating stretches of cobbles that demanded respect even from a 4x4 Nissan. But the awfulness of the road had done nothing to inhibit the sprouting of new houses and chalets beside it. Every clearing along the river bank had its picnic benches and tables, its campfire marks, its drifts of rubbish.

Peter was a live wire, a restless knot of energy unable to keep still or quiet for a moment. He was Jewish, and made a good living as a dealer in parts for cars in Târgu Mureş. Some years before, he had hired an English tutor for six months, as a result of which he spoke the language rather more fluently than Grigore. They fished together a lot and Grigore was endlessly amused by his perpetual chatter and motion. 'She has three mobile phones,' Grigore said, laughing. 'Sometimes she speaking into all at the same time. Not she. He.'

Peter told many jokes: Romanian jokes, Jewish jokes, but mainly gypsy jokes. When I said something about the river looking a little coloured after the recent rain, Peter said: 'It is not the rain. The gypsies have been washing. It happens once each year.' He and Grigore cackled. They never tired of mocking the gypsies for their idleness, their dirtiness, their incurable dishonesty and fecklessness, their fertility. Calin laughed dutifully at the jokes but did not make any himself. He told me his father had represented a group of gypsies whose homes in Târgu Mureş had been destroyed in one of the frequent and vicious outbreaks of racial violence. A Romanian judge had thrown out the gypsies' claim, whereupon Vasilie had taken it to the European Court and won compensation.

Calin had just finished his second year studying law at the celebrated University of Cluj. Very tall, very slim, with glasses and neat hair brushed back, he had a thoroughly wholesome look to him, combined with an air of idealism. Although he had followed his father's path thus far, he was not sure about the law as a career. He was concerned that the first loyalty of lawyers had to be to their clients rather than to truth and justice, and that this would sometimes conflict with his conscience.

I asked him if his fellow students were interested in the past, in what had happened under the regime. He said the old people talked about it all the time, like it was yesterday. Some thought it would be good if Ceauşescu were still the boss because he gave everyone somewhere to live and a job, and now many people didn't have a job and couldn't pay the rent. It was at this point that Peter made his comment about the fishing being better then. Calin laughed, but became serious again. 'We watch the documentaries on TV, we know what happened. But for us it was another time.'

**MINISTERUL AGRICULTURII, PADURILOR SI DEZVOLTARII RURALE**
REGIA NATIONALA A PADURILOR
ROMSILVA

Seria RNP, Nr. ...**009377**...
Directia silvica .....*Munev*.........
Ocolul silvic.......*Gungliv*........
Gestionar delegat ....*Cota Galafhou*

*Chitanta: 0011618*

### PERMIS DE PESCUIT
in scop recreativ/sportiv in apele de munte
Perioada de valabilitate
*29. 06 2008*

Domnul ......*TOM FORD*...................... cu domiciliul in localitatea
*Anglia*........, str...............nr...........judetul (sectorul)...................
Posesor al buletinului / cartii de identitate, seria.........nr....................,...emis/emisa de................................, poate exercita pescuitul in scop recreativ/sportiv, in urmatoarele zone gestionate de Regia Nationala a Padurilor Romsilva .....
*Fond pescuit Gunghiv superior de la confl. cu Gurghiv cu pr. tancel in amonte la confl. cu pr. Negra. Pescuitul interzis in amonte de pr. Negra aval de pr. tancel si toti afluentii.*

Efectuarea pescuitului in scop recreativ / sportiv se face numai in conditiile, cu mijloacele si in perioadele prevazute de lege. Posesorul acestui permis este obligat ca de fiecare data cand practica pescuitul sa aiba asupra sa documentele privind identitatea sa, pentru a fi prezentate organelor de control, la cerere.
Nerespectarea prevederilor referitoare la practicarea pescuitului in scop recreativ / sportiv atrage anularea acestui permis, precum si raspunderea materiala, contraventionala sau penala, potrivit legii.
Pescuitul recreativ/sportiv in apele de munte mentionate mai sus, este permis a se exercita cu undita sau lanseta tinuta in mana si folosind, in exclusivitate, momeli artificiale.
Se pot retine numai pestii cu lungimea minima de 20 cm la pastrav, 22 cm la coregon si 25 cm la lipan. Pescuitul recreativ/sportiv in apele de munte este permis numai in timpul zilei, de la rasaritul pana la apusul soarelui.

Emitent
Nume si prenume ......*Cota Galafion*..................................
Semnatura si stampila.................................................

Fishing licence, Romania, 2008

It was a blazingly hot day but the Gurghui was thickly wooded, the air over it deliciously cool and moist. Away from the picnic sites, it kept itself to itself in the private way some rivers have, its secrets communicable only to those prepared to get close to it. Peter had brought a large wooden box with a barbecue inside it and enough meat and salad to feed a rugby fifteen. While he worked on the feast, the rest of us dispersed to fish. I went upstream, ducking low under the trailing branches of the willows and alders, slipping and sliding on the rocks, the current welling up against my waders.

By now I was a little more accomplished in the Romanian technique. The river was in too much of a hurry to bother with proper pools. You had to look out for the little pockets of water below or between the boulders, where the texture of the flow changed and there was enough depth for fish to hold a position out of the main force of the stream. There was no room to cast in the conventional back-and-forth manner; it was a question of flicking and flipping the flies into a possible holding place, and trying to keep them there long enough for any fish to take notice.

I slithered and dodged quite a way, catching the odd trout here and there, not many and none of them of any great size, but enough to keep me happy and alert, and for the time to fly. I was aware of nothing beyond the pervasive, gently percussive sound of the water, its shifting rhythms, the play of sunlight through the trees, the darting of warblers and – twice – the flash of a kingfisher. Then, suddenly, I realised how hot, thirsty and hungry I was.

Back at the picnic site Peter was crouched over the fire. A trestle table was covered in plates of tomatoes, peppers, salad, onions, and the fiercely hot little green chillies that Romanians love to chew while they wait for their meat. At the next table a tall lad with razored hair was sitting with a group of girls, drinking beer and Coke, talking and laughing. The lad was Peter's son,

Kristi. He and the girls were celebrating the end of their university exams. Most had studied medicine, although Kristi was going to be a dentist. Peter tapped his own crooked, yellowed gnashers proudly. 'He is very good. He is repairing my teeth for nothing.' I told Peter about some recent root canal work I had suffered, and how much it cost. 'Kristi will do for you, he is needing the practice.'

Calin gave me a can of beer that had been cooling in the water. We ate blackened chunks of coarsely minced pork and beef, shaped like sausages but without skins. I sliced mine and made a thick sandwich with tomato and onion. Peter urged more meat on me, and then more, until I felt that if I didn't eat again for a week, that would be soon enough.

A couple of the girls in Kristi's group went for a paddle. The rest joked and laughed. Their youth and happiness and shared sense of eagerness and excitement were palpable, and I felt rather old and wistful. I noticed one of the girls parodying the fly-fisherman's casting actions. Her performance prompted convulsions of hilarity.

Later on I fished again, until I was too tired to fish any more. Grigore, disgusted at the lack of sport, had long since given up. By then we were high up the stretch of the Gurghui on which fishing was allowed. The valley had closed in and the shadows had lengthened. The river was dark and uncommunicative. Ahead lay the Castle.

Although everyone called it the Castle or the Château, it was in fact a hunting lodge built in the 1920s for the second of Romania's four kings, the Hohenzollern Ferdinand I. It stands to one side of a clearing in the forest, a long dark building, pine on the outside, cherry and oak inside, with high chimneys rising above steep shingled roofs. The hunting theme is insistent, particularly downstairs. Velvet chairs and polished tables rest on legs made of antlers. The gilded mirrors are bordered with more antlers. Stags' heads with gentle, glassy eyes rear out from the panelled walls. A stained-glass huntsman in red hat, green jerkin, burgundy leggings and yellow boots marches across the dining-room window, jabbing a spear at a white stag, his dog following at his heels. In one of the forest scenes decorating the enormous tiled stoves, a hunter stands with a falcon on his shoulder, dog at his side, cherubs floating above.

The air inside is cool, smoky, resinous. Although queens, princesses, countesses and royal mistresses came to Lăpuşna, the atmosphere is still resolutely masculine. One pictures the morning of the shoot: men with moustaches, in jackets and breeches from the best tailors in Vienna or London, polished boots scrunching the gravel, cigar smoke hanging in the air; dogs yelping and scrabbling; beaters waiting at a respectful distance; King Ferdinand's Director of Royal Hunts, Colonel August von Spiess (who styled himself Oberst August Roland von Braccioforte zum Portner und Höflein), deep in discussion with the local foresters on the prospects for the day.

Deep forest stretches north, east and south from the Castle and is alive with capercaillie, lynx, boar and lesser creatures. But the prizes here are the great beasts, the red deer and the bear. It is on them that Colonel von Spiess's mood – and the foresters' jobs – will depend. If the bag at the end of the day includes a stag or two, or a bear taller than a man, then there will be feasting and songs of celebration, and the tipping will be generous. If not . . . well, no one is indispensable.

Including kings, as it turned out. Although Ferdinand himself managed to last to a respectable age and a royal burial with full honours, both Romania's subsequent monarchs – Carol II and Michael – were forced to abdicate. The replacement of Romania's short-lived monarchy by the People's Republic in 1946 changed many things, but not the tradition of preserving the special places for the select few; or, in the case of the hunting lodge at Lăpuşna, the select one, a man possessed by a passion for killing animals that spilled well beyond the boundary of mania.

No story about Ceauşescu and hunting was too fantastic to be disbelieved. It was said of him that he machine-gunned deer from a helicopter; that when he got bored with killing the native Romanian brown bear, he imported a pair of polar bears and shot them; that when he was in a hurry to get back to affairs of state in Bucharest, a suitable trophy would be immobilised with drugged food and shot lying down; that he employed a team of taxidermists whose job was to stretch the skins of his victims before they were submitted to the annual prize-giving organised by the *Conseil International de la Chasse et de la Conservation du Gibier*.

Lâpuşna was merely one of his many hunting grounds. He came once or twice a year, some years not at all. It all depended on the bears. The task of the staff there was to search the forest until they found one worthy of the Great Leader's attention, and then to educate it into becoming a convenient target. Trails of food were laid to bring the animal down to a clearing cut a little way outside the fenced compound enclosing the Castle.

The leader's shooting box

On one side of the clearing, facing the trail from the hillside, was a little wooden cubicle with a window, and a ledge on the inside at a comfortable height for a man to sit and rest his rifle. A high-voltage light was fixed above the window, on the outside.

Neat little notches were cut into the fir trees where the trail reached the clearing, so that the height of the animal could be accurately measured. In autumn, when bears feed hard in preparation for hibernation, the food supply was increased. Hunks of freshly dismembered horse were spread on the ground. The foresters watched from the cubicle. Once they were satisfied that a regular feeding pattern had been established, and that the bear was big enough, the call would be made to Bucharest.

The underlings and Securitate men came first. In the lodge, empty since the last visitation, linen was aired, carpets were cleaned, the forest of antler legs and animal heads dusted, the great glazed stoves packed with logs and lit. At the appointed hour the black motorcade would sweep up the valley from the airport at Târgu Mureş, or the presidential helicopter would swoop from the sky. The villagers of Lăpuşna stayed indoors and crossed themselves. The foresters and beaters uttered their prayers.

In the late evening, as dusk gathered, Ceauşescu would take the short walk from the lodge to the clearing in the forest. Here, away from the petty problems and irritations of his office, deep in the eternal Transylvanian forest, he was in his true element, the element of the hunter. He would chat to the chief forester, then take his seat in the cubicle, laying his favourite Holland and Holland .375 on the window ledge. There was a telephone there in case some emergency demanded his attention. Behind him the forester murmured into a two-way radio, keeping in touch with the watchers in the trees.

The Leader settled in his chair. Outside, the light was fading, the forest growing grey, seeming to close in. He was in no hurry. He knew well enough that impatience was fatal. The animals must be allowed to take their time. He was a hunter, a man of the forest, after all. If these men had done their work, all would be well. If not . . .

He felt the forester's hand touch his arm. At once he was alert. He gripped the rifle, raised it, working the butt against his shoulder. He listened. There was silence; then a muffled snuffling, the whisper of grass and sticks underfoot. The snuffling became louder, mixed with grunts and the sounds of teeth and claws at work. He hoped the bear was eating where the horseflesh had been put down, next to the water-trough, and hadn't moved off to one side, which would make the shot trickier. The source of the sound seemed fixed. Slowly he turned the rifle towards it, spreading his elbows on the ledge so that the balance was right.

He nodded to the forester, who flicked a switch. The clearing was flooded with light. There, 20 yards away, standing on its hind legs, was *Ursus arctos*: eight foot high, 600 pounds in weight, the remains of the last evening meal it would ever eat gripped in its paws, strings of horsemeat between its teeth, blinded and frozen by 1,000 watts of electric light in its eyes. The bear's heart was just where a man's would be. The finger squeezed.

The trophy

And then, if everything went to plan, the lights would burn late in the lodge's dining hall as the boss's marksmanship was toasted and toasted again. In the morning he would be gone, taking the body of the beast with him to be delivered to the presidential taxidermists. The grates would be brushed, the smashed glasses swept up, the dust sheets spread, the doors locked, the gates to the compound padlocked, a collective sigh of relief heaved. Until next time.

In the end the hunter became the hunted. Ceauşescu suffered the fate that he himself had meted out to such a remarkable number of dumb beasts (with a smile, Romanians swiftly renamed the *Conducator* – meaning the Boss or Master – *Impuscatus*, the Shot One).

The Castle at Lăpuşna entered an uncertain phase. When I stayed in the compound in 1990, as a result of some potent string-pulling by Grigore, the place was deserted apart from a caretaker couple. I was quartered with Ioan Varlam in one of the chalets near the lodge, where the caretaker's wife heated our water in a wood-burning ceramic stove and served a succession of delicious meals. Her husband showed us around, taking a particular pleasure in pointing out the remains of the horse carcasses littered across the clearing where the bears were shot, some of the bones picked clean and dried to a dusty grey, others with scraps of flesh still attached. I was able to wander where I wanted and to fish the stretch of the Gurghui that ran past the compound gates, which was strictly out of bounds to other anglers. The gates were kept locked and casual visitors were brusquely turned away.

Subsequently, I learned, the Castle was taken over by an English businessman with extensive interests in Romania, and used by him as a holiday home. By the time of my return it was being run by a travel agent from Târgu Mureş, partly as somewhere to enter-tain her family and friends and partly as a commercial weekend and holiday retreat. She showed us around the inside, laying heavy emphasis on the luxurious authenticity of the fixtures and fittings and the moderateness of her charges, although it wasn't possible to see a lot because of a power cut. She said the roof was in a poor state and she was having trouble finding the craftsmen to cut and fit the thousands of wooden shingles needed to repair it.

I asked her if people still came to shoot bears. She said they did, although she had nothing to do with the arrangements, which were made between hunting agents and the Ministry. With the price of a trophy bear carcass at $20,000, hunting had become a significant currency earner for the Romanian government. There were occasional scandals: King Juan Carlos of Spain had caused some outrage by bringing a party that accounted for nine bears (the King himself bagged a pregnant female). The argument for it was always the same: the hunting paid for conservation, and conservation worked because Romania had by far the biggest population of bears in Europe, at around 6,000 . . . which doesn't alter the fact that shooting a bear is a horrible thing to do, and the further fact that anyone who regards it as sport has more in common with the late Nicolae Ceaușescu than they might care to admit.

Later Grigore was scornful about the travel agent and her sales pitch. 'He did not impression me,' he said. 'She', I corrected him. 'She. She is not having the proper respect for that place. It should not be used for holidays. And he have not enough money to make it right. She.'

It was late evening by the time we left. The bouncing, crumbling road back to Reghin took us past several sites where low, windowless, whitewashed buildings were arranged in rows in a manner reminiscent of a prison camp. They were intensive farming units, for pigs and chickens. All the time I was in Romania I never saw a pig in the open (pretty much the same applied elsewhere in eastern Europe). They are all imprisoned in the dark, either upright, their heads clamped in bars to stop them biting each other; or, in the case of sows weaning piglets, on their sides, unable to get up. Romanians, Poles, Czechs, Slovakians and Hungarians eat a great deal of pig meat themselves and, with the help of EU investment funds, foreign companies (principally the American hog giant, Smithfield), have been busy snapping up industrial farms wherever possible, to take advantage of minimal welfare standards.

I attempted to interest Calin in the issue of animal suffering. He said it was important to protect the wild animals, to keep the rivers clean, to clamp down on poaching and pollution. But the notion of being concerned about the treatment of pigs and poultry clearly struck him as absurd.

# Chapter 18

## *What's in a name?*

To almost half its population, and indeed to an entire nation, Târgu Mureş is not Târgu Mureş at all but Marosvásárhely, which in Hungarian means market town on the River Maros (Mureş). Historically it is the cultural and economic capital of the Székely region, the Szeklers being a Hungarian people who settled this remote enclave of the Carpathian basin a thousand years ago. Isolated from the main Hungarian centres of population, they were charged by the Kings of Hungary with the defence of the eastern borderlands against assorted invaders: Bulgars, Cumans, Tartars, finally Turks. In return they were granted privileged social status, exemption from taxes, and near autonomy.

Over time they came to regard themselves as the 'true' Hungarians, their sense of nationhood strengthened by their geographical separation from court and, later, parliament, and by the proximity of the Romanians, whom they despised. To this day, the Szeklers continue to constitute a majority in the region. But in Târgu Mureş they are outnumbered by Romanians, largely due to Ceauşescu's policy of enforced settlement of Romanian workers there. Politically, the Hungarians have lost the town. Spiritually, they continue to regard it as theirs.

In March 1990 – less than three months after Ceauşescu's over-throw, and three months before I arrived there – long-standing tensions between the two communities in Târgu Mureş exploded into violence. There were pitched battles outside the cathedral in the main square in which several people – most of them Hungarians – were killed and 300 or so were injured. Two distinct accounts of the trouble were heard. The Hungarian version was that Romanian ultra-nationalist groups bussed in hired thugs masquerading as miners, with orders to smash peaceful Hungarian protests against decades of oppression. The Romanians maintained that their neighbours were trying to exploit the general collapse of central control to press demands amounting to de facto autonomy within Transylvania, and that the people had sponta-neously risen to defend their town.

The tendency of the BBC World Service to favour the Hungarian version outraged the many educated Romanians who listened to it. As a result I – a visiting Englishman then working for the BBC – found myself being harangued at every opportunity about what really happened on those two nights of bloodshed, and about the arrogance of Hungarians in general, their disdain for Romanian culture and history, their inability to accept that they had twice lost Transylvania by backing the Germans in world wars, and that they were never going to get it back.

Many of these harangues were delivered by Grigore's wife, Dana. She was small and slender, with a Gallic look about her, her brown hair cut short and parted like a boy's. Her dark-eyed face was lined, her teeth and fingers yellowed with nicotine. Although her habitual expression was sombre, she had a ready sense of humour which responded best to the comedy of mischance and misfortune. Before she laughed she would duck her head forward, then jerk it back, mouth open, eyes shining.

On her father's side, Dana's family originated in France. Her mother came from a Romanian family long established in Transylvania, at least seven of whom had been Greek Orthodox priests. Back in Habsburg days one of these priestly forbears had refused to obey orders from Budapest to conduct school teaching in Hungarian only, and had been hanged for his defiance.

Dana's family history and her Romanian blood had moulded a strong cultural antagonism towards the Hungarians. But that was nothing compared with the implacable, unforgiving hatred she harboured for Ceauşescu and his regime. Her father, a lawyer, had spent nine years in a labour camp in the 1950s for the crime of having belonged to the National Liberal Party before it was purged. Grigore freely admitted to having been a Communist Party activist in his youth and to having kept his membership thereafter for reasons of expediency. When I asked Dana if she had ever been a member, a whole history of suffering and hatred was written in the quick, angry shake of her head.

She lectured me frequently and at length about the fearsome complexities of Transylvanian history. We talked in French, which she spoke better than me, although hers was rusty from long disuse. Sometimes my head would reel from the strain of trying to grasp how the Daco-Roman people had come to co-exist with the Hungarian usurpers. (This, of course, was the official Romanian version, in which the Roman Emperor Trajan's occupying force had become assimilated into the aboriginal Dacian stock.) One of her favourite themes was the brutality of Magyarisation under Habsburg rule, which trampled on Romanian culture and demanded that everyone take a Hungarian name.

Grigore tended to keep out of these discussions. He employed many Hungarians at the factory he managed; he said they were generally good workers, and he claimed to have a number of Hungarian friends. He was aware, I think, that the persistent beating of the Romanian drum in my ear might be counter-productive. Typically, he devised a more subtle means of education.

István Horváth was a Hungarian manager with Grigore's company. He had a stringy, undernourished appearance, a dark, suffering countenance, lank black hair, and a shaggy moustache that he was forever twisting and tugging. He smoked incessantly and seemed to throb and twitch with resentment at the hand fate had dealt him. He was an educated man – we too communicated in French – and a capable manager, Grigore said, but not much liked by the workers.

For István, to be Hungarian in Romanian Transylvania was to be a victim. His disdain for Romanians and their culture was absolute. The notion that his ten-year-old daughter should be taught in a Romanian school, or have to mix with Romanians in any way, was abhorrent to him. His view was that history and Hungary's enemies had conspired to steal Transylvania from its rightful inheritors. The Romanians were interlopers, peasants, barbarians, capable only of ruining the treasure that had dropped into their lap. But István was determined that Hungary's spiritual ownership would be defended to the last. 'Arise Hungarians' had been Petőfi's cry, and István had answered it. He had been on the streets during the riots that spring and he knew what had happened, which was that the barbarians had attempted to terrorise the superior race. (Grigore, he pointed out, was on a business trip to Italy at the time.)

He had another passion, which was more sympathetic, although, on occasions, tiresome. Denied freedom in the city, István found it instead in the mountains. Here, in climbing boots, alpenstock in hand, he could breathe the pure air, stride by the lakes, share the crests with the chamois, be looked down on only by the eagle. In the mountains István need bow to no one.

His particular affinity was with the Retezat Mountains, which form part of the last great massif of the Carpathians that extends from the Iron Gates in the west to the valley of the Siret in the east. Only the peaks of the Tatras are higher than those of Retezat, Cibin and Făgăraş, which together constitute a mighty 200-mile-long barrier, hemming in the north of the Danube plain and facing down the rugged mountains of Bulgaria on the other side.

Up to the tree line, at around 6,000 feet, these southern peaks are characteristically Carpathian, swathed in forests and split by valleys containing tumbling streams. But above that line they have a grandeur of their own. Sharp, bare schists bound by looping ridges rise from great screes jumbled with lichen-covered boulders. There are meadows spotted with huge stones, in whose lee orchids and saxifrages burst forth in the brief period when the snow has melted. In the shallow bowls between the outcrops are Alpine lakes, which sparkle like sapphires when the sun is out, and frown granite-grey under cloud.

Grigore had appointed István to guide me on an expedition to Retezat. It had an unpromising start. It was teeming with rain when I arrived at István's flat, which comprised two rooms of a crumbling, single-storey house in one of Târgu Mureş's less favoured back streets. He had already warned me at some length of the dangers the mountains could pose to the inexperienced in severe weather, and I rather assumed that we would now confirm the cancellation of the trip. But István was ready, with a rucksack almost as tall as himself.

'*Pas de problème*,' he said airily when I asked him for the third time if it would be safe to go. '*Ici il pleut. Mais en Retezat, qui sait?*' He smiled reassuringly. '*Nous verrons.*' He picked up his rucksack, gasping with the effort. It seemed excessively large and full for what was planned as a two-day trip.

István with wife and daughter

The explanation appeared – István's wife and daughter. Would I mind if they came too? Of course not, I replied after a moment. István was delighted. His wife, he assured me, spoke excellent English and would be a great help in conversation. Mollified, I repeated to her, in English, what István had just said. She registered incomprehension. I tried again. She shook her head emphatically and said: 'No Engleesh.'

Heavily laden, we set off in my car through the pounding rain. István lit a cigarette and I opened the window a couple of inches to let the smoke out. István's wife leaned forward from the back seat and muttered in his ear. He asked me if I would shut the window as she was very sensitive to the cold. I did so, and asked him if he would mind not smoking in the car.

For almost all of the long drive south-west István held forth on the Transylvanian/Hungarian/Romanian question. Initially I tried to challenge some of his assertions, but I was brushed aside. At one point I asked him if it was really desirable that his daughter could speak no Romanian, had no Romanian friends, and was forbidden to learn anything about the country in which she had lived her whole life. István shook his head good-naturedly.

'*Mais, Tom, vous ne comprenez pas. Elle est Hongroise, pas Roumaine.*'

We followed the valley of the Mureş, through Alba Iulia and past Sebeş, until we reached the confluence with the principal river of Retezat, the Riul Mare. The weather had cleared to some degree; the mountains ahead formed a dark, massive barrier, their tops lost in the cloud. We made for them, passing close to Sarmizegetusa, the mountain capital of the kingdom founded by the Dacian conqueror Decebalus. István had no interest in its stirring history. He maintained that the Dacians never existed, that the land was empty when the Magyars arrived, and that it was only much later that primitive men dressed in sheepskins – the advance guard of the Romanian horde – had infiltrated from the south-east.

We drove up the valley of the Riul Mare. The stream was wretchedly shrunken, and after some miles the reason became apparent. Blocking the narrow defile through which it flowed was a gigantic plug of earth and rocks, the Riul Mare dam. We approached it behind a string of dust-shrouded earth-movers which were shuddering up the twisting road to dump their loads at the tops. The hillsides all around were torn and gashed where the soil and rock had been ripped away. Abandoned machinery and wrecked vehicles littered the slopes.

The road ran up one side of the ravine, then crossed the dam. I dodged between thundering diggers and trucks, feeling the car's wheels slip on the pebbles and sticky mud, trying to avert my eyes from the dizzying drops to the river on one side of the dam and the lake on the other. István entertained me with an account of how a lorry carrying 30 dam workers had slipped off the road. '*Trois cents mètres,*' he said with relish, pointing down.

He had arranged for us to stay at a hostel overlooking the lake. Two fierce-looking cocks and a pair of abundantly wattled turkeys were competing for position on a dungheap at the side of the building as we arrived. The turkeys spotted us and high-stepped towards the car, scarlet dewlaps flapping. István's daughter cringed in terror and burst into tears. An old man appeared and shooed the birds away. He greeted us with wild enthusiasm, as if we were the first humans to come this way for many a year. His face was silvered with stubble and his yellow eyes were reddened by webs of broken blood vessels. He ushered István and me into a down-stairs room, one corner of which was filled by a wood-burning stove emitting terrific heat. A fat old woman with matted, strag-gling grey hair sat opposite the stove, looking like a toad. The room stank of sweat, cooking and alcohol.

'*Je crois qu'il est ivre,*' István whispered. He mimed swigging from a bottle. I nodded. '*Mais nous avons de la chance de trouver une chambre.*' '*Absolument,*' I agreed.

Conditions in the bathroom upstairs were basic verging on squalid. The lavatory was surrounded by a pool of liquid. Someone had disconnected the down pipe from the basin. The walls were mouldy and the bath itself, standing on a black, dank floor, was horrible.

We were shown into the bedroom next door, which was an improvement. It contained a large antique wardrobe, colourfully decorated with floral motifs, a table, and two beds set a yard apart. István indicated that the Horváth family would occupy one. The other was for me. I looked forward to the night with foreboding.

While Mrs Horváth made ready to prepare the evening meal, István and I descended the precipitous road to the lake. It was a depressing sheet of water, trapped between steep walls of loose rock. Lorries roared in all directions, gears grinding, throwing up long plumes of dust. There were two or three anglers casting spinners into the water. István, who was a fisherman in a minor way, joined them. I made a few desultory casts where the river flowed into the lake. There was no sign of fish life.

Back at the hostel, I immediately regretted having accepted István's offer to provide the food. Laid out on the table were a loaf of stale bread, a slab of greasy processed cheese in a cellophane pack with the words 'Denmark – Food Aid' stamped on it, a pot containing a slimy brown substance said to be pâté, and a tin of pork luncheon meat from Finland, also stamped 'Food Aid'. I ate what I could, which wasn't much, and surreptitiously swallowed a sleeping pill along with a couple of slugs from a bottle of malt whisky that I had concealed from István. Rather to my surprise I slept peacefully, with the three Horváths an arm's length away.

Breakfast was the same in its essentials as supper. István collected the leftovers and packed them away to serve for our lunch in the mountains. I suggested taking one of three bottles of beer that I had been given by Dana. '*L'alcool est mauvais dans les montagnes,*' István said sternly. '*Nous buvons de l'eau de la rivière.*' I slipped the bottle into my fishing bag.

Leaving Mrs Horváth and daughter to amuse themselves as they might, we set off in the car. My spirits began to revive as the dam and the lake disappeared from sight behind us. It was a dewy, refulgent morning, the sunlight flooding across a brilliant sky, although trails of cloud were curled around the highest ridges ahead. For a few miles the unmade road was open and easy. We passed another hostel, markedly better appointed than ours; reserved, István said resentfully, for Romanians with connections.

Further on, the road became alarming. Squeezed between a soaring wall of rock on one side and a plunging gorge on the other, it was no more than a foot or two wider than my car. I began to sweat with the strain of trying to keep the wheels out of the worst of the ruts. Every so often the undercarriage thudded horribly against the ridge of compacted mud and rock down the middle. István sat at my side issuing a stream of advice and encouragement, puffing at his cigarette, tugging at his moustache and occasionally leaning out of the window to adjust the wing mirror to improve his view of our rear end. Twice I stopped, confronted by seemingly impossible stretches of bare, jagged rock. István urged me on, until I ordered him out of the car. I inched forward, dimly aware of the crashing of the water below, acutely conscious of my pounding heart and the mist creeping across my spectacles.

After what seemed like hours, the road came to an end in a clearing in the trees at a height of more than 5,500 feet. Three hardy individuals watched us as we got out. They wore thick woollen cardigans, rough grey trousers, and boots. One had on a beret, the other two wore shapeless brown felt hats. Their horses stood behind them, packsaddles bulging. They told István cheerfully that they were off to the pastures to tend their sheep for the summer. He asked them how they liked the life. They laughed, shrugged their shoulders, looked at each other. What other life was there?

'These are good people,' István said as they bade us farewell. 'It is a hard life but good for them.'

He lifted his rucksack on to his shoulders, exhaling sharply. I asked him what was in it, apart from lunch. He explained that one must not take the mountains lightly. A sudden storm, a fall – one must be ready for an emergency. It was therefore necessary to have a tent, spare clothes, medical supplies, cooking utensils, blankets and so on. What about maps? I asked. He looked at me scornfully and tapped his head. The map was here. He knew these paths as

Mountain men

well as the streets of Târgu Mureş. He held out his hands towards the bare ridges above the trees like a priest officiating at communion, inhaled deeply, then strode forward. I followed with my fishing bag over my shoulder, my bottle of beer within, and my rod in one hand.

The path led down into a gulch, over a small stream, then up a steep slope in a series of zigzags. To our left a much bigger stream descended in haste from the distant lakes. The path, marked by blobs of yellow paint, continued to ascend. The trees thinned and became progressively smaller. To begin with I had some difficulty in keeping up with István. But halfway up the first slope he slowed drastically. I noticed that he was stealing frequent rests, leaning for a moment on his thighs, head down. When we reached the top of the first ridge he pulled off the rucksack and crumpled to the ground, drawing quick shallow breaths. His face was grey and shiny with sweat.

'We are going too fast,' he said accusingly. 'It is foolish to hurry in the mountains.' I offered to take the rucksack, but he dismissed the idea. 'It would be too difficult for you. You are not accustomed to the mountains.'

Thereafter the way became easier. Tremendous views opened up in all directions. Across the gorge, screes of bone-white boulders had spilled down, broken by streaks of green grass and ferns and darker clumps of stunted rhododendrons and dwarf pines. Further on, naked ridges thrust serrated edges into a cottony mist. Our side of the valley was gentler, scattered with colonies of sturdy little trees and shrubs. Clusters of pale saxifrages and purple bell-flowers brightened the lees of the boulders. Bony, fawn-coloured cattle wandered through the grass, the bells at their necks clanging softly.

Mountain lake

We came to the first of the lakes, Lia. There were two or three tents at the far end, the flat ground between them and the water disfigured in the usual Romanian way by bottles, rusty cans and scorchmarks from campfires. I scrambled down to the shore and began to cast while István went off to chat to the campers. When he rejoined me he said: 'I think we will not fish here.' I said I thought it looked promising. 'They say the dam workers were here yesterday. With nets. They took away enough trout to fill this. That is what Romanians do.' He patted his rucksack. 'We will go on.'

I again offered to take the rucksack, but István waved me away. 'The mountain air is making me better. I should not smoke so much.' He lit a cigarette. 'Yes, fifty or sixty a day. It is too many.'

The next lake, Ana, was a place of fond memory for István. The previous year he had caught a trout of nearly two kilos here. He assured me that there were many more just as big. I wandered along the leeward shore, casting my flies towards the middle. The weather was showing the first signs of a change for the worse. Dark clouds were hurrying in from the west, turning the water from glacial blue to slate grey as they passed in front of the sun. Sharp gusts of wind wrinkled the glassy calm of the surface. I looked back and saw István winding in a well-conditioned trout of about eight ounces.

We ate a lunch whose austerity was only partially mitigated by my beer. As he munched his slice of stale, cheese-smeared bread, István reflected on the deteriorating state of the weather. He said it would not be safe to attempt the rest of the eight-hour round trip he had originally envisaged. I was rather relieved to hear it. I climbed up the hill behind us. From the top I looked down on to the largest of the Retezat lakes, Bucura. Beyond it towered the jagged heights of Peleaga, rising to nearly 8,000 feet. Stretched across the distant skyline, like a sheet on a washing line, was the ridge known as the Bucura Saddle.

I lay on the soft grass, feeling the breeze against my cheek. It was cold enough for my breath to hang in the air momentarily. I dozed on a pillow of heather until an odd sound, a tinny, rhythmic tinkling, roused me. Using field glasses I searched the slopes for the source. A movement caught my eye. I made out a line of horses, with tiny figures astride them, in the middle of the Bucura Saddle. They must have been ten miles or more away, mountain people on their way to remoter pastures deep in the massif. I could not begrudge them their last link with the outside world, the music from their radio cheering them as they followed the path between the boulders.

István was already on the move as I came downhill. He gestured dramatically at the pass leading from Ana up to the next lake in the chain. A mist with a menacing, metallic texture was leaking through it and spreading over the neighbouring screes. István said something about hailstones the size of eggs, and hurried forward. We managed to keep in front of the mist, István almost trotting as the gravitational pull of the rucksack propelled him down the slope.

Near the car we overtook a party of three young men who had walked 30 miles or so from the Jiu valley in the east, skirting Peleaga and Lake Bucura before hitting the same path as us. They caught us up as we were getting into the car to begin the dreadful journey back to the dam, and begged us for a lift towards their destination for the night, a campsite near Sarmizegetusa. I asked István to tell them that the car was not up to carrying them and their gear, which he did with relish, brushing aside their appeals. He settled in his seat, twiddled his moustache, lit a cigarette and adjusted the wing mirror. We soon passed the three walkers plodding dispiritedly down the road.

'*Ce n'est pas une grande tragédie pour eux*,' Istvan said cheerfully. '*Une distance de vingt kilomètres seulement*.' A few moments later the storm broke, blotting out the mountains and sheeting the slopes with rain.

In the evening I explored the Riul Mare above the dam and managed to catch a trout about three inches long. The fish István had caught earlier brightened our evening meal considerably. I had managed to commandeer a separate bedroom in the hostel and went to bed early. I was kept awake for some time by the drunken yells of the caretaker couple in the room below me and the periodic baying of the sheepdog tethered outside my window. When I did sleep, I was bitten extensively by bedbugs, and there was a further disturbance towards dawn when a car pulled up and a group of men began hammering at the door and shouting. Soon afterwards the cocks struck up a penetrating crowing, joined a little later by a horrible belching antiphony from the turkeys.

István's provisions took their final bow at breakfast. I commented irritably on the various noises in the night. He said he had heard nothing. In the mountains, he said, he always slept well. We returned to the lake for a last fling before returning to Târgu Mureş. This time I followed a smaller stream that flowed in from the west. Ten minutes' walk took me out of sight of István, the lake, and the dam into an enchanted valley. The crests of the enclosing hills were covered in spruce and pine. Below, sweeping down to the stream, were banks of grass spotted with grub-like sheep. To left and right rose escarpments, each bluer and less distinct as they stretched away into the distance. A mass of green blocked the farther end, its summit hidden in thin grey cloud. I swung my binoculars across it and saw a silver gleam, a cataract by which the stream issued from the mountain.

I came upon a clump of wild strawberries and half-filled my cap with them. I ate them beside the stream, watching a peregrine falcon circle above, so slowly as to seem to defy all laws of gravity and motion. After a time I felt strong enough to face István again.

The drive back was hot and tiresome. Near Haţeg we jumped a two-mile queue at a petrol station, as I was legally entitled to by virtue of having coupons bought with dollars. Two or three Romanian drivers protested furiously as I slid up to the pumps in front of them, which delighted István almost as much as it mortified me. In Sebeş we contrived to mislay the main road. I drove like a madman to make up for lost time, and was congratulating myself on the daring manner in which I had overtaken two huge trucks and a bus when the passenger in the car in front flagged me down. I stopped, assuming some emergency had arisen. The man sauntered over, smiled ingratiatingly, and asked if I wanted to change money. As I stared at him, the two trucks and the bus roared past.

Such behaviour, István observed, was typical of Romanians. Wearily, I admitted that I had never had such an experience in Hungary. He relapsed into silence, fingering his moustache. By then we had entirely run out of things to say to each other. What surprised me was his complete lack of curiosity about me and my life – or anyone else's – in England. The only question I can remember him asking about Britain concerned the extent of the domestic airline network. Having put me right on the Transylvanian issue and introduced me to the wonder of the mountains, he had done all that could be expected of a good Magyar.

I asked after István when I came back to Târgu Mureş in 2008, even though I had no great desire to pick up where we had left off, or to reacquaint myself with the hangdog look, the moustache tweaking, the yellowed teeth and ashtray smell. Grigore did not even suggest a reunion. He said István was still living in the town, still smoking, now working for a Hungarian company – 'she is happy about that' – still bemoaning the unfairness of everything. He admitted his ulterior motive in landing István on me all those years before. 'Was black propaganda,' he said, laughing.

As for the ethnic divide, it was no longer the burning issue. The two communities remained separate and distinct. Hungarian schools, the Hungarian university, the Hungarian newspaper and club, all proclaimed the superiority of the Magyar way with every appearance of pride and conviction. But the people themselves had learned to rub along together in a way difficult to imagine two decades before. Mihály Spielman, the Hungarian director of the magnificent Teleki Library in Târgu Mureş, told me that the new generation had no interest in the old history, only in making money. 'And not just money,' he said, shaking his head. 'It must be Euros, always Euros.' The last two elections for mayor had been narrowly won by the Romanian candidate, and he said it was difficult to see how a Hungarian could win again.

The market forces had done much to erode ancient antagonisms. Significantly, an increasing number of Hungarian parents were choosing to send their children to Romanian schools at secondary level, in the knowledge that future jobs and prosperity would depend on a proper command of the language. Grigore told me he had recently interviewed a Hungarian woman for an engineering job: 'He very nice, intelligent, good qualifications, but he not read Romanian. She. I said, please, I am wasting my time.'

The two governments now talk to each other with wary courtesy, keeping off the question of the rightful ownership of Transylvania. There are even moves afoot for Hungarian and Romanian academics to get together to look for common ground between two versions of history so far apart that an outsider is surprised to find they apply to the same place.

Even so, dealing with the other side is very different from respecting the other side, and it is difficult to imagine Hungarians ever being able or ready to consider Romanians as being on an equal footing with themselves. A visit to Debrecen, the Hungarian city closest to Transylvania, helps explain how vast and deep is the sense of Magyar superiority.

Debrecen could not be mistaken for a Romanian city. Its graceful, clean, orderly centre is gathered around the northern end of a wide boulevard that extends from the railway station in the south to the Great Church with its twin clocktowers and eight clock-faces. There is none of the atrocious traffic din and general grubby confusion that blights all Romanian conurbations. Instead, a splendidly smart little tram clatters up and down every few minutes, making buses and even taxis quite unnecessary. At dawn every morning the cleaners are trundling about in their machines, hoovering up the litter and washing the paving slabs so that they sparkle in the morning sun. The fine old houses to either side of the boulevard and around the square in front of the church – now mostly converted into shops, bars, restaurants and hotels – speak of a long history of prosperity and cultured living.

The Reformation in its Calvinist form took a firm grip on the hardy, hard-working people of Hungary's Great Plain. Debrecen grew into a great centre of Protestant learning, heavily influenced by religious teaching from Switzerland, the Netherlands and England. The Reformed College, which stands a little way behind the Great Church, was founded in 1538 by high-minded pastors and teachers determined to build on the city's reputation as 'the Calvinist Rome'. Despite its remoteness and the notorious difficulty of getting to and from it, Debrecen stood squarely in the mainstream of the Protestant movement in Europe. The oak stairs leading up to the library and the oratory of the school have been worn into hollows by the feet of generations of scholars eager to grapple with the secrets and challenges of science, natural history, philology, philosophy, mathematics and – above all – religion. Biblical translations and commentaries flowed from the local printing presses. Debrecen and its school were to be counted with Geneva and Wittenberg as centres of educational excellence and doctrinal orthodoxy.

It was in the Great Church that Kossuth stood in 1848 to declare Hungary's independence from Habsburg tyranny; and it was in the oratory of the Reformed School that the first and short-lived National Assembly gathered. And while Hungary was making a stand for liberty and enlightenment, and could count among its sons a host of intellectuals, poets and statesmen who commanded respect across Europe, what did Romania have to offer?

Vlad the Impaler.

# Chapter 19

## Grigore's story

One day in 1986 the Comrades came to call on Grigore in his office. He was then director of Prodcomplex. It was one of the biggest companies in Târgu Mureş, with 3,000 employees, making furniture, carpets, glassware and other household items. 'Mr Lungu,' they said, all regretful smiles, 'you know the rule.'

Everyone knew the rule. Ceauşescu had decreed that no one who had family living outside Romania could be in charge of a major company. A few years before, Grigore's younger brother, Toti, his wife, and their infant daughter had left Bucharest to settle in West Germany. Not long afterwards they were joined by the mother of Grigore and Toti.

Their emigration was perfectly legal. For each Romanian of ethnic German origin permitted to move to the fatherland, Ceauşescu received a bounty of 4,000 deutschmarks. After oil sales it was his chief source of foreign revenue. It was typical of the regime's mentality and method of operating that, whenever such transactions were completed, any members of the family remaining behind were automatically classified as suspect and penalised.

Grigore smiled back at the Comrades. It was true that his mother's side of the family were originally German Schwabs, but Grigore regarded himself as wholly Romanian. So did Dana. The Comrades were not to know that both of them had made a pact, years before, that they would not leave Romania unless their lives there became utterly intolerable. They believed that, eventually, the tragedy that had overtaken their country would end. 'It is simple,' Grigore wrote to me. 'I was convinced that the comedy would finish one day and I wanted to see with my own eyes.'

Toti's situation was very different. His wife taught French at a school in Bucharest, hated Romania, and longed to leave. As for his and Grigore's mother, she thought of herself as being a German in exile, and looked down on Romanians to the extent of trying to forbid her sons to speak Romanian at home. Despite an age difference of ten years, the brothers were very close to each other. Grigore did not try to dissuade Toti from leaving even though he knew there would be consequences for himself. When I asked him about it, the old pain was evident in his face. 'I was not happy,' he said. 'But what can I do? She is my brother.'

He was summarily removed from his position as director of Prodcomplex and lost the perks that went with it. Grigore's first inclination was to leave the company altogether. He was a highly trained theoretical and practical engineer, fluent in German and Hungarian and competent in English, with extensive business experience and contacts, both in Romania and abroad. He would have been a prized asset to any company. But then an official at the Ministry had a quiet word in his ear. The rule was the rule, nothing could be done about that. But Prodcomplex was an important company and it needed Grigore. It would be better for everyone, the quiet voice said, if he stayed.

So he took over a unit within Prodcomplex set up to develop new products and processes. Under Grigore's leadership it flourished, testing and patenting many original systems. Then in 1989 the Comrades came calling again. They had received letters — anonymous, naturally. Comrade Lungu was in possession of important commercial secrets. His brother and mother were living abroad. What if he decided to join them, taking his secrets with him? Secrets that were the property of Romania would be at risk.

The Comrades had a proposal. A conference was to be held

shortly in Târgu Mureş, to be attended by important figures from the commercial and business sectors. If Mr Lungu were to address the conference and tell the delegates what a great man Ceauşescu was, how Romania had progressed in leaps and bounds under his wise and inspiring direction, how golden was the future shaped by his guiding hand etc etc, then all doubts about his loyalty would be erased. Look, to make it easy, they had even composed his speech for him.

Grigore addressed the conference. But he delivered his own speech, in which he dwelled at length on the technical detail of the various manufacturing processes he and his team were working on. He failed to mention the Great Leader. 'They were *vairy* angry,' he told me, laughing. 'But what can they do? And then Ceauşescu is shot.' Laughter exploded from him.

With chaos threatening on all sides, the official from the Ministry approached Grigore again. The situation had changed once more. The old rule – many old rules – no longer applied. Democracy beckoned. The free market was coming. Would Mr Lungu care to be reinstated as director of Prodcomplex? 'I said yes. It was a big mistake. Maybe the biggest mistake I make in my life.'

When I first came to Târgu Mureş, Grigore was back in charge. By Romanian standards he had rejoined the elite. He had a salary of £70 a week, a spacious flat with a video and two German-made televisions, a new car, a cottage in the country. He had also been readmitted to the town's inner circle, the 'Târgu Mureş Mafia', as he called it, half-humorously. He knew everyone who mattered. He could get petrol when the petrol stations were shut, meat when the shops were empty, beer when the bars were dry. As I found, Grigore was a very useful man to have as a friend.

What I did not realise then, because he never gave me a hint of it, was that he was under enormous pressure. His big mistake was that, instead of getting out of the state system and grasping one of the business opportunities opening up all around, he spent five years toiling in vain to save a bloated, doomed, industrial dinosaur from going to the wall. Dana also worked at Prodcomplex, and toiled with him. Grigore now admits that they neglected other aspects of life, including their son, young Grigore, who had a troubled adolescence.

In the end they both got out, and Prodcomplex crumbled. Dana opened a shoe shop in town, which did well for a while. Together she and Grigore looked at other possibilities. In the end they started a small company making furniture moulded from polyurethane. After an uncertain beginning it did well. Grigore oversaw the technical side and shaped the business strategy. Dana did the books. Young Grigore left his difficult times behind, took a university degree in management, and did the legwork. Then Dana, a habitual heavy smoker, developed cancer. She had surgery and treatment, was in remission for a time before the disease came back and killed her.

She was Grigore's second wife, he her second husband, and they had forged a strong partnership. When they were together, they never touched or gave each other intimate signs of affection, which at the time struck me as curious. I now think that this was simply their way, that of a couple who had been through much and had been strengthened by it. Grigore talked about her easily enough – how they had built the business, the building of their new house, the progress of her illness. Whatever he felt about his loss, he kept to himself. He gave every appearance of enjoying life, relishing the way in which 'young' Grigore was taking the weight off his shoulders, allowing him the time to potter in his garden, to sunbathe on his lawn, to go fishing when he felt like it.

I missed Dana very much. I still remembered my first evening in their flat. After Grigore and I had watched the football, he went off somewhere and she gave me supper in the kitchen with the other television on, showing the news. There had been a big anti-government demonstration in Bucharest that had been broken up by men with clubs. There was an interview with the student leader of the protest from his hospital bed, where he lay heavily bandaged.

'He is saying that it was a peaceful demonstration, for democracy,' Dana translated. 'Then these miners come with big sticks. But they are not miners, they are Securitate, like in the old days. Now this student is beaten up, in hospital and under arrest, just like with Ceauşescu.'

The scene changed to an office with a large, shiny desk. Behind it, rubbing his hands and smiling shiftily, sat President Iliescu. Dana jabbed her finger angrily at the screen.

'Ah, here is Iliescu, the great democrat. He will now say that this demonstration is not democratic. That the miners are showing the anger of the people. Iliescu is a Communist. He was with Ceauşescu. He does not know the difference between truth and lies.' Iliescu's eyes darted away from the camera. His hands jumped about. 'He is lying,' Dana cried, waving her cigarette. 'This great democrat. We have killed Ceauşescu and now we have him . . . the same.'

Grigore came in. She greeted him with a vehement summary of the news. He smiled at her and spoke to her quietly. To me he said that the students were looking for trouble, that they didn't like the results of the elections because Iliescu had won. 'Maybe he was a Communist. The same like me. Now I think there are no Communists in Romania.'

Dana took great, visible pleasure in dusting off her French for my benefit, and engaging me in long, serious conversations about the situation. On the way to the hunting lodge at Lăpuşna, we stopped for an al fresco lunch in a grove of silver birches close to the River Gurghui. She was wearing a T-shirt over a blue bikini that suited her figure well. I told her I had been reliably informed in Poland that Romanians were so short of food they had been forced to resort to cannibalism. At the time we were eating pork in a wild mushroom sauce with boiled potatoes, and drinking beer.

She laughed, then her face became grave again. '*Vous devez être plus sérieux, Tom. Pour nous, c'est une affaire à prendre très sérieusement. Pour vous, pour les autres pays de l'Europe, la Roumanie est un pays de barbarisme.*'

I made the mistake of mentioning the assault on the students in Bucharest that had aroused her to such fury on the night of my arrival. The fury returned, this time aimed at me. This was a matter for Romanians. Who was I to condemn them? Had they not got rid of Ceauşescu? Did I know what Ceauşescu was like then? What life was like? No, I did not. Had there not been sacrifices . . . many sacrifices? Did not Romania deserve a chance?

Of course, I replied hastily. It was just that some people in the West suspected that Romania's democracy was a façade. That choice of word was another mistake. Dana's cigarette danced under my nose. '*Qu'est ce que vous pouvez comprendre de ces événements? Vous ne savez rien de . . . de . . . de . . .*' She banged her fist on the table as she searched for the word. '*. . . du cauchemar de la Roumanie. Vous, vous . . . ah!*' She turned away in disgust at my ignorance.

Two other couples had joined us for lunch. Grigore sat at the far end of the table talking conspiratorially to the two husbands and dispensing glasses of his home-made *tuică*. One of the wives murmured something to Dana who turned back to me. She pointed at the river. 'What about a swim?' she suggested.

'*Non, non, je n'ai pas de . . .*' I pointed at young Grigore's swimming trunks.

'*Ça ne fait rien. Tu peux nager nu.*'

I could feel my face going red. '*Non, merci. Je suis heureux de rester ici.*' She laughed at me in delight and said something to the other women. The news spread and the whole table burst into hilarity at my so-English reserve.

Dana would often denounce the iniquities of the past, but if anyone dared extend criticism of the regime to the country itself, or to its people, she would turn on them in a flash. Neither she nor anyone else would talk about the complicity Ceauşescu and the Party had deliberately nurtured between themselves and the people, the way in which this had worked its way throughout society and corrupted all other relationships. Family members had spied and informed on other family members, friends on friends, colleagues on colleagues. Almost everyone had, to a greater or lesser degree, been implicated in actions and events of which they had cause to be ashamed.

There was an unspoken collective agreement that these matters should not be discussed. Everyone, including Grigore and Dana, was doing their best to disassociate themselves from certain aspects of the past. One way, useful when dealing with an inquisitive outsider, was to classify the whole experience using the word Dana had used: *un cauchemar* . . . a nightmare . . . as if an entire country and its people had been forcibly transported into a parallel reality beyond the understanding of non-Romanians.

On the last night of my return visit, I reminded Grigore of what Dana had said all those years before: that as an outside I could not begin to understand the Ceauşescu nightmare. We were having dinner at the smartest restaurant in town, its smartness reflected not in the food – which was ordinary enough – but in the service, which was remarkably slow, and the conspicuous affluence of the other diners. The lamp-lit setting, among trees in a garden, the atmosphere of ease and money, the pop of corks, the swish of the waitresses – all might have been choreographed to show the gulf between present and past.

'It is true, what Dana say, that it is not possible for you to understand what it was like then.' Grigore's face was furrowed by the effort to find words; and, perhaps, by the weight of the subject. 'Also how it could happen here. How we could let it happen.'

We changed the subject and talked about fishing for some time. In a few days Grigore and a friend would be driving to Germany to pick up Toti on their way to Lapland for their annual month-long fishing trip. Grigore was looking forward with relish to the enormous numbers of trout and grayling they would catch.

Later he returned, briefly, to the past. 'You want to know how this could happen? I tell you. It was a combination. Force and . . .' it took him some time to find the word '. . . anxiety. That is how they ruled us.'

# Chapter 20

## Delta

On the farthest edge of Europe, the river that runs through so much of the continent's history comes to its quiet, diffuse end. The most dazzling of the Danube's many historians, Claudio Magris, sees the delta as 'one great dissolution . . . a great death . . . a death that is also incessant regeneration.'

Magris addresses the problem facing any writer who tries to convey a sense of this place: 'the inadequacies of our perceptions, our senses atrophied by the millennia . . . our antique severance from the flow of life'. 'The immense chorus of the delta,' he writes elsewhere, 'is to our ears only a murmur, a voice we cannot catch, a whisper of life which vanishes unheard.'

The camera has its own inadequacies. You can record views of channels of water, walls of reeds, lines of willows, a heron or a cormorant standing guard on a branch, pelicans turning like coins against the sky, old boats blackened with pitch, a sunset, a mist-laden dawn. But the lens keeps missing the point. The geography of the delta, its relentless, uncompromising flatness, conspires against the eye as well as against language. You see the channel and the reeds or trees that confine it, nothing beyond. The prospect broadens as you enter one of the lakes, but the detail dissolves and you are left with flat water, beds of lilies, clods of weed, the grey reed line around the edge, trees smudged against it, everything flattened by the conquering immensity of the sky.

The essence of the delta is contained both in the illusion of infinity and in its fine details. Only the mind can encompass both. It is like a vast musical structure – Beethoven's *Diabelli Variations*, perhaps, or Brahms's *Handel Variations* – built on a small, simple theme. In the delta's case, it is the theme of water. Like us, it is 90 per cent water. Its major channels are its arteries, the connecting arms its veins, the multitude of creeks and ditches its capillaries, the marsh and reedbeds its tissue.

How wonderful it would be to glide bird-like over it, maintaining a flight path over extended distances with no more than an occasional wing-beat, changing direction at will. But even then you would only skim the surface. You would probably miss the boar, otters, mink, ermine, hares, wild cats and other animals of the reed islands and marshes and thickets. You would spot the big, less shy birds – eagles, herons, pelicans, cormorants – as well as the waterfowl, but you would be lucky to catch a glimpse of the more self-effacing among the 180 resident species, such as the rail, the marsh harrier or the bittern. Closer to the water you might see a spray of little roach escaping from a pike, but for the rest of the fish species – carp, zander, catfish, the very occasional sturgeon – you would have to take their concealed presence on trust.

Then there are the people. They are certainly visible, but their lives would be more unknowable than those of the sturgeon or the sea eagle; unless, that is, you were prepared to stop for good and learn not just the languages (Romanian, Ukrainian and Russian to start with), but also how to live on a floating island of reed, how to lay nets across the feeding paths of fish, how to track boar, how to tell a red-breasted goose from a white-fronted one before shooting it.

For Magris, this insoluble problem was illustrated by a momentary encounter with a Lipovan fisherman, Kovaliov Dan, and by the sighting of a young man he calls Nikolai, who gets off a boat and smiles shyly as a girl kisses him on shore. To justify its existence,

Magris says, the book ought to be able to tell their stories. But it cannot, so it falls back on 'summaries, on a precis of conquests and the fall of empires, anecdotes from the Council Chamber, conversations at court or in Parnassus, the minutes in international commissions'.

In other words, the writer – always inadequate, always missing most, and the best part, of any story – is reduced to a condition of more-than-usual helplessness by the Danube Delta. On the other hand, it's a long way to go and not even try . . .

Arriving in June 2008, I was 30 years or so too late. I had carried a picture of the delta in my mind for a long time. In this picture I lodged in a shack on one of the *plaurs*, the islands of living and dead reed. I was looked after by a Lipovan boatman, one of the blue-eyed, blond-haired, bushy-bearded race of Old Believers who had migrated south from Russia nearly 300 years before to escape the persecution of the Russian Orthodox Church.

Danube boat – old style

Conditions in the imagined shack were very basic. There were bugs, and mosquitoes as big as bats. At dawn, perhaps even earlier, we would push off across the still, black water in a pitch-blackened, sharp-nosed boat redolent of fish, smeared with dried slime and blood and spangled with scales. We would creep over the black water, along channels and across lagoons, until we reached the spot where the carp, the pike or the catfish – I was not choosy – lurked. It was a silent journey, apart from the dipping of the boatman's oars, the purling of the water against the boat, the rustle of stirring reed-heads, the croaking of frogs, the call of cuckoos and the bustle of ducks and coots.

When Grigore first came to fish the delta, in the 1970s, that was pretty much how it was. He was up at 3 a.m. to meet his Lipovan boatman who then rowed for three or four hours to get to the place (and three or four hours back). One year Grigore brought with him an outboard engine that he himself had adapted from a petrol-driven wood-saw. Unwittingly he thus became one of the pioneers of the mechanical revolution that swept away the old, very slow, very arduous order so that when my turn finally came, I had to recompose my mental picture fast. The silent rowing boat was supplanted by Grigore's and Toti's jointly owned pride and joy, a gleaming white 20-foot craft powered by a 60-hp engine capable of skimming the water at 30 kilometres an hour; which was not part of the original scheme at all.

The petrol-driven engine destroyed for ever the delta's most potent quality: its silence. But at the same time it's worth recalling that the peace that still reigned when Grigore started coming was more the peace of the hospital ward than that of a pristine wetland wilderness. The process of taming the delta that had begun with every virtuous intention a century and a half before had eventually brought it to its knees.

The Lipovan exiles from Russia arrived here around the middle of the eighteenth century, and for a long while were left to their own devices. They learned the habits of the fish, particularly the migrating sturgeon. They built slim boats with shallow draughts to ease their way along the silty channels. Fishing was the main business but they hunted birds and animals as well, and built villages on the few spits of dry land, where they kept animals and fowls and grew crops and fruit trees. The water was their element and they were attuned to the delta's secret, shifting ways. No one bothered them. To the west, wars raged, dynasties were forged and toppled, the flames of rebellion were fanned and brutally doused, alliances were made and broken, territories were conquered, borders were redrawn, kings were crowned, deposed, assassinated. None of it made much difference to the Lipovans. They stayed loyal to their ancient Russian liturgy, bowing to the floor and crossing themselves with two fingers; and they kept laying their nets.

But it was inevitable that in the Europe that emerged from the ruins left by the Napoleonic Wars, the potential of the Danube would arouse interest. The river reached from the heart of Europe to the Black Sea. The Black Sea offered a route to the Bosphorus, and the Bosphorus to the trading world beyond.

In Budapest Count István Széchenyi looked across its waters and decided to make it his business to subdue the river so that it might serve the rebirth of the Magyar nation. Between 1830 and 1846 Széchenyi made ten journeys up and down the Danube, some lasting months, accompanied by engineers, potential investors, fellow visionaries and a fair number of tourists. His mission was to persuade anyone prepared to give him a hearing – in England he bent the ears of the Duke of Wellington, Palmerston, Sir Robert Peel and Lord Grey, among others – that the conversion of the Danube into a major east–west trade route would have a dynamic effect on the economies of the whole continent. Among much else,

Széchenyi supervised the blasting of a way through the rapids and cataracts of the Danube's most notorious blackspot, the Iron Gates near Orşova.

Much was accomplished, and Széchenyi's Danube Steamship Company worked the river regularly – if not very profitably – between Linz in Austria and Galati in Romania, the last river port before the delta. But the grand vision of a Danube trade route foundered at the delta. Below Galati the river split into a web of tortuous channels as it sought the sea, none of which could be relied upon to take cargo vessels. From one year to the next they would change course or silt up to the point of being impassable. A single storm in the Black Sea could pile up enough sand to block the way through entirely.

In the 1840s Britain – the world leader in this kind of enterprise – sent a Royal Navy survey team to assess what should be done to address this deplorable situation. The team looked at the three principal channels: Chilia to the north, Sfântu Gheorghe to the south, Sulina in the middle. Sir Henry Trotter of the Admiralty reported to Parliament on what they found as they approached the mouth of the Sulina channel:

> . . . a wild, open seaboard strewed with wrecks, the masts of which, sticking out of the submerged sandbanks, gave to the mariners the only guide to where the deepest channel was to be found; while the banks of the river were only indicated by clusters of wretched hovels built on poles, and by narrow patches skirted by tall reeds, the only vegetable product of the vast swamp beyond . . .

Nothing daunted, the Admiralty recommended that the Sulina channel offered the best prospect. Over the next 20 years it was dredged, embanked, straightened and significantly shortened. Sulina itself – hitherto a decayed, lawless outpost of the Ottoman Empire

– became the Black Sea port. The project was a co-operative v.
by the European powers, and a pan-European Commission was
established to oversee the commercial development of the river.
It set up its headquarters in the inland port of Galati, where the
presence of the Commissioners and their families bestowed on
the town a prosperity and cosmopolitan gentility not found elsewhere in the region. There were parties, musical soirées, visits to
the best addresses, and excursions into the countryside to inspect
the curious customs of the natives and down to the delta to look
at nature.

But despite the Commission and the great investment, the
Danube trade never flourished as pioneers such as Széchenyi had
envisaged. The river was too long. It passed through too many
countries that were too inclined, at difficult moments, to put
their own narrow interests before the common good. And, for
all the efforts to tame the river, it remained too unruly. Most
winters saw floods that made long stretches unnavigable for
weeks. Even at times of normal flow the upstream passage was
agonisingly slow for the big barges, which in places had to be
towed from the bank by locomotives. At its height the volume
of goods shipped on the Danube was less than a fifth of that on
the Rhine.

But the endeavour was not abandoned, and the Danube
Commission continued to wave the flag of co-operation between
nations until that ideal itself fell face down in the dust in 1939.
Thereafter a new imperative held sway. Romania and Yugoslavia's
Communist leaders clasped each other in comradely bear-hugs
and agreed to pool resources in order to harness the power of the
Danube at the Iron Gates. In 1972 the dam across the gorge and
its two attendant hydro-electric plants were opened. One of
Europe's most dramatic natural wonders was lost for ever, as was
the island of Ada Kaleh, the famous walled Turkish enclave with
its mosque and web of twisting alleys.

.nched Grigore and Toti's boat from a slipway at the edge
.ulcea, a little way downstream from where the Chilia channel
splits off to the north and just above the separation of the Sulina
and Sfântu Gheorghe channels. Mrs Ethel Greening Pantazzi, the
American wife of one of the Danube Commissioners stationed in
Galati in the period before the First World War, left a charming
picture of Tulcea then: 'with its quaint windmills slowly turning
their wide brown wings on the hillsides . . . the slender minarets
side by side with the round church domes'. The mosque and the
church are still there, and apparently some Turks as well. But the
windmills have long gone, and the quaintness and charm have
been submerged beneath the racket and disorder inescapable in
every Romanian town and city.

The waterfront at Tulcea churned with activity. A rusting ferry,
weighed down by trucks and cars, was heaved by a smoky tub of
a tug in an arduous arc to the far bank. Towering Russian and
Turkish cargo ships cleaved downriver, bound for Sulina, sirens
booming. Barges heaped with sand and gravel, bristling with scrap
metal and machinery, crept towards their berths. Past casualties
of the river trade – barges, stubby coasters, derelict pleasure boats
– lay abandoned on the mudbanks between the jetties and wharves,
like drunks suddenly overtaken by the urge to sleep. Multitudes
of smaller craft – launches, inflatables, dinghies – cut angles across
the water, engines buzzing and growling.

As the elder brother, it was Grigore's privilege to steer us out
of Tulcea. Subsequently he and Toti shared the wheel, and neither
I nor Toti's daughter Ada – who completed our quartet – was ever
invited to take a turn. Ada, who was slim and strong and outdoorsy,
was put in charge of the anchor. I made no useful contribution to
the management of the boat.

Grigore at the wheel

With the aid of a brisk current we headed seawards, the twin propellers ploughing deep, curving furrows behind us. There were anglers everywhere: in boats tucked into the reeds, or stationed on the banks where there was shade from the ferocious sun. Far away a flock of pelicans wheeled against the blue sky like a handful of black and silver buttons thrown towards the sun. Through my binoculars I fixed on three eagles swaying on the thermals. The cormorants watched us, unmoving, from their stations in the trees, but the herons retreated with heavy flaps of their wings as we approached.

No vermin-infested shack awaited us but a well-appointed *pension* on the waterfront at Crişan, the last major settlement on the Sulina channel before Sulina itself. The address of the *pension* was 57, which sufficed, as there was only the one street, extending the six-kilometre length of the village. Since no road runs to Crişan from anywhere else, there is no traffic to watch out for except bicycles, the odd scooter and the occasional horse.

Number 57 was roughly in the middle, a ten-minute walk from the hub of the settlement which consisted of the one bar/restaurant and the one shop. Crişan was bounded to the front by the channel, here about 250 yards wide, and behind by a few fields, grazed by horses and cattle, and a wetland of bog and reedy, weedy ponds from which, soon after the fall of darkness, a tremendous massed chorus of frogs burst forth as suddenly as if someone had flicked a switch.

But Crişan was no hick backwater. The channel was as busy as any well-used through road, and the village was growing fast. The old houses – single-storey wooden structures with verandahs and reed-thatched roofs – had originally each been allocated land for orchards and vegetable plots and a paddock for the beasts. These gaps were being rapidly filled by two- and three-storey holiday houses and *pensions*, to cater for the swelling tide of visitors.

Instead of a beaten mud floor, a palliasse and an oil-lamp, I had a room to myself with en-suite shower and lavatory, and a little balcony from which to listen to the frogs. The dining-room was downstairs, where the proprietor – an incomer from Bucharest – swapped fishing tales with Grigore and Toti while his wife served fried eggs and sausage for breakfast, and chicken or catfish steaks with boiled potatoes for supper. There was a verandah at the back, cluttered with fishing tackle where the fishermen gathered to discuss fortunes and prospects. In front, on the other side of the street, was a landing-stage where, each morning, the proprietor's wife was to be found cleaning catfish. She stood in the shallow water, sleeves rolled up, hair pulled back, slashing and twisting and rending until the surface of the landing-stage was dark and slippery with blood and slime.

We checked in then headed off, following a canal that cut away to the south-west from the main channel, until we came to a fork where we anchored. The water flowing down one arm was khaki, thick with suspended silt; down the other it was clear, looking

Cleaning catfish for supper

black only because of the black mud beneath. We cast spinners into the mingling of the two streams. Toti's rod was the first to bend. '*Barsch*,' he grunted as the fish flashed in the water. I asked Grigore what *barsch* might be. '*Barsch* is . . .' He hesitated. '*Barsch* is . . . *barsch*.' It proved to be a perch of about half a pound. We caught some more, all about the same size. Then Toti got something a bit bigger, a long, slender silver fish with a lot of sharp little teeth which I didn't recognise.

After a time the *barsch* stopped biting. We followed the dark, clear flow to a lake, but it was so clogged with weed as to be unfishable. We nosed past huge expanses of lilies, searching for ways into clear water, but they all had nets strung across them that sagged just below the surface between stakes driven into the mud. Grigore took the boat into a lagoon where he had had success before, but the weed was just as bad there. A single pelican was hunting along one bank, paddling slowly through the water, jabbing with its bill, occasionally tilting back its head to adjust the catch. Despite its outlandish appearance, the bird's performance looked highly efficient, even menacing.

Back at the *pension* I was introduced to a delta regular armed with a great array of rods, reels and boxes of tackle. He was a striking sight as he waddled about the place wearing a turquoise Adidas vest and a pair of outsize white shorts, both garments stretched to the limit and beyond by a vast barrel of a stomach rugged with hair. More hair curled up and over his mighty arms and shoulders to a neck like a section of a severed tree trunk. His head was completely smooth, like a dinosaur egg, his face nut-brown and creased with smiles, blue eyes bright with laughter as he peered over the top of gold-framed glasses.

He was catching his share of catfish. But catching these requires the angler to spend many hours sitting motionless in a boat waiting for a bite, ideally at night, just when the mosquitoes are hunting. Grigore and Toti were not interested; nor — having once had a bellyful of it in Hungary — was I. We wanted pike. The great bald head shook slowly. No one was encountering pike, no one knew where they were.

Next morning we roared upstream to a point where the Sulina channel intersected with the original course of the river. We diverted on to the Dunărea Veche, the Old Danube, then followed a cut north-east through marsh and waterlogged willow forest until we reached a big lake. This was Brogdaproste, the south-ernmost of a group of 20 or so lakes and lagoons contained in a great swathe of wetland between the Sulina and Chilia channels. Two years before, Grigore said, he and his friend the doctor had landed 90 pike between them here in one afternoon. But now the lake was thick with fibrous weed and there was not a pike to be seen.

We went back to the Old Danube and along it to a village curiously named Mila 23, a well-known Lipovan settlement. I asked Grigore how the Lipovan fishermen were faring these days. Well, he said. They were all building themselves new houses, with electricity and running water. So the fishing is good? I asked naively. He laughed in the slightly dismissive way Romanians tended to adopt when questioned about the old days. He said they were all guiding tourists now. Why go fishing when there was easier money to be made? They're not stupid, you know.

A few miles due south of Crişan, about midway between the Sulina and Sfântu Gheorghe channels, was Caraorman, a Ukrainian village set among dunes of fine white sand. A little way from the village, on the edge of a basin excavated to one side of the canal, stood the gaunt shell of a factory with a block of apartments, half-finished and abandoned, next to it. Under one of the legion of Five Year Plans drawn up to realise the vision of Nicolae Ceauşescu, this was to have been the Caraorman Glassworks, another glorious milestone along the path mapped for Romania's Industrial Revolution. Instead, its fate has been to provide haunts for bats and nesting sites for birds, and to commemorate the remarkable folly of the little man with the big ideas.

Ceauşescu was challenged by the delta. Something must be done, he resolved, to drag this unproductive expanse of bog and water into the era of progressive socialism. What use to the Greater Romania were birds and fishermen with long beards who spoke Russian? Factories and blocks of apartments must rise. Conveyor belts and machines must be installed. Industrialisation must triumph.

It was pointed out to the Leader that the peculiar geography of the place might make some aspects of his vision problematic. Very well, he reflected. Let factories and apartment blocks be built where possible. Elsewhere let the waters be constrained and engineered to enable crops to be grown and fish to be farmed.

Over the 25 years of Ceauşescu's rule, almost a quarter of the delta was drained and reclaimed for agriculture, aquaculture and forestry. Vast areas of wetland, with their breeding sites for resident and migrating birds, were lost. Spawning grounds for sturgeon and other fish were obstructed or destroyed. Pollution from fertilisers, herbicides, pesticides and farm wastes of every kind poisoned the waterways. Over the same period the whole Danube system was turned into a network of conduits to remove the filth of half the continent. The heavy industries of Romania, Bulgaria, Yugoslavia, Hungary and Czechoslovakia poured their toxic waste into the Danube and its tributaries without restraint. By 1989 both river and delta were desperately – some thought terminally – sick.

But rivers are difficult to kill. Their capacity for self-healing and regeneration is one of the wonders of the planet. All they need is some respite from attack, and in the case of the Danube that came with the collapse of the Soviet Bloc. In Romania, the glass factory at Caraorman and much else were overtaken by the whirl-wind that spread from Timişoara in the winter of 1989 and sent Ceauşescu spinning on his way.

Within a year the Danube Delta had been designated a UNESCO biosphere reserve. Work soon began on dismantling the most damaging of the dykes and dams so that the polders could revert to wetland. The aquatic food chain struggled back to life. The enormous discharge of nutrients, particularly phosphorus, which had caused the spectacular and disastrous eutrophication of the Black Sea, was sharply reduced thanks to improved waste-water treatment upstream and the enforced abandonment of much of the intensive agriculture. The closure of many factories and mines, combined with tighter pollution controls introduced under the aegis of the EU, sustained the recovery.

In the past 20 years the delta has been dragged back from the brink. Water quality in the channels and lakes is generally adequate. The backwaters and lagoons swarm with shoals of fry, and although fishermen bemoan poor catches, fishermen usually do. The dynamics of fish populations are at the mercy of many factors, of which water quality is just one. Out at sea the water is clearer, the incidence of algal blooms is down, and the abundance of the phytoplanktons, phytobenthos and macrozoobenthos at the bottom of the food chain is slowly improving.

But while the delta may have its health back, it will never regain its lost innocence. That would require total protection from pollution, engineering and other obvious forms of abuse, and from us. It is not going to happen. It is already not happening. The delta is too valuable. While the scientists and ecologists appeal for human intrusion to be restrained, beady-eyed politicians, administrators, regional developers and deal-makers have gone to work. In the age of cheap travel, expanded leisure time and ready money, the delta has been transformed from wilderness into investment opportunity.

The accessible sections are under occupation. Hotels and *pensions* have sprung up on every spit of dry land. Redundant steamers have been spruced up and transformed into floating pleasure palaces. Villages like Crişan and Mila 23 have doubled in population, and each has its waterside petrol station. In the summer season the power boats snarl up and down the waterways all day long, filling the air with the whine of engines and the smell of benzene. The hallmark big birds – the pelicans, egrets, herons and cormorants – spend the daylight hours hiding or fleeing from grotesquely over-powered craft steered by paunchy men in swimming trunks and baseball caps, with one hand on the wheel and the other cupping the inevitable mobile phone. They are not there to fish or paint or enjoy the beauties of nature, but to sweep at maximum speed wherever they are allowed to go, their wash slicing the water and slapping against the reedbeds. Those areas of the delta not designated as reserves are now a free-for-all.

*       *       *

The old way of life was in headlong retreat, but not every vestige had yet been erased. Occasionally we would pass one of the traditional slim, black rowing boats piled with nets or reeds, being pulled along by an old man under a straw hat, and leave it bouncing in our wake. Grigore and Toti were much too delighted with their new toy to be bothered about noise or disturbance to wildlife. From their point of view, the boat simply expanded their horizons, gave them freedom. Grigore said there were proposals to impose stricter speed limits and require the use of much quieter electric engines away from the main channels and canals. In the meantime everyone's first impulse was to open the throttle.

From the abandoned glass factory at Caraorman we took a narrow cut into a big, triangular lake, Puiu. There was another lake, Lumina, immediately to the north, and the map indicated there was a channel between the lakes. Grigore and Toti seemed to have convinced each other that Lumina must be where all the fish had retreated. Two or three years before, Grigore related, the doctor had had a great day there fishing for pike. In the evening, however, he found that the creek he had taken to get in had closed behind him (a familiar delta phenomenon as the rafts of reed shift position in the wind). In fading light he had searched in vain for another exit before resigning himself to a troubled night with only the mosquitoes, the nightingales and the frogs for company. Overnight the breeze dropped and in the morning the creek was open again.

This tale struck me as reason enough to leave Lumina alone. But the questing spirit of the brothers was aroused. We nosed our way around the northern shore of Puiu, looking for a break in the reeds. At length we found one that opened into a twisting channel squeezed between willows. Grigore cut the engine and we paddled. A convoy of carp ghosted beneath us, grey silhouttes against the black mud. The way ahead narrowed so that it became impossible even to paddle, and we had to pull ourselves along by grabbing at overhanging branches. Eventually we ran gently aground 20 yards short of the open water of Lumina.

Ignoring Ada's protests, Toti, determined to drag us through, seized the rope and jumped sideways for the bank. He sank up to his knees in the mud, took two floundering steps, and was up to his waist. Ada and Grigore yanked him back on board, his lower half plastered in black ooze. We retreated, and soon the reassuring throaty chug of the motor asserted itself again.

Only at such moments does the delta provide a reminder of its epic indifference to the specks of humanity buzzing around it, and cause to remember that this is a world where we really do not belong. It may tolerate us, or it may turn against us and swallow us into its moist, quaking being. We reflect that it would take us a lifetime just to be on terms with it, and then only if we had access to the wisdom and experience of the generations that came before us. We may sigh regretfully at the invasion of the motorboats, but we would not care to be out here on our own, in a rowing boat, trying to find our way home with bad weather brewing.

For obvious reasons, very little is heard in travellers' accounts of the delta's darker moods: the dreadful storms that sweep in from the Black Sea, flattening the reeds and churning the waters into foaming yellow seas; the raging floods swamping villages and washing people and livestock away; the Crivat, the vicious wind from Ukraine, that drives snowstorms across the ice. The lives of the delta people are a closed book, more or less. Mrs Pantazzi observed complacently that the region was 'the refuge of the homeless, the fugitive, the victims of religious persecution . . . an immense puzzle of nationalities', and sailed on. Sacheverell Sitwell sketched a quick impression of the 'quivering lagoon that glittered and trembled in the heat'; but instead of lingering with the Lipovan fishermen, he was much more interested in Galati and its community of Skoptzi, the weird sect of self-castrators who believed that Christ was mutilated rather than baptised by John, and that the way to paradise lay in ecstatic prayer and the excision of the sexual organs.

Claudio Magris is the best of an unsatisfactory bunch of guides. As his boat 'wanders like an animal' among the branches of the river, he at least acknowledges the complex narratives vested in the reed-thatched houses, the ramshackle villages, the blackened boats; even though he hasn't the time to pause and unravel them. A story by one of the giants of twentieth-century Romanian fiction, Mihail Sadoveanu, gives a glimpse of the untold story. Entitled *A Fishery*, it describes a visit in driving rain to a fish-processing centre on the Sulina channel. Sadoveanu observes the Lipovan fishermen:

> . . . with faces made harsh by rain, wind and sun . . . bareheaded, with matted hair; their trousers were rolled up to the knees; their clothes were nothing but tatters, braided jackets smeared with scales and grease, breeches smeared with scales, grease and mud . . . rain and Danube water was streaming from the tops of their heads into every last seam of their clothing . . .

Inside the building, sturgeon, carp, perch and other fish have been sorted into heaps. Cleaners with razor-sharp knives cut and gut. Outside, more boats laden with fish arrive. Some of the fishermen squat in a corner tearing chunks from a loaf of black bread and swigging from a bottle of *tuică*. Shouts in Russian are heard from an approaching boat. The master of the fishery, a Greek, says the boatman is Nechita, a ne'er-do-well notorious for poaching and suspected of darker deeds, including murder. 'The administration, mayor, sub-prefect, gendarmes have no existence here,' the Greek says. 'No one can penetrate these wilds.' Later they pass

Nechita's boat again, moored near his house on a raised sandbank. They see a tall, slender young woman come out to greet him. He knocks her down and beats her with his fists. They leave.

In the late 1990s a group of Romanian ethnologists began a two-year project to try to find out how the fishing communities of the delta had adapted to the new order introduced after Ceauşescu's overthrow and the award of UNESCO biosphere status. They found that a cultural chasm had opened between the fishermen, with their inherited understanding of the delta and traditions of exploiting it, and the ecologists from outside, who were empowered to use force, if need be, to impose their conservationist regime. In the jargon of ethnology, the coercive methods of the authorities and the lack of communication with villagers had engendered 'a self-victimising mentality on the part of the delta people which does nothing but register failures, frustrations and subversive techniques'.

At a deeper level, the researchers found that the delta people had lost, or were fast losing, their inherited 'mental maps' of their homeland. Traditionally the delta was their territory, in that they belonged there. But by its nature it could not be the property of anyone, and thus no one could be excluded from it. Over time their mental maps of the important places – where fish spawned or wild boar retreated – had blurred into copies of the tourist maps. The reference points had become the places tourists were interested in. The territory had become biosphere, reservation, property; patrolled by guards in fast motor-boats. Faced with dispossession and exclusion, the delta people could drink, moan, emigrate or dream of emigrating (they favoured comparably watery destinations like Canada), seek factory jobs outside the delta, turn to serious (often violent) poaching, or enlist in the tourist service industry.

The Delta Biosphere Declaration of 1993 stated that the right of the people 'to preserve their specific customs and traditional economic activities is guaranteed'. No more. Now the Reserve

Administration 'makes proposals for paying compensation . . . in case of economic contraction or the suspension of traditional activities as caused by restrictive management measures'. In other words, step aside, fishermen of the delta. Your day is done.

Grigore and Toti were not in the least interested in any of this. Their view was that times changed, and you either changed with them or suffered the consequences. Wallowing in regret for the passing of a way of life was an indulgence strictly for romantics or EU-funded researchers who would recoil from actually living that hard, uncomfortable life. It was as pointless as bemoaning the disappearance of the scythe and the horse-drawn plough.

Picnic in the delta – Grigore, Toti, Ada

On the whole we were a relaxed, happy party. The bond between the brothers was close, and they took evident delight in being together. Language obstacles meant that Toti and I hardly communicated at all, and I found out very little about his youth or his time in Bucharest before leaving for Germany. I'm not sure I would have got far even had I been able to speak German or Romanian.

Toti was shy and reserved, and did not give the impression of being a ready sharer of confidences.

Ada was six years old when the family left. Before this trip she had been back to Romania just once and, although she spoke Romanian to her father and uncle, she regarded herself as entirely German. She seemed embarrassed by her origins; or maybe this was a defensive posture adopted to deal with German prejudice against Romanians, whose reputation elsewhere in Europe does not stand high.

Ada's English was good and she seemed to like talking to me as well as rolling my cigarettes, which she did with a deftness I could not emulate. She was 30 and had just qualified as a doctor, having previously spent several years at university studying chemistry. She had never had a job, and Grigore enjoyed contrasting what he regarded as her mollycoddled upbringing with the worldly progress of young Grigore, who'd recently been in Alma Ata negotiating a possible export link with Kazakhstan.

She had a boyfriend who was also a doctor. On their holidays they went rock-climbing together, and she told me that she found the flatness of the delta oppressive rather than intriguing. Ada said she was glad she had come, but did not think she would be doing so again. As for fishing, she regarded it as an existential mystery not worth the trouble of studying. While we stood casting our spinners, she would sit reading, making notes in a little notebook, taking occasional pictures and peering through the binoculars at the birds.

On our last afternoon the crushing heat and lack of fish action drove us back to the *pension* in Crişan, and thence to the bar up the one road. While we sat there drinking cold beer and discussing for the umpteenth time where the pike might be hiding, the sun vanished. When we came out, the sky to the north was heavy with thundercloud, darkening by the minute. A hot, moist breeze huffed spasmodically, silvering the willows. Threatening rumbles were audible from the direction of Ukraine.

The brothers decided the fishing omens were favourable. Ada said she would give the proposed outing a miss and stay in her room to read. I didn't like the look of the sky, or the noises coming from it, but I didn't want to be thought a wimp so I hopped into the boat.

We roared off down the canal towards Caraorman then cut off somewhere else, I wasn't sure where. We anchored and immediately began catching *barsch*. Daggers of lightning stabbed down from the heavens, which had assumed the colour of granite. The brothers were not at all daunted by the pyrotechnics or the timpani rolls of thunder or the rain, which was soon descending like a cataract. They shouted and laughed and swigged from their bottle of *tuică*, swallowing as they cast, the water streaming down their happy faces. Their delight was infectious. Each time one of our rods bent, and one or other of us felt the familiar, jagging resistance of a perch, we would chorus '*Barsch!*' and watch for the flash of the pearly belly in the water, and the twist of the striped olive-green flank and red fins.

The weather cleared overnight and the sun was shining again as we made our way back upstream to Tulcea.

Evening sun on the delta

When I recall the delta now, I cannot help thinking of the mysteries and secrets I never touched, of the many meanings that eluded me. I can hear noises: frogs at night, cuckoos at dawn, reeds whispering at any time (even when I could not feel a breath of wind on my cheek), herons beating their wings, water lapping against the sides of the boat, our spinners plopping into it, the buzz of our reels. Most of all, the din of the engine.

# Chapter 21

## Lost world

Everyone knew the Countess, Grigore said. She had always been there: back in the days of the King, before Ceauşescu, during Ceauşescu. Now she had survived Ceauşescu. I asked if she was a real countess. Of course a real countess. But she sold flowers. He told me where to find her.

She sat in the shade, on a wooden chair next to her barrow. On the barrow were pots of tulips, daffodils and roses, bundles of herbs and lavender, little bunches of dried flowers in baskets. She wore a cheap print dress, a far cry from the silks and chiffons of her youth. Her old face, tanned and lined by age and the outdoor life, was dominated by a jutting beak of a nose and narrow, clear blue eyes. Her snow-white hair was gathered into a wispy bun. There was something about her, an air of distinction.

I introduced myself in bumbling French, on the assumption that if we had a language in common that would be it. She was clearly nonplussed for a moment, then answered in English.

'You are not French, I think?' I admitted it. 'You are English.' I admitted that as well. 'I prefer to speak in English, if you would be so kind. My French is very bad. Yes, I am the Countess Teleki.' She corrected herself. 'I am a Countess Teleki. There are many Telekis. But here in Romania, I am the only Teleki, I think.'

The name is a thread through 400 years of Hungarian and Transylvanian history. Generally speaking, they were a brainy, bookish lot, prone to eccentricity, neuroticism and attacks of typical Magyar melancholy. As was expected of their class, they offered themselves in the service of their country, but tended to make their mark – if they made one at all – in other spheres.

For example, Count Sámuel Teleki served as Chancellor of Transylvania towards the end of the eighteenth century, and seems to have performed his official duties conscientiously enough. But his passion, energy and wealth were expended on rampant bibliomania. He hunted down the rarest manuscripts, incunabula and early printed books – among them the fourteenth-century Bible known as the *Koncz-codex*, the *Liber de Homine* printed in Bologna in 1475, Erasmus's edition of the New Testament printed in Basel in 1519, and a copy of the United States Declaration of Independence. The Count displayed his treasures in his baroque mansion in Marosvásárhely, now the Teleki Library in Târgu Mureş, outside whose gates the Countess set up her flower stall.

A later Count Sámuel Teleki forsook his government post and life of ease to become an African explorer. He led the expedition that discovered the Jade Sea, and named it after his ill-starred friend, the Archduke Rudolf. (Much later Lake Rudolf was renamed Lake Turkana.) A cousin, Count László Teleki, was the erratic representative of Kossuth's short-lived revolutionary government in Paris, where he fought duels, conducted love affairs and wrote forgettable plays, eventually returning to Hungary where he committed suicide in despair at the re-imposition of Habsburg tyranny.

Susceptibility to despair was a family trait. In Hungary's darkest hour – darker even than the crushing of the Revolution of 1848 – the last of the Telekis to hold public office retired to his rooms in Budapest and wrote a letter dated 2 April 1941 which he addressed to Hungary's quasi-fascist dictator, Admiral Horthy. The previous day Horthy had acceded to Hitler's demand that Hungary join an unprovoked invasion of Yugoslavia, despite the opposition of his Prime Minister, Count Pál Teleki.

'We have become word-breakers out of cowardice,' Teleki wrote. 'We have sided with the villains. We will be the most miserable of nations. I did not hold you back. I am guilty.' He signed his name and then put a bullet through his brain.

Count Pál Teleki makes a fleeting appearance in *Between the Woods and the Water*, the second volume in Patrick Leigh Fermor's uncompleted trilogy about his walk from Holland to Constantinople in the 1930s. Leigh Fermor met him in Budapest, and Teleki – whose preferred calling was not politics at all but geography and cartography – was soon charting the Englishman's way into Transylvania, suggesting routes and offering introductions among the web of Teleki cousins.

It is characteristic of Leigh Fermor that he places the most generous possible interpretation on Teleki's suicide, and makes no mention of his less sympathetic side – for instance, his enthusiasm for eugenics, his vigorous, private anti-semitism, and above all his disastrous obsession with reclaiming Transylvania (the carrot dangled by Hitler). All the aristocrats who crop up in Leigh Fermor's narrative, and there are many, are of the same stamp. The young counts are handsome (or at least striking in looks) and their countesses beautiful and accomplished, the old counts interestingly eccentric and their countesses exquisitely dressed and immensely charming. Everyone is intelligent, sensitive, humorous and steeped in history and culture. They dance beautifully, shoot unerringly, have impeccable manners, and talk brilliantly. There are no acts of meanness or cruelty. Nothing is said of their idleness or the chasm separating them from their downtrodden retainers, who – when they do appear – are cast in the roles of devoted servants or happy, singing, dancing, fiddle-playing rustics.

Although academic historians may frown on its lack of gritty social realism, Leigh Fermor's realisation of the sunlit curtain call of the Central European aristocracy has not lost its power to dazzle and beguile. It conjures up a world of great houses standing in magnificent parks, with limitless estates extending beyond the soaring limes and spreading oaks; young men with high foreheads and distinctive noses, dressed for hunting or polo, or for dinner beneath sparkling, many-tiered chandeliers; young women in sumptuous satin and imported *couture*, shading pale complexions under their parasols; ballrooms alight with precious stones and polished boots, pulsing to the waltz, the galop, the *csárdás*, heels clicking, medalled chests bowing, bosoms heaving, intrigues swirling.

The seductiveness of this portrait – real or not – is intensified by our awareness that this whole world was about to crash. Within a few years the counts and countesses who had entertained the young Englishman would be scattered to the four winds. The castles and manor houses and shooting lodges would be ransacked and left to fall into ruin, or bombed and blasted, or commandeered in the pursuit of war, while the estates were marched over by successive armies.

One of the most beguiling episodes in *Between the Woods and the Water* unfolds at a leisurely pace in the Mureş valley in western Transylvania, where forests of oak, beech and ash roll down over the hills to where the broad river winds its way between wavering lines of willows and fields of maize. It is high summer, 1934. Not so far away the first of the convulsions that will tear Europe apart is being felt. Occasional rumbles reach the manor house where the Englishman is staying, but his head is too filled with old history to pay much attention to the ugly new history being made across a border or two. He is only 19, after all, an age for romance and seizing the pleasures of the moment.

He is there at the invitation of a new friend whom he calls István: 'Cultivated, tall, fine-looking, with a hawk's nose, a high forehead and wide clear blue eyes like a francolin's, he was a brilliant shot, horseman and steeplechaser, and a virtuoso in all he took up.' Nothing out of the ordinary there. Together they explore the woods, help bring in the harvest, catch crayfish in mountain streams, meet witches and gypsies, visit neighbours, organise picnics and dances, romp in a hayrick with a pair of peasant girls after swimming naked across the river, and talk through the night as the moon wanes, the stars shoot, and the nightingales sing.

With István's connivance, the Englishman pursues a heady love affair with Angéla, who lives nearby − 'she was a few years older than I, and married, but not happily'. The three of them borrow a car and embark upon a Transylvanian tour to Gyulafehérvár (Alba Iulia in Romanian − Leigh Fermor generally uses the Hungarian names out of deference to his Hungarian hosts), Koloszvár (Cluj), Marosvásárhely (Târgu Mureş), the Saxon towns and villages, through Szekler land. The Englishman is intoxicated by this medieval landscape of valleys, streams, canyons, endless woods, Roman salt mines, vineyards, hop fields, stately citadels and churches and crooked gabled inns; and by its dense tangle of peoples and history.

The idyll comes to an end at a railway station where the girl, recalled unwillingly to the real world, threads button-holes of roses and tiger lilies into her lover's shirt before boarding the train that takes her out of his life for ever. The friends watch the train disappear until all they can see is 'a feather of smoke among the Maros trees'.

The Countess Gemma Teleki did not know the book, but she recognised the description of István at once. His real name was Elemér Klobusicky. 'Oh, yes, everyone knew Elemér. He was in everyone's house. Good family, good manners, very good company. He played bridge and tennis, he rode horses. He was amusing, everyone liked him. He married after the war, I think, and was living in Budapest.'

I asked her about Leigh Fermor's previous stop, at Zam (also in the Mureş valley), where his hostess was called Xénia. The Countess's memory was sharp. 'I don't remember that name, but I remember her. She was often very much excited . . .' the Countess tapped her head and gave me a toothless grin '. . . but very pretty.' There was something else about her, something that happened later. The Countess shook her head as the memory swirled and faded.

I decided to make an excursion along the Mureş valley to see what had happened to the places where Leigh Fermor had stayed. His first stop was Kápolnás (Căpălnaş), the country residence of Count Jeno Teleki – 'a tall, spreading, easy-going middle-aged man, with gold-rimmed spectacles and a remarkably intelligent, slightly ugly and very amusing face' – happiest among his books and his enormous collection of butterflies and moths. The Countess recognised him at once, and smiled at the description in the book. 'We were at Sáromberke so we did not see those

The Teleki mansion at Kápolnás, photographed 1990

Telekis often,' she said. 'They were a long way away and a different branch of the family. But I remember him well. He was big and loved his food, but not as much as his . . . butterflies, I think you say in English.'

Once grand, now decrepit, gates led to a large, rectangular, mediocre house which rose from a wilderness of wildly overgrown shrubs and rampant undergrowth. Yews were advancing up the stone steps of the double staircase that led to the balustraded terrace. In front of it was a still, scummy pool beside which stood a stone stag, antlers intact, eyes and nose missing. A notice at the gate stated that the place was a psychiatric institution. Some of the inmates, in pyjamas and rough sweaters, wandered between the weed-choked box hedges, muttering and twitching.

To my embarrassment, the porter insisted on escorting me inside and intruding on a meeting of the hospital staff that was taking place in a downstairs room. One of them, presumably the director, turned on me. 'No tourist,' he shouted, shooing me out. He saw my camera. 'No photograph. Is not permitted.'

Xénia's *kastély* at Zam had been turned into another psychiatric establishment. This time I was turned away at the gates by a stern female janitor in a blue uniform. I wandered along a high, spiked boundary fence, trying without success to secure a view of the building through the trees. From Zam I went upstream to look for István's *kastély*. The map in *Between the Woods and the Water* suggested it should be in or near Guraszáda (Gurasada), but I explored the village in vain. Eventually I accosted a young woman who was tidying the graveyard of the little church. '*Kastély kaput*,' she said, pointing to a slope above the village. I saw at once what I had missed before – not a grand mansion, in fact not a building at all, but trees: cypresses, wellingtonias, catalpas, copper beeches, horse chestnuts, limes; trees planted long ago when members of the Hungarian nobility were brought up to admire and imitate the English park of Capability Brown.

Entrance to Guraszáda, photographed 1990

I set off through the back streets to find it. I had Leigh Fermor's book open on the seat beside me, and knew at once when I reached it: 'A flattened arch through massive ochre walls gave on a court-yard where gigantic chestnuts still dropped their petals and the pigeons on the cobbles underneath would suddenly take off with a sound like the wind.' I drove in and stopped in the shade of the chestnuts, where the cobbles were edged with weeds. On one side of the courtyard a flight of fan-shaped stone steps led up to a pair of flaking green doors. An arcade ran along one side of the building, with a door at the end giving access on to a loggia. There was a fanlight over the door, the green and purple panes noted by Leigh Fermor still intact. Below the loggia extended a thicket of bamboos, their slender stems and sharp leaves swaying and rustling in the breeze.

A stout matron appeared, addressed some words of Romanian to me, and waddled off. Shortly afterwards another woman arrived. She was middle-aged and friendly, and spoke some English. She said the house was in the hands of the Ministry of Agriculture and been used for some kind of research work, although not recently. She acted as caretaker and had a key. Inside, the rooms were bare, except for a few chairs and a desk. The plaster was crumbling and the ceilings were stained with damp. Every surface was pale with a thick layer of dust. There was nothing obvious to recall the family that had lived here so long; except, possibly, the armorial escutcheon mentioned by Leigh Fermor — a bow with an upward-pointing arrow — which I forgot to look for until it was too late.

Weeds had taken over the courtyard where sheepdogs and their puppies had welcomed István and his English guest. The stables and barns were abandoned, and the coach-house where the carriages and sleighs once stood was now an empty recess. There was, however, still a storks' nest stuck precariously on the roof, and the chestnuts still cast cool shade, and the house martins swished from sunshine to shadow and back.

The caretaker showed me a path leading from the courtyard down the slope to the park. She knew the Latin names of the trees: *taxodium, catalpa, quercus, taxus baccata, carpinus*. Seen from below, the bamboos formed a pale green sea, over which the tiled roof of the house and the pillared loggia gazed protectively. We came to an avenue of beeches whose branches met overhead, excluding the sunlight and creating a cool, ecclesiastical space. It led to the family grave, which had been overwhelmed by vegetation. My guide told me that it had been smashed and defiled when the Communists took over. They had held a party, she said, dancing on the graves of their feudal oppressors. The story had a familiar mythic ring.

She herself knew nothing about the family apart from their name. She and her husband had come to live in a modern house on the edge of the park long after the Klobusickys had gone for good. She gave me an excellent lunch of grilled chicken and beer and freshly picked raspberries, and we talked of the usual things: Ceauşescu, prices, democracy. I asked her if anyone else had ever come, asking the same questions as me. There was one, she said, another Englishman, a few years before. He was tall, white-haired, older than me. He told her that he had stayed here a long time ago, that his friend was the son of the house. She had left him with his memories.

That all happened in the summer of 1990. Later I learned some more as a result of writing an article for the *Financial Times* about the Leigh Fermor connection. Some months after it appeared I received a long letter from the writer, in blue ink and not easy to decipher. He disclosed that the 'Xénia' of the *kastély* at Zam and the 'Angéla' with whom he had wandered hand in hand through Transylvania were one and the same. She had, he said, left Zam at the end of the war and been forced to share a small flat in Budapest with 'a fiendish woman' whom she had eventually killed with a carving knife. According to Leigh Fermor's account, she was acquitted at her trial on the grounds of provocation.

As for István/Elemér, he had also moved to Budapest where he made a living translating English books, living in a flat in a 'workers' suburb'. Leigh Fermor kept in touch, visiting three or four times over the years. On the last occasion István was in hospital after having a stroke. He didn't recognise his visitor, but when Leigh Fermor mentioned that he was going back to his home in Greece, István said he must be sure to look up his old friend, Patrick Leigh Fermor.

'What a sad story about Countess Gemma Teleki,' he said towards the end of the letter. 'I never went to Sáromberke, alas.' He was close, as it is only a few miles from Marosvásárhely: a long, low, handsome house in pale apricot stucco – with white

The Countess Gemma Teleki's house at Sáromberke

reliefs over doors and windows and a mellow mansard roof with sleepy eyelid windows – standing back from the road behind a formal garden intersected by gravel paths and the inevitable box hedges.

In 1934 the mistress of Sáromberke, Gemma Teleki, was 26. She was a Teleki by birth, her father acknowledged as the pre-eminent authority on the breeding of horses in a country where there were many experts on the subject. 'It was his passion,' she told me. 'He wrote a book which he called *Horses*. He went to Cambridge, you know. It was he who taught me to speak English. He used a book called *Brush Up Your English*. He was a good teacher, very kind.'

She laughed throatily, smoothing the wisps of hair away from her ears. 'He read many English books to me. His favourite was *Three Men In A Boat*. When he was coming to an amusing episode he would begin to laugh. Then I would laugh as well. You know, my daughters say I speak Oxford English because I say spectacles instead of glasses. Or perhaps it should be Cambridge English.'

Her husband was Count Károlyi Teleki – 'Many Telekis married other Telekis,' she explained, 'because there were so many to choose from.' But the marriage, like Angéla's, was not happy. They divorced, and he lived at Sáromberke for a while with his second wife before leaving for Hungary and, subsequently, Canada. The Countess Gemma chose to stay, to be with her mother and father, sharing a cramped flat in the Teleki Library in Târgu Mureş. At some point, I wasn't sure when, her three children went abroad as well.

To be Hungarian aristocrats in post-war Romania was to present easy targets for official bullying. For several years the Countess and her parents remained cooped up inside the library, denied passports to leave and cut off from the rest of the family. After the deaths of her mother and father, the Countess moved into a basement room in Lupeni Street, not far from the library. She had a friend with a small market garden out of town, where she would drive each morning to collect the flowers before setting up her barrow. I visited her several times, both there and in her dark room which was crammed with books and mementoes and boxes of photographs and letters. She had no television, radio or telephone, and spent much of her spare time reading, and writing letters to her friends and children and grandchildren.

Perhaps tactlessly, I asked the Countess to come with me to Sáromberke to show me around and tell me the history. She refused politely; there was too much sadness associated with it, she said, so I went on my own. The house had been converted into some sort of college for agricultural students. Its fabric was visibly decayed, the outbuildings were full of rubbish, the box hedging had been smothered in bindweed.

A couple of miles up the road from Sáromberke was another, much grander, Teleki mansion, Gernyeszeg (Gorneşti), a great pile in cream-painted brick built around a deep, rectangular courtyard, with a mighty central clocktower roofed in red copper or

Gernyeszeg

zinc. The drive crosses high above a moat on a stone bridge and leads to a vaulted corridor giving access to the interior of the *kastély*.

A sign at the gate stated that it was a sanatorium for children with tuberculosis. The moat had pretty much drained away, leaving a couple of shrunken pools bright green with pondweed and algae. A stone statue lay face down at the water's edge. The parquet floor of the vaulted corridor was buckled and ridged. Damp stained the walls and ceiling. Beyond the courtyard the gardens had gone completely to ruin. But the trees – limes, copper beeches, cedars of Lebanon, oaks, sycamores – were magnificent, seeming to proclaim a lofty disdain for the dereliction around them. Facing the house along the road, rising like a green rampart, was a line of seven enormous willows. Pigeons flapped among the branches and cawing rooks fought over nesting sites.

As I strolled through the park I understood all too well why the Countess had preferred to stay away from these decaying, unwanted leftovers from an age that now seemed incredibly distant. But I never heard one word of complaint from her about her fate.

'I learned many things from my father,' she said proudly. 'He taught me always to remember what was good, and to ignore the bad things. There have been many sad events and difficult times, but what is the use of thinking about them? Many times my children have asked me to leave here, but how could I learn to live in Vienna or Canada or America? I am an old woman. I was born here and I have always lived here. My life is here. I am close to where my children were born and where I had so much happiness with my father and mother.'

In her cheap dress and battered shoes, alone in a dark, damp room, she remained every inch a Hungarian noblewoman. But – uniquely among the Hungarians I met – she bore no grudge over the fate of Transylvania. 'Yes, I am Hungarian,' she said. 'I was born a Hungarian countess and I shall die one. But now this is Romania. We do not like it, but we must accept it. That is what my father taught me.'

The last time I saw her, she gave me some apricots and a tiny arrangement of dried flowers. I asked her if there was anything she wanted. She said: 'I would like some gardening magazines. English gardening magazines. The English are the best gardeners in the world.'

When I got home I posted her a bundle of issues of *The Garden*, the Royal Horticultural Society's magazine, but I never heard if she received them.


Gemma Teleki died in 2000, aged 92, without leaving Târgu Mureş. Two or three years before she died, she gave an interview to Hungarian television which astonished people by its fluency and the clarity of her memory, and touched them with her dignity and generosity of spirit. Patrick Leigh Fermor called hers a sad story, but – although there was certainly much sadness in it – it struck me more as uplifting. I still think of her as one of the most impressive people I've ever encountered.

Returning eight years after her death, I went to see the director of the Teleki Library, Mihály Spielman, who had known her quite well. He filled in some of the facts and dates I was missing. He told me that she had regarded it as her sacred duty to keep an eye on the library. 'It was her family's legacy to this town,' he said. 'She was an example to us all.' I learned from him that both Sáromberke/Dumbrăvioara and Gernyeszeg/Gorneşti had been legally restored to surviving Telekis. There were plans, he understood, to restore them, perhaps create a museum. But he wondered who would pay. It would cost several fortunes to refurbish them, and the Telekis were no longer rich. How could they be, when everything had been taken from them? And, besides, why would they want to live in such places now?

Both looked very much as I remembered, just scruffier, and both were being used for the same purposes as before. But the Klobusicky manor house at Guraszáda, which I also revisited, now looked beyond hope of repair or redemption. The massive outer walls of the courtyard were ravaged by decay, the ochre plaster-work crumbling, holes gaping in the tiled roofs. The courtyard itself was a sea of weeds. One of the chestnuts was dead, the others had fallen victim to disease. The storks had gone, their nest blown away. The fan-shaped steps leading up to the front door had subsided and buckled. The verandah roof had fallen in at intervals, exposing laths like smashed ribs. Several windows were broken, although the green and purple fanlight over the door leading to the loggia was still intact.

When I arrived a man was in the act of padlocking the door. He let me in. It was obvious that the place had not been inhabited or regularly used for years, quite possibly since I was last here. The parquet floors rolled in waves, the walls sagged with moisture, the sky was visible through the roof. Outside, the wilderness

Guruszáda, 2008

was closing in fast, swallowing walls and outbuildings. The branches of an acacia rested comfortably across the main roof. Shrubs and brambles reached for the windows. The bamboo grove had almost engulfed the loggia where Leigh Fermor and István sat through the summer nights, smoking hand-rolled cigarettes, breaking off every now and then from their eager conversation to watch the Perseids glitter in the dark sky.

I sat at the top of the steps overlooking the courtyard for a while, feeling an ache of regret. For so long, 200 years or so, this house had been the beating heart of the village. It had seen such life, heard such laughter, stood for a kind of permanence and security for so many, a kind of guarantee that, here at least, the order of things went on as before. Now the heart had stopped beating. How could it have been allowed to die? How could it have become so useless, so unwanted?

The only signs of life left were the cooing pigeons; the martins which still made their nests beneath the disintegrating eaves; the butterflies twitching through the sun-warmed air; the bees feasting on the flowers of the acacia. And the trees, the great trees, that had guided me here before. It would take more than the passing of an era to bring them down. They rose high above the scene of desolation all around, looking out across the valley of the lazy, twisting Mureş, to the sweep of woods beyond.

## Chapter 22

### Poles apart

At half-past nine on a Sunday morning the congregation of the Catholic Church in Lesko was emerging in a strong, steady stream. It took a good while for them all to disperse into the streets of the town, which stands on a hill above the River San in the south-east corner of Poland. As the last of them strolled off, the bells were summoning the next intake for ten o'clock mass – the third of the day, with three more to follow.

By ten-thirty, when I returned from visiting Lesko's synagogue and Jewish cemetery, the church was full and the worshippers had spilled into the open space outside, where all the benches were taken and there was standing room only. The voice of the invisible priest came loudly and insistently from speakers fixed to the wall. The crowd was quiet and attentive, even the children, and the responses came in confident unison. It was an impressive spectacle. The Jews of Lesko are no more, but the Catholics are there in force.

To an outsider, the continuing grip of the Catholic Church on Polish society, 20 years after the overthrow of Communism, is one of the wonders of modern Poland. I asked the manager of the hotel where I was staying a couple of miles upriver why so many people went to church. 'They are hypocrites,' she said scornfully. 'They think it is not important how they behave during the week because they make confession on Sunday.'

Jurek Kowalski, 1990

My friend Jurek Kowalski had a more charitable, perhaps more perceptive, explanation. He, his wife Wiesia, and their daughter Ania, are all regular church-goers. Jurek told me he had the usual problems with matters of faith and the after-life. But his commitment to the Church as an earthly power for good was unshakeable. Polish society, he said, had a desperate need for a powerful, binding influence to counter the forces pulling it apart. Mainly for historical reasons – war, conquest, subjugation, genocide, loss of sovereignty and territory, migrations and emigrations – Poles had little sense of community or shared identity. Polish politics had become extravagantly divisive, parties feeding off the promotion of envy and suspicion, and on the fingering of hate figures: Russians, Germans, gypsies, the EU, homosexuals, and so on.

The Polish mentality, according to Jurek, was to assume that everyone was cheating. Faith in institutions or in ideals of probity and service was almost non-existent. People relied on their families and their cronies and if they thought they could get away with cheating they would. Free market economics and the widening chasm between the fortunate few and the excluded many had further eaten away at the idea of nationhood. Only the Church,

Jurek believed, could bridge these divisions, treat the wounds, speak with a single Polish voice.

He talked a lot about the history of his country. One recurring theme was that it was impossible for someone from England to understand the lasting psychological and spiritual effect of the almost unbroken sequence of conquest and tyranny that constituted Poland's past. In particular, I could not be expected to grasp the nature of the scars left by the enforced migrations of its people. It seemed that there was hardly a family in Poland that did not look back on some trauma of slaughter, dispossession or uprooting.

Jurek's own family was no exception. One strand on his mother's side had originated from near Kielce, in what was known as the Kingdom, the eastern portion of historic Poland annexed by the Russians as a result of partition in the eighteenth century. Rule from Moscow was periodically challenged in gallant, hopeless uprisings, the last of which — in 1863 — was crushed in the customary brutal fashion. In the aftermath, thousands of Poles were dispatched to die in labour camps in Siberia, and thousands more emigrated. Many others sought refuge in Galicia, the southern sector under Habsburg control, among them Jurek's forbears on his mother's side, who settled near Jasło, not far north of the Carpathian mountains.

His paternal ancestors were themselves Galician but migrated east, to the borderland near the River Bug, from where they were forcibly removed into Russia during the First World War, to the Volga, where they were interned. Jurek's grandfather and grandmother met as schoolchildren during this period of exile. After the war they returned to what was once more sovereign Polish territory, as a result of the establishment of the expanded Second Polish Republic (also including Lithuania and the western part of Ukraine). The family speciality was farm management, and Jurek's grandfather was in charge of estates close to the

Bug. He also owned his own farm south of the town of Hrubieszów.

The respite did not last long. Under the terms of the Ribbentrop–Molotov pact of 1939, the Russians again took control of eastern Poland – including the territories of eastern Galicia and Volhynia – and set about obliterating the Polish influence there. At least one million Poles, mainly middle-class professionals and their families, were deported or murdered. Two years later Germany invaded Russia, and Soviet savagery was exchanged for the more refined, but equally horrible, Nazi model. All the time, awaiting their opportunity, was a pack of Ukrainian nationalist groups who considered Volhynia and eastern Galicia to be theirs and were resolved to rid them of foreign interlopers.

The German occupiers were content to leave much of the dirty work to sympathetic Ukrainian militias. In Volhynia 200,000 Jews died; and early in 1943 the so-called Ukrainian Insurgent Army, the UPA, embarked on a carefully planned genocide against Polish villages. Deploying tactics learned from their Nazi instructors, they attacked settlements, murdered the inhabitants, looted anything of value, then burned the houses. The slaughter spread south from Volhynia into eastern Galicia. Scores of villages were destroyed and thousands of Poles were killed, often after torture, often with gruesome cruelty. The massacres continued even after the Red Army swept back on its way to Berlin. The Russians had no more qualms than the Germans about getting rid of Poles, and had their own particular reasons for liquidating the remnants of the educated bourgeoisie.

In all it is believed that at least 60,000, and possibly as many as 100,000, Polish people were murdered by Ukrainian nationalists. Jurek's grandfather and his family survived on their farm for three years, finally fleeing west to Lublin, where they stayed. Jurek's father, Andrzej, went to university there, but after some kind of trouble with the Communist security police, he completed his law studies in Kraków. Eventually he became a lawyer in the town of Krosno, in south-east Poland, Jurek Kowalski's home town.

Krosno's most celebrated son is Ignacy Łukasiewicz, who not only sank what Krosno firmly believes was the world's first oil well (in 1854, a few miles south of the town), but also invented the oil lamp. Several hundred specimens of this useful household item can be admired in the municipal museum. Also on display in the museum – more as a matter of record than pride – is a photograph of another local notable: Władysław Gomułka, one of the founders of Polish Communism and a long-serving Party leader. The photograph is not flattering – it makes Gomułka look like a bespectacled, hairless reptile in a suit – and there is no statue or commemorative tablet to him to be found anywhere. For those with long memories, however, there is a discreet memorial of a kind: a building on the main square, now a doctors' surgery and pharmacy, previously the police headquarters where enemies of the state were quietly disposed of.

Krosno's fortunes have waxed and waned over the centuries. The fine old houses on the main square mostly date from the sixteenth century, when the town flourished on the proceeds of the Hungarian wine trade. The oil boom initiated by Łukasiewicz fostered an era of prosperity that lasted until the convulsions of 1939. When I was there in summer 2008 it was clearly thriving, the old town spankingly restored, the rest of it humming with commercial activity. But when I first came, in May 1990, it was very different: shabby and uncared for, full of drunks and down-and-outs, fearful of what the future might hold.

Jurek Kowalski was then in his late 20s. He had a plump-cheeked, boyish face that made him look younger than he was; and a quiet, careful way of talking that made him seem old and wise beyond his years. He was a highly serious fellow, but the seriousness was shot through with a very Polish sense of the absurdities and contradictions inherent in every situation, which would show itself in smiles and quiet laughter. He worked immensely long hours for very little money as a doctor in Krosno's hospital, where he saw plenty of the desperation rife at all levels of Polish society. His recreation, which he also took very seriously, was fishing. A passionate, highly skilled angler, he had captained the winning Polish team at the world fly-fishing championships in Finland in 1989, and had previously competed in England.

He was waiting for me in his flat in a cluster of forbidding grey-and-mustard-coloured blocks rising from a scar of wasteland on the edge of town. 'It is typical of this country,' Jurek said severely when I commented on the unlovely display of puddles, mud heaps, piles of aggregate, rolls of rusty wire and lumps of metal outside. 'Polish people are very untidy.' We drove east from Krosno to Sanok, a half-dead provincial town known for its bus factories. 'They are the worst buses in Poland,' Jurek told me. 'Maybe the worst buses in the world.' They bore the name Autosan, although more often than not this was invisible underneath their crust of filth and carbon. You saw them everywhere, wheezing along the road with their rear ends enveloped in smoke or broken down at the side, the passengers standing around in attitudes of weary resignation.

At Sanok we crossed the broad and stately San, the river Jurek had fished all his fishing life. Ahead was the Bieszczady, the region of forested hills and dark valleys that fills Poland's far south-eastern corner. On the higher Bieszczady hills the trees give way around the summits to meadows of thick, waist-high grass, so that from a distance they suggest the tonsured heads of monks. The beech forests are full of animals, including lynx, wolves, bears and European bison (exterminated in the wild in the 1920s and subsequently reintroduced using animals bred in zoos). Not many humans, though.

* * *

The Bieszczady extends to the border with Ukraine. A rifle-bullet's range inside the border is a settlement called Smolnik. Visitors come to see the ancient, beautiful wooden church that stands in a grove of ash, lime and acacia trees on top of a low hill. Bees nest at the top of the flattened square tower, and the man who sells drawings of the church and other knick-knacks outside the door will show alleged claw marks along the side, left, he says, by a hungry bear that tried to get to the honey.

The church looks down on meadows where, in summer, the grass is cut in oval patterns. Woods rise steeply beyond the meadows. The landscape is very pretty, very empty. There is nothing here to suggest that a mere 70 years ago it was full of people and flourishing communities. There were watermills and brickworks, leather workshops, a dairy, a network of farms and businesses. There were even oil wells a couple of miles north, outside the town of Lutowiska, where more than half the population was Jewish.

In 1942 most of the Jews of Lutowiska were murdered by the Gestapo, and the rest were dispatched to the extermination camp at Bełżec. That episode was a prelude to a period of guerrilla conflict that consumed the region until the end of the war and beyond. As the Russians came from one direction and the Germans retreated in another, Ukrainian UPA separatists pursued a vicious, hopeless campaign for the independence they had been promised by Hitler.

Damned beyond redemption in Polish and Russian eyes for their collaboration with the Nazis, the UPA fought on from their bases in the Bieszczady mountains even after the rest of shattered Europe was at peace. In 1947 a UPA unit ambushed and killed the Polish war hero General Karol Świerczewski. The Polish army responded with a massive incursion which crushed the insurrection for good.

A dark chapter followed. The people of the Bieszczady were mainly Boyks and Lemks, ethnically linked with the Ukrainians but – as a result of their isolation in their remote enclave below the Carpathians – culturally distinct. This distinction was lost on the Polish and Russian military commanders and their political masters. They saw this pastoral peasant society of farmers, shepherds, wood-carvers and loggers as a bunch of collaborators and traitors that must be expunged. Under the terms of Operation Vistula the entire population of the Bieszczady was cleared out: 150,000 Lemks were removed to the Soviet Union; 80,000 Boyks were 'resettled' in Poland, many of them in Silesia, the coal-rich region in the west handed over by Germany in the redrawing of borders agreed at Yalta.

Initially the Bieszczady – now almost empty – was incorporated into the Soviet Ukraine. A few years later Moscow decided to hand it back to Poland in exchange for a much more useful strip of coal deposits close to the border to the north. Subsequently the abandoned villages of the Bieszczady, mainly of wooden buildings, were razed. But even the most fervent members of the Polish Central Committee retained a certain superstitious reluctance about attacking consecrated ground, and the churches – both Orthodox and Uniate – were allowed to stand, and were handed over to the care of the Roman Catholic Church.

So the church at Smolnik still guards its hill, and the bees still nest in the tower and graze on the acacia flowers. The construction is strong, and there is no obvious reason why these mighty interlocking beams, black with resin, should not be standing in another 200 years. Its principal function these days is as a visitor attraction for the swelling numbers of tourists coming to the Bieszczady, although a service is held once in a while in honour of its dedicatee, St Hubert, the patron saint of hunters.

The communities that built the church and sustained it have gone almost as if they had never been. The ground they stood on has been reclaimed by woods and meadows. The departed way of life has left few obvious traces. But there is one, visible in early summer. Here and there, against the green of the forest, splashes of white and cream show, where the orchards of apple, pear, cherry and plum trees planted long ago still blossom.

The church at Smolnik was looked after by a family of foresters, the Bartniks, who lived across the valley. Jurek had known them since he was a boy; he and his father stayed with them when they came from Krosno to fish the San. Their house, built of wood and painted green, stood in a clearing. Pigs foraged in a pen at the back, next to a plot bursting with fruit and vegetables. Hens and geese patrolled the yard at the front.

'These are simple people,' Jurek said as he unlatched the gate. 'They have a simple life but a good one, I think. They have enough to eat, they don't drink too much, they go to church, they work hard. I think they are happy . . . more happy than most people in Poland.'

We were welcomed by the senior member of the family, Julian Bartnik, and his wife Maria. She gave us coffee, then a splendid lunch of fresh tomato soup followed by grilled pork with boiled potatoes and spinach. The table where we ate stood on legs made of antlers. The chandelier above the table and the candelabra on the walls were fashioned of the same material. The chairs were covered in deer hide, the floor with boar and wolf skins. From the window the forest rolled away, the viridian of the conifers mixed with the light spring green of the beeches.

Through Jurek I asked Julian Bartnik what effect the collapse of the old system had had on hunting. He smiled, showing a few, well-separated tooth stumps. Before, of course, it was reserved for the Party elite and their cronies. Periodically they would sweep down from Warsaw in a fleet of limousines, exchange their shapeless suits for jackets and hunting breeches, fracture the silence with gunfire, get drunk, stuff their faces, have their photographs taken with piles of animal corpses at their feet, toast their marksmanship and Marxist–Leninism from silver flasks shaped into hunting horns. Tito came once, and – as befitted his international stature – was allocated a bison to shoot. The Polish Prime Minister of the day was only given a bear, which Bartnik himself had to shoot for him.

These days, he said, the ex-Party men were much too busy pretending to be good capitalist democrats to spare time for hunting. But the market was taking up the slack. Sportsmen came from Germany, Austria, America, Switzerland, waving their dollars and brandishing their firearms. A few months before, he had been instructed to arrange for a bison to be conveniently situated. A hunter arrived from Zurich, shot the beast as it grazed, and airlifted it home in his helicopter. The charge was $10,000.

When we left I tried to explain how touched I was by their hospitality. 'They say the door of their house is always open,' Jurek said. 'To me, to you, to anyone. They say that life is short, and if you are lucky and have food, you must share. They ask if you have in England our saying, that a house is blessed by having a guest?'

I shook my head, feeling rather ashamed.

'In our cities we are losing it too. But in places like this it is the rule. Everything they have comes from God and is for all people.'

It is easy for us to forget or overlook how vital our rivers once were, how much of a country's history flowed through them. Poland's great river, flowing 600 miles from the Carpathians in the south to the Baltic in the north, is the Wisła, or Vistula. For centuries it served as a great, free-flowing artery, making possible the emergence of the port of Gdańsk (Danzig as was) as one of the richest and most powerful commercial hubs in Europe.

Each spring, with the melting of the mountain snows, the river ports along the Wisła and its tributaries – including the San, the Dunajec and the Bug – came to life. Great rafts known as *skuta* were made ready. The corn, harvested the previous autumn on the estates of the noble landowners and stored through the winter, was loaded into the silos thrusting up from the oak decks. The rivers were swollen, yellow, foam-flecked, surging with irresistible force. At the last moment the passengers would be taken on; often they were members of the grain-owning dynasties, desperate to exchange the monotony of life in the country for the excitement of the city for a month or two. The convoy would sweep away, the groan of the timbers competing with the roar of the water and the cries of the rafters as they dug their poles down.

Sixteenth-century Danzig was five times the size of Warsaw, three times that of Kraków, bewilderingly cosmopolitan, phenomenally wealthy, its culture as golden as the corn that nourished it. Visitors were awestruck by the splendour of the public buildings and merchants' mansions, and by the scale and energy of the commercial life. In the marvellous chapter on the grain trade in *God's Playground*, Norman Davies's history of Poland, he depicted the port as:

an anthill of work, prosperity and culture, common enough in Italy or the Netherlands but unique in Poland. As such it undoubtedly presented a superlative attraction, a materialist Mecca, to which the Polish nobleman was drawn and tempted – to buy and sell, to be ruined or make his fortune, to load himself with trinkets and luxuries for his house and family, to hear the news and gaze at the sights, and at last, relieved and exhausted, to sail against the currents of the Vistula on the long, slow journey home.

Those currents continued to flow, strong and clean, long after Danzig's heyday was over. Salmon and sea-trout forged their way upstream from the Baltic, seeking their ancestral spawning grounds, all the way to the Tatras and the Dunajec, where my friend Adam Gebel caught his first salmon some time in the 1920s. But post-1945 the age of hydraulic ambition dawned. All over Europe, all over the world, rivers were dammed to power developing industries, and to light and heat peoples' homes. The construction of a succession of dams on the lower Wisła, and two immense hydro-electric barriers – one downstream from Warsaw, the other upstream from Kraków – blocked the way to the spawning streams. Gross pollution resulting from Poland's post-war industrialisation completed the job of wrecking the river.

Over the past ten years or so, the Wisła has been on the convalescent list, as measures to tackle the worst of the effluent pollution have taken effect. But no one has proposed taking away the dams, and the river's spirit remains broken and shackled. In Kraków the summer flow is non-existent. Confined by walls of concrete, the Wisła is more reservoir than river. If it could cast envious eyes to its tributary in the east, the San, it surely would.

The San is born in the foothills of the Ukrainian section of the Carpathians. For 50 miles or so its sinuous course defines the border between Poland and Ukraine. Not far from Smolnik it turns west then north-west, after which it flows in the shape of a back-to-front S through south-east Poland to join the Wisła near Sandomierz.

In the 1960s the decision was taken to dam the San where it emerged from the Bieszczady via a steep defile at Solina. Two barriers were installed, creating two reservoirs, one very big, one much smaller, both very deep. Until then, the river had tended to flow warm and murky through the summer. Now the water coming into the reservoirs was stored and cooled, and the silt retained. The water released from the turbines stayed cool, even in the hottest summers, and generally clear. Unwittingly the engineers charged with constructing another epic symbol of socialist dominance over Nature had created a perfect habitat for trout and grayling, and the San was transformed into the best fly-fishing river in Poland and one of the best in Europe.

Fishing there should have been one of the angling highlights of my 1990 expedition. In Jurek Kowalski I had as my guide a brilliant fisherman, streets ahead of and miles above me, who knew every bend and pool of the stream. But the weather is a great leveller of fortunes. Fierce and unseasonable heat (it was early May) kept the fish deep and out of sight, and as jittery as cats. There were moments, though.

One morning we drove from Krosno in pitch blackness to the stretch of water immediately below the second dam. The dew was heavy on the grass and the grey half-light was filled with the growl of the turbines and the roar of escaping water. Stars still pricked the paling sky as we tackled up. The water was black and smoked with trails of mist. It was also extremely cold and strong-flowing, as I found when I tried to wade out. Despite the liberal application of solvent, the rubber waders I had brought with me leaked badly, and my teeth were soon chattering.

I began casting towards the far bank, where the trees rose steeply, coal-black against the sky. Little by little the day came to life. As the rim of the sun rose into sight I felt a twitch at my fly, then the solid resistance of my first Polish trout. It was not very big, and I held it in my hand for a moment to admire the red and black spots speckling its olive-oil flanks before letting it slip away. I got another, slightly bigger, then a third, big enough to kill but too lovely to warrant it. Then a much bigger fish took with a violent thump at the limit of my casting range, making me lose my footing for a moment. Everything went slack, and when I retrieved the fly I found it had snapped at the bend in the hook.

By now the sun was blazing across most of the river. The fish would only take in the band of water that was in shadow, which narrowed and narrowed until it vanished altogether. After that there were no more plucks or twitches or thumps. The full rising of the sun sent the San to sleep, and it was time to pack up.

We stopped at a pre-fabricated house near the turbines. It was divided into two, and served as the living quarters for the men employed to check and adjust the water flow. There was a shed outside, from which came the noise of a machine. We looked in. A thin wiry man was bending to feed a slender section of wood into it. Drifts of shavings covered the floor. The man's face lit with pleasure when he saw Jurek.

His name was Tadeusz Korecki. 'He is a good fisherman,' Jurek said. 'Once he was Polish fly-fishing champion, but now he prefers to go sailing on the lake. When he is not making pencils.'

Korecki ushered us into his side of the house and made coffee and a pile of spam sandwiches. Smoking incessantly, he explained that he made 20,000 pencils a month, almost doubling the wage he got for sitting above the turbines watching the dials. Dirty plates were piled in the sink. Ashtrays heaped with butts stood on every surface. The tattered rug was grey with cigarette ash and spotted with food stains. He said his wife was working as a nurse at an old people's home in Naples. The implication was that tidying the place would have to wait until she got back.

He showed me the book on Polish fly-fishing written by his and Jurek's friend, Józef Jeleński. Jeleński was living in Libya then, consoled in his exile by his cabinet of fly-tying gear – the one thing in his life, so Jurek said, that he managed to keep in order.

\*     \*     \*

Permit for the San, 2008

Eighteen years on, the San was exactly as I remembered it: big, broad, flat, stately, powerful. But much water had flowed by in Poland. Lech Wałęsa had become President Wałęsa and then ex-President Wałęsa. Solidarity had vanished from the scene. Governments of varied political complexions had come and gone. The Kaczyński twins – two limbs of the same ultra-reactionary, rigidly Catholic, viciously intolerant being – had enjoyed their brief spell at the helm (although one, Lech, remained as president). Poland had joined NATO, then the EU. Despite the exodus of workers to Britain and elsewhere, the country's economy was booming.

At a local level, Tadeusz Korecki was dead. Józef Jeleński was back in his homeland, battling to keep the Raba alive. Jurek Kowalski was no longer a fresh-faced hospital doctor but a medical adviser for GlaxoSmithKline, based in Warsaw, with a house there and another in Krosno. His secondary career, in the administration of fishing, had also blossomed; he had served as both president and vice-president of FIPS-Mouche, the body that organises competitive fly-fishing across the world. Jurek's hair had gone ash-white, his face had rounded out, and the years of hard work had left him looking a touch weary. But I soon found that he was the same, softly-spoken, perceptive, serious commentator on the human comedy that had made him such good company before.

He reported a revolution on the San. Although the local branch of the Polish Fishing Association had managed to hold on to the lease, it had – under Jurek's influence, I suspected – introduced a novel business model. The prime section, seven kilometres from the lower dam down the first significant tributary, was designated as gold-star water on which fish could not be killed. The number of permits was strictly limited, a premium price was charged, and foreign anglers were encouraged to come and take them. These changes had aroused bitter opposition from local anglers, accustomed to getting their fishing cheap from the state and being allowed to kill every fish of any size. But by the time I returned with Jurek, the storm had passed and the political waters were comparatively calm again.

Jurek had arranged permits for us on the special section, but – as before – the weather gods were not kind. This time the problem was not tropical heat but rain and tempest. Throughout the three days I was there, heavy, moist cloud never stopped rolling up and over the Bieszczady Mountains, delivering downpours with distressing frequency. The San was running clear but very strong, and the atmosphere was saturated with moisture, so that every now and then layers of mist would form suddenly across the surface, thickening silently and swiftly to obscure the patterns of water and shroud the pines; then, just as suddenly, dematerialising.

Jurek's other duties allowed us just one day's fishing together. The conditions were too testing for me, although he got one cracking trout of 42 centimetres that lit his face with delight. Before he left for Krosno he entrusted me to the care of a party of French anglers who were staying at the hotel where the permits were issued and where I was to stay on for a couple more nights. Most of them were members of the French youth team, there to prac-tise in advance of the world championships in Portugal. They had a manager, but the undisputed kingpin of the party was an Arab called Said: tall, rangy, with hawkish nose and sparsely bearded, jutting chin. Said was a core member of France's adult team, and – like my Slovak friend Peter Bienek – had been in New Zealand for the 2008 championship. He had come to the San to help with the coaching and for some relaxed fishing of his own. He spoke excellent English and was effusively genial to Jurek and me. Flashing his swift smile, he said I'd be welcome to tag along after Jurek had gone. There was room in the van, I could fish with them the next day. No problem.

That evening, with Jurek departed for Krosno, Said invited me to join the French for dinner. I sat next to him, opposite his brother-in-law Jackie. Jackie was the pack joker, with a little grey quiff that bounced up and down above his quicksilver brown face as the cracks and insults sparked back and forth. I couldn't follow any of it, so Said and I talked about fishing. No other subject seemed to interest him at all – certainly not me or my life, except where fishing was concerned – although he did let slip that he was married with two grown-up children and was an economics lecturer at a university in Lyons, or perhaps it was Lille.

He talked at length about New Zealand. What a country! What rivers! What fish! He had broken two rods there, one of them on the biggest trout he had ever seen. His mobile, aquiline face registered awe and disbelief that he, Said, could have been defeated in such a manner. Pah! The trout was on but he could not hold it. It was too strong, like a buffalo. Bang! The rod went, the trout was gone. He laughed, and asked me if I'd ever been to New Zealand. No? The look he gave me over the ridge of his nose suggested that it was just as well. I might have suffered something a lot worse than just a broken rod.

He was indisputably a demon on the water. In the morning we went to a pool towards the bottom of the special section, which was big enough for all the French to fish together and – equally important – remain within earshot of each other. Said, probably acting from a generous but misplaced hope that he could teach me something, invited me to fish close to him. But I was thoroughly intimidated by his air of Gallic superiority, so I made excuses and set off upstream before making a perilous crossing of the river, the water up to within a couple of inches of the top of my waders. The badinage between Said, Jackie and the others followed me like a Greek chorus.

As so often in fishing, the promise of the far bank proved illusory. It was deeper than it looked and it took me some time to find a shelf of rock shallow enough for me to fish from. By then

Said had progressed far enough up the middle of the pool for him to be able to give me a full commentary on his regular successes. 'Oh, nice fish. Grayling, I think. Yes, another grayling. I have eight now. This is big grayling, forty centimetres, I think. On the dry fly, very small, size twenty. On the drift. You must have the drift correct, Tom. I think maybe your fly is dragging. The grayling will not take if the fly is dragging.'

Thunder boomed and the rain came down in sheets. When it slackened, the fish near me began to feed at the surface on a sudden hatch of olives. I hooked two, lost them both, and hated myself. Later Said offered me some sandwiches and I felt ashamed of the dark thoughts I had harboured towards him. The day wore on, punctuated by storms, and I longed for it to end. I began to wonder how many of the ribald comments echoing across the water were about me. None probably, but I still felt humiliated by my failure, like a hack golfer who'd accidentally strayed on to the fairway at Augusta.

As we were packing up, three Polish anglers turned up, waiting to get on the water after us. They were noticeably unfriendly, even when the French party's Polish guide tried to talk to them. Said commented on this dumb hostility. I suggested it might arise from resentment that foreigners, French foreigners, were helping themselves to the cream of Polish fishing. He considered the idea then shook his head. 'It is not just the fishermen,' he said. 'I find all Poles are the same.'

Said and his gang left for home before dawn the next day. Deprived of the attentions of the more thickly gelled and gallant of the French lads, the two pretty girls who shared duties at the hotel reception desk completely lost their sparkle. I was the only guest left, and evidently a poor substitute for the Gallic charmers. I had no transport, so I bought a permit to fish the unrestricted stretch of the river, which was within walking distance of the hotel. But by the time I got there in mid-afternoon, the weather had worsened again. There was a deluge as I was tackling up, which at least had the effect of thinning the throng of fishermen; and a second soon after I had completed a hazardous wade into the middle of the river to address a gathering of grayling that were feeding purposefully along the far side.

With the rain hissing malevolently against the surface, I retreated to the cover of a picnic shelter on the bank and watched as the river perceptibly rose and thickened. Eventually I packed up and went back to the hotel. In the evening I walked back to the bridge leading to Lesko.

The San in the mist

Mist blanketed the San. A couple of hardy souls were still fishing, dark smudges in the gloom. The water was a grey, elemental, implacable force, and I was heartily glad not to be in it.

I left the next morning, taking the bus from Lesko to Kraków. I had a dead man to ask about.

*   *   *

Jurek made the introduction. I had driven him from the San via Krosno to Skoczów, a scruffy town in the foothills of the western Carpathians. A fishing competition was being held there, after which Jurek — as captain of the Polish fly-fishing team — was due to announce who would be going to Wales later that year to defend the title won in Finland in 1989. On the way he told me he intended to drop two of the winning team for getting drunk and misbehaving. 'We are representing our country so we wish to do well,' he said in his careful way, 'but we have a bad reputation in other countries for cheating and playing tricks and getting drunk on vodka, so it is important that we behave well.'

Arguments over Jurek's selection resounded through the thin hardboard walls of the hotel late into the night. In the morning he looked pale and withdrawn, and the other fishermen avoided him. After breakfast we went outside. The figure waiting for us there would have attracted attention anywhere. In that setting, and at that time, he was as exotic as a Ghanaian chief in tribal robes. He had on a wide-brimmed grey felt hat with a black band, a black silk vest, baggy white tracksuit trousers, white Reebok running shoes. He had a scrubby beard and shoulder-length hair gathered into a pony-tail, and was leaning against a red Honda jeep — itself a startling sight among the clapped-out Fiats, Ladas and Trabants.

He and Jurek evidently knew each other. They shook hands in a guarded manner. The newcomer was introduced to me as Janusz Wanicki. He lit a cigarette and began to talk to me in fast, fractured English. He said he was an artist. I looked at the jeep. 'Not in Poland. You think Polish painter drive Japanese jeep? I live in Finland. You ever been to Finland? Fucking strange country. Finnish people are mad. But rich. So much fucking money.'

He said he worked as an art conservationist at a museum in a provincial town called Tampere, and supplemented his income by painting portraits of public figures. 'I paint nearly every bastard in the government. They pay good because the bloody Finns don't know how to paint.' I gathered that Janusz had been attached to the Polish team for the fishing championships the year before as fixer and unofficial guide. He was now taking a year's break and had brought his Finnish wife to live in Kraków. 'My wife Tarja, she like Poland. She love horses, so every day she is riding. I hate fucking horses but I like fishing, so she rides and I go fishing. Is good arrangement.'

Janusz owned a flat and a house in Kraków and was thinking of buying a house in Zakopane as well. But he was in no hurry. He liked the English; he said it would be good if we went fishing together. Jurek had already arranged for another Kraków fisherman, Andrzej Fox, to accompany me on a trip to the Dunajec, but as there were doubts about Mr Fox's English, it was agreed that Janusz would come as well. He had the language, and the jeep.

He picked me up a week later from outside Leszek and Isa Trojanowski's house in Kraków. Isa, clearly shocked, said there was a girl waiting for me, but it was only Janusz, who had freed his hair from its rubber band. Racing south towards the mountains, we passed immense queues of cars at the few petrol stations. Janusz laughed heartlessly. 'For this fucking people anything is better than to work,' he commented. At Leszek's suggestion I had brought my petrol can with me in the hope of finding the fuel I would need to get to Czechoslovakia. Janusz stopped ahead of one of the queues and marched into the petrol station with my can. 'Polish people are very generous,' he said when he came back. 'If you don't bullshit them. Or if they don't know you bullshit them.'

We met Andrzej Fox at Łopuszna, a village on the upper Dunajec a few miles east of Nowy Targ. He had queued for 13 hours to obtain enough petrol to get his ancient Fiat 126 here from Kraków. He was grey-faced with fatigue, limping badly, and looked about 70, although he was actually in his 50s. As feared, he spoke very

Fishing companions: Janusz Wanicki and Andrzej Fox

little English, and that little cost him dearly. He would squeeze out a few words, his worn face puckered with concentration, then abandon the sentence, blowing out his cheeks in frustration.

But there was one area of English terminology in which Andrzej moved easily. Little Chap, Wickham's Fancy, Greenwell's Glory, Partridge and Orange, Tup's Indispensable – the names of trout flies were no mystery to him; in Andrzej's view it was in fly-fishing that Britain had made its major contribution to world culture. He was filled with reverence for the traditions of the chalkstreams of Hampshire and Wiltshire, and he regarded the great authorities – Halford, Skues, Grey of Falloden – as his spiritual leaders.

Andrzej had an old salmon reel made by Hardy Brothers of Alnwick which had a cracked drum and had not been used in decades. He carried it with him, and loved to slip it from its bag and display it to a fellow enthusiast as if it were a fragment of the True Cross. His holy book was a Hardy catalogue of the 1930s with colour plates illustrating the company's range of flies, rods, reels and accessories, garnished with testimonials from customers from across the globe, praising the efficacy of Hardy gear in deceiving and subduing mahseer in India, rainbow trout in Lake Taupo and the Tongariro, golden dorado in the Parana, giant tunny off Newfoundland, as well as more mundane species closer to home.

It had been arranged that Janusz and I would stay in a complex on the edge of the village originally built as a holiday centre for the families of miners or steelworkers or some other privileged category of workers. For some reason – probably to do with his conspicuous lack of money – Andrzej put up at a cheap boarding house elsewhere in Łopuszna. Even though Janusz and I were the only guests in this sepulchral block of wood and concrete, we still had to share a room, which was dominated by a huge Soviet-made television as big as a chest of drawers. When Janusz switched it on, it hummed and whined for some time before conjuring up a picture of nightmarish greens, purples and yellows. Much of the downstairs was occupied by a spacious restaurant which opened only to provide the two of us with an austere breakfast of cold sausage, cheese and stale bread, accompanied by a tureen containing diluted hot milk and flabby noodles. Janusz turned away from it with a shudder; milk and noodles had unhappy associations for him, he said.

I never managed to extract a coherent account of his past. He had been born somewhere in the Bieszczady, I gathered, and his father had spent some time in prison: 'It was usual thing, telling people how Communists are bastards.' He had a brother who was a loyal party member – 'Fucking shit, he is still Communist, can you believe?' – and at some stage there had been a Polish wife before the Finnish one. Janusz was deeply nostalgic about his time as an art student in Kraków. He would play, over and over again, a tape recorded at a student concert, a medley of obscene and subversive songs evoking smoke-filled basements, pale faces bent over guitars, voices harsh with cynicism asking what they had done with our world. One song – an account of a rich Italian's sexual adventures with the simple lasses of Kraków, sung in a drunk, tuneless voice to a crude guitar accompaniment – would make Janusz shout with laughter. 'My wife Tarja, she hate that fucking song,' he would say, rewinding the tape.

Janusz's attitude to Poland was complicated. He disliked what he saw as expat disloyalty: 'Many Poles are now abroad and making shit about their country . . . I hate them.' But his own exile had nourished a deep sense of anger and disgust at what he found on his return. He railed against the poverty, the dismal hotels and restaurants, the queues, the prevailing down-at-heel shabbiness of everything. He was contemptuous both of the authority of the Church and the explosion of political debate. Freedom was an illusion. What Poland needed was a more authoritarian form of Finland's materialistic paternalism. What it would get, in Janusz's opinion, was chaos and corruption.

He did his best to condescend towards Andrzej. But Andrzej's view, which he sustained with great determination, was that in the matter that had brought us together – namely fishing – he, Andrzej, was the master and Janusz the pupil. (As a foreigner, I had special status.) Wherever we went in Janusz's jeep, Andrzej would keep up a flow of fish-related discourse. Since I could understand none of it, I had no difficulty in switching my mind elsewhere, but Janusz would quickly become restive. He would stare in silent exasperation out of the window or attempt to drown Andrzej's voice with rock music from the cassette player. Sometimes he would listen for a while, then interrupt, or laugh derisively, or try to make some point of his own. But Andrzej always knew too much for him, and would overwhelm him with expertise.

Andrzej should have been a thumping bore but somehow managed not to be. Once he realised that we shared his enthusiasm for our little adventure, he disarmed us with his passion. He knew every yard of the Dunajec and its delicious tributary, the Białka, and was able to take us places we would never have found on our own.

The Białka

The weather remained too hot and thundery for us to do much good on the Dunajec, so we concentrated on the Białka. Andrzej would direct Janusz on to a rough track leading off a country lane through pines and spruce until, with magical suddenness, the stream appeared, and Janusz would jump down and cry out with delight.

However hot it was, this most giving of little rivers did not let us down. But our last visit was cut short by a furious thunderstorm that turned the water milky and unfishable within half an hour. Janusz decided we needed decent hot food, so we drove to Zakopane and stopped at a *szałas*, a barn that had been converted into a grill/bar. There was a blazing fire at one end, with rough tables and benches along the walls, and the place was packed with sweating, red-faced Polish holidaymakers. A band of Highland fiddlers in loose shirts, embroidered waistcoats, woollen leggings and leather boots was tuning up. They began to play as our beers arrived, and at once several couples leaped up and began whirling around the floor. One broad-shouldered young man flung his girl this way and that, then abandoned her briefly in order to be sick in the corner and down a tumbler of vodka before returning to grasp her again.

The climax of the show was a performance by two members of the band of what Janusz – yelling in my ear – informed me was the dance of the robbers. The pair of them half-squatted, hands on hips, elbows thrust out, circling each other, slowly at first, then accelerating to a frenzied finale, urged on by deafening yells and stamping from the largely drunk audience.

Zakopane the next morning presented a dispiriting spectacle. It was drizzling persistently and the surrounding mountains were hidden by cloud. The town itself was pockmarked with deserted construction sites. Squads of holidaymakers in boots and anoraks wandered up and down the main street. Wet horses munched in their nosebags, the plumes on their harnesses drooping over their ears, while their grooms sat smoking under their little bowl-like black hats, leggings streaked with ash.

We had come back to meet a celebrated man of Zakopane, the world fly-fishing champion, Władysław Trzebunia – or Trzebunia-Nebies, to give him his full Highland name. Andrzej knew him of old, and Janusz had become friendly with him in Finland. His triumph there had transformed his life. Having previously worked as a bouncer at a bar in Zakopane, Trzebunia had been offered the position of angler-in-residence at a famously exclusive lodge on one of Norway's most prestigious salmon rivers, where he could earn enough in three months to fund a life of ease back home for the rest of the year. He had the air of a man well aware that he had been blessed with an amazing stroke of luck and determined to make the best of it, but with the grace to be thankful every day of his life.

He ushered us into his spanking new house, and he, Janusz and Andrzej settled down to talk about fishing. The television was on, showing the Sky Sports channel, a rare novelty anywhere in those innocent times. I watched a report on the county cricket championship in England. Atherton, an occasional leg-spinner, had taken four wickets for Lancashire against Leicestershire. New Zealand were playing Middlesex at Lords. I felt a very long way from home. I didn't realise then how rapidly the distance was already shrinking.

The others agreed that we should all fish the Dunajec next day. We drove from Łopuszna to Zakopane to meet Trzebunia, then all the way back through Łopuszna to the river. 'Two Poles, three fucking opinions,' Janusz commented as the journey unfolded. The stretch was in the shadow of the Three Crowns, the jagged outcrops just upstream and across from the monastery at Červený Kláštor (where, three weeks later, I found myself fishing the same water from the other side). The river foamed and raced along with an urgency I found slightly alarming. Trzebunia waded straight out, his sturdy legs braced against the current, his rod held high. He forged his way from rock to rock, dropping his weighted nymphs behind each one, only holding his position to play and land a fish, which happened often enough.

I watched him for a time, marvelling at his technique and concentration and sure-footedness, then wandered upstream looking for somewhere less public and turbulent. I passed Andrzej, who was wading the quick water and looking as if he might be swept away at any moment. He caught a decent grayling and waved precariously at me. Further up I spotted Janusz, who – in a characteristic show of disdain for the regulations – had waded across to Czechoslovak territory. I came to a quieter reach, fringed by a meadow touched with the yellow of buttercups and celandines, where I caught a chub followed by two decent grayling, and felt slightly pleased with myself.

Back where we had started, I was accosted by a rickety unshaven old man with an errant left eye who smelled strongly of drink. He berated me at length about something, and then turned to Trzebunia, who was wading to the bank. A terrific row flared immediately. Janusz appeared and told me that the ancient was complaining about my having two rods with me, which apparently constituted a serious breach of the rules. Trzebunia was objecting violently to this perceived lack of courtesy to a distinguished visitor. The two of them shouted at each other for a while, then the old man stumbled away. But the strength of his emotion was too much for him, and he turned back to renew the attack.

By now Janusz was laughing helplessly. 'The old man is drunk,' he explained to me eventually. 'Władysław is calling him a dickhead. He ask Władysław who is the dickhead. You see him hit his chest? He say he have medals and Władysław have no medals. Władysław say they are dickhead medals. That old man is as drunk as four arseholes.'

That evening I said goodbye to Andrzej Fox. I gave him a dictionary of English flies and he gave me a selection of his own patterns, including one with a stiff, iron-grey hackle that I used to great effect until I lost it up a tree beside the Ilva in Transylvania. We had a final supper in Nowy Targ, during which Andrzej described how he once floated down a stretch of the Dunajec on his back, with his head under water, to ascertain how an insect might look to a trout. He had even collected a handful of mayflies and eaten them, in case they had some special flavour that he could reproduce (he said they tasted of nothing). Andrzej seemed taken aback when Janusz and I burst out laughing. Then he laughed too, and ordered more beer, becoming ever more voluble in the grip of his piscatorial mania.

On the way back to Kraków, Janusz said: 'Andrzej is mad. He goes in river to be like fish. He eat fish food. Maybe he thinks he *is* a fish. But I like him OK.' He pulled on his cigarette. 'But he make me want to get drunk like hell.'

I didn't guess it but drink was Janusz's fatal weakness, as it was at that time for so many Poles. On occasions, particularly at weekends, it seemed the whole country was drunk, getting drunk, or nursing a hangover. The drunkenness was gross, brutal and shockingly public. Spirit distilled from almost anything was the cheap, universally available ticket to hilarity and oblivion. Drunks were a major hazard on the roads, weaving and lurching along, clutching their bottles, singing and yelling and falling over. Many were overcome before they reached home and lay down to sleep, the bodies scattered along the verges like casualties of a retreating army.

These sights filled Jurek Kowalski with shame. They acted as pitiful reminders – as if he needed reminding – of the great lie he had grown up with: the system that promised health and prosperity for all, and heaped degradation on them instead. He told me that he had been called out one evening to a factory near Krosno where one of the workers had been injured in an accident. When he got there he found the whole workforce was drunk. They were singing, shouting, sleeping, fighting and swigging vodka, while the untended machinery clanked and roared.

Jurek would have an occasional beer, no more. With me, Janusz drank beer only, about the same quantity as me. He was savagely sardonic about Polish alcoholism. 'On Sunday morning,' he said, 'the Polish worker wakes up with bad head from vodka. He feels so bad he beats wife, then he go to Mass to say sorry to God for beating wife, then he go home, drink vodka, sleep, then beat wife again. Then he go to church again, go home, drink and go to bed.'

On the day I met Janusz for the first time, he, Jurek and I had a late lunch together in the hotel restaurant in Skoczów. At seven o'clock that morning a kiosk in the street outside was already dispensing the first beers and shots of the day, and by mid-afternoon the town was lurching with drunks.

A youngish couple on the edge of complete alcoholic collapse were slumped at the table next to ours. The man, stubble-chinned, red-eyed, hair matted, filthy and reeking, rolled around in his chair, pushing his glass across the surface of the table with the care of a chess player. His wife – either still short of or beyond the speech-lessness phase – began to shout at us as we sat down. Gulping at her glass, she staggered over and pawed at my neck and shoul-ders, the stench of sweat and spirits billowing from her. Janusz pushed her away. Her husband swayed upright, brandishing his glass. Suddenly rediscovering the power of speech, he said he was unable to finish his drink. Would the gentlemen care to buy it from him? Half-price, a bargain.

A youth came in, and together he and a waitress herded the pair out of the door. Our food came and we started eating. The lad returned and apologised for his parents' behaviour. Janusz said not to worry, it wasn't his fault. His apologies became more effu-sive. He grinned and laughed, then sat down and asked for a drink. Janusz grabbed him by the collar and shoved him out into the street. He was no more than 14.

When I came back to Poland I reminded Jurek Kowalski of this scene. He told me that kind of frantic, public drunkenness had become much rarer. The problem of excessive drinking still existed, no doubt, but it had retreated behind closed doors.

By a nice twist, the talking point in the newspapers now was not Polish drinking but English drinking, specifically the antics of English males on stag weekends in Kraków. Why, I was repeatedly asked, did they drink beer like that? The phenomenon aroused bewilderment among the new generation of Kraków professionals, who favoured *caffè latte* or a glass of Chilean Merlot over spirit distilled from potato peelings, and who were generally too young to remember much about the old days of alcoholic frenzy. It was Kraków's misfortune that, in its eagerness to draw in visitors and service their requirements, it had not yet devised a way to keep this particular British export out.

I came across one of these bands of brothers after arriving in

Kraków on the bus from Lesko. There were six blokes, all in jeans, trainers, and black T-shirts bearing the legend STEVE'S STAG DO CRACOW 2008. Nicknames were printed in red: Lex Dangle, Boney Lips, and so on. They loped along the pavement, shoulders swinging, bellies swaying, barging into each other as they rehearsed football moves, oblivious to the stares. It was four o'clock in the afternoon and they seemed to be sober, although not much more attractive for it. No doubt they would be hitting the bars around the Rynek later, ready to give 110 per cent effort to ensure Steve had a send-off to remember the rest of his married life.

I had to catch the train to Prague that night, but I had a few hours spare to see if I could pick up any remaining trace of Janusz Wanicki. By then I knew what Jurek Kowalski and Józef Jeleński and one or two others had heard, which was that he had died eight or nine years before, in Finland. Of drink, they said, nothing more specific than that. They talked about Janusz fondly, but as if he came from a distant place and time. Jurek told me that when they were all in Finland for the 1989 World Championships, Janusz had been drunk every day. He said Janusz could speak Finnish fluently, but when his wife's parents – who disapproved of him strongly – came to visit, he would pretend that he couldn't speak or understand a word. I remembered him telling me about social life in Finland: 'When Finnish people invite friends for dinner, they come, they say hello, they sit down and eat and don't say anything, then they say goodbye and go home. Is not easy for Polish person with these fucking strange people.'

The address I had for him was in a quiet residential street across the river from the Wawel. I'd gone there on my final evening before leaving Poland for Czechoslovakia. It had been a wearyingly long day, devoted to celebrating the First Communion of Leszek Trojanowski's younger son, Wojtek, then aged ten. The service itself took place at the Capuchin Church, where I stood in the throng at the back while a flock of children – boys in white suits, white shoes, white gloves and white bow-ties; girls in white lace with garlands of white plastic lilies – made their vows in front of a battery of whirring and waving video cameras. Afterwards we went back to Leszek and Isa's house where breakfast, lunch and tea were served at intervals of two and a half hours, none of the meals accompanied by any alcohol save for one glass of pink Asti Spumante to toast Wojtek's new status in the world.

In the evening I'd galloped round to Janusz's flat, yearning for beer. I described to him the events of the day. He alleged that the children were under orders from the priests to report their parents if alcohol was consumed at First Communion celebrations. 'And if they are given money for presents, they must give half to the Church.' He handed me a glass of cool Löwenbräu. 'The Church has so much fucking power in this country! Too much power. Is why people drink so much, because Church make them feel so bad. *Nastrovje.*'

Eighteen years on, I didn't recognise the building and no one answered when I rang the bell. Finally an elderly woman appeared from next door and summoned a man who spoke some English. He remembered the name Wanicki. Some kind of artist, wasn't he? He'd moved to a street near the Castle. Agnieszki Street, he thought. I went back across the river and found the street, which was narrow and dark, lined with shops and grimy nineteenth-century houses divided into flats and bedsits. I rang the bells of the flats at number 2, to which I had been directed, but received only blank expressions and shakes of the head.

To kill time, I wandered back to the river and walked along the embankment among the cyclists, runners and dog-walkers. Chess players sat at chequered tables in the municipal gardens, studying their pieces. In theory I was heading downstream, but there was no perceptible flow in any direction. Rubbish floated in rafts against concrete retaining walls, bobbing gently on the ripples stirred by the breeze.

Normally the company of almost any river is enough to keep my spirits up. But the thought of what had happened to Janusz, and of the sparkling water we had fished together, and the sight of the inert, dirty Wisła swilling around in its concrete prison, combined to fill me with an ache of sadness. So I left the broken, unwanted river and walked through the Planty gardens to the railway station. There were three English girls in front of me in the queue at the ticket counter, backpacking somewhere. They were discussing the disappearance of Madeleine McCann, and knew it all, young as they were. Of course it wasn't fair to accuse the parents, but they agreed that there was something not right there. And the bottom line was you never left a child on its own, simple as that.

Quite suddenly the past, a time when three-year-old girls could sleep safely in their beds, seemed a long time ago.

# Epilogue

Six weeks after I came home from eastern Europe, the American investment bank, Lehman Brothers – crushed under a burden of debt greater than most countries' GDP – went bankrupt. Other mighty institutions tottered. Some fell. The soothsayers said the global economy was entering a dark valley; some said it was the darkest since the Great Depression of the 1930s.

Prophecies as to the fate of the countries I had just left behind varied from the dire to the apocalyptic. There was a feeling that one or more of them – Hungary was the favoured candidate – could follow Iceland, where the collapse of the banks had precipitated the implosion of the entire economy.

For their part, the people of eastern Europe looked on in bemusement as those in charge of the advanced industrial economies released unheard-of sums to keep their banks and other institutions from sinking beneath the waves. Time and again they had been lectured by sharp-suited economists from the IMF and the World Bank on the paramount virtues of liberalising trade, balancing budgets, and leaving the private sector to run the business, and the market to decide the winners and losers. Now they were witnessing government intervention on a colossal scale. The figures were beyond comprehension.

It was no wonder panic was in the air. For the previous ten years or so – roughly half the period since the downfall of the Communist regimes – the countries of the former Soviet Bloc had experienced constant and rapid economic growth. The dismantling of the old command structures combined with a strong, steady flow of investment from the west had released a vast reservoir of talent, energy and ambition, setting countless entrepreneurs on the move. Wages, living standards and consumer spending rose and kept on rising. The promise of convergence with the levels of prosperity in western Europe, which had seemed so remote in 1990, had become an article of belief.

Now everything seemed at risk. There were forecasts of currencies collapsing, governments defaulting on debts, runs on banks, chaos on stock markets, financial meltdown to be followed by political chaos. The shallow foundations of the new democracies seemed in danger of being swept away, with incalculable consequences for peace and security.

It did not happen. Nemesis kept its distance. But the impact was severe. Except in Poland, the biggest and least debt-burdened of the economies, growth stalled and recession bit. State spending projects were cancelled, social spending was cut, taxes rose, unemployment soared. In Hungary – where the *forint* fell by a fifth against the euro, leaving millions of people and hundreds of businesses who had taken out loans and mortgages in foreign currencies facing ruin – the ostensibly socialist government introduced an austerity programme that prompted a seven per cent fall in GDP within a year. Throughout the region the squeaking of tightening belts mixed with groans of protest and cries of anger.

In Târgu Mureş, Grigore Lungu's furniture company laid off half its workforce. Business in Ukraine – one of its developing markets – was described by Grigore as '*katastrof*'. Exports elsewhere, particularly to Italy, slumped, but the company survived. Gábor and Márta Hegedüs's marina at Tiszafüred stayed afloat, although unemployment in the town rose above thirty per cent. Márta told me business was down, but not by as much as they had feared. She thought 2010 would be as bad again, but maybe after that things would get better. Peter Bienek reported a steep fall in sales of fishing tackle. Žilina's dependence on car making had exaggerated the effects of the recession, but he was hopeful that the worst would soon be over. 'People must still go fishing,' he said cheerfully.

In the circumstances it was perhaps not surprising that celebrations to mark the 20th anniversary of the overthrow of Communism in eastern Europe were generally subdued. The tone seemed to be set in Poland, where the initial plan for a ceremony in Gdańsk was abandoned after anti-government protests by the few shipyard workers to have survived the withdrawal of state support for ship-building. The event was switched to Kraków, where public wrangling over Russia's refusal to accept responsibility for the slaughter of Polish army officers at Katyn in 1940 served as a reminder of grievances and tensions going way back beyond the recent history.

We Europeans were invited – most insistently by the journalists who had witnessed the momentous happenings first-hand – to contemplate this miracle of our time. But the problem with any miracle is recalling the reality that preceded it. When I was in Kraków in 2008 I commented to someone I met on the petrol shortages I had experienced in 1990. 'What shortages?' he demanded roughly. I described to him the scenes at fuel stations that I had recorded in my notebooks. He shook his head. There was no crisis, he said. Many problems, for sure, but not that. I was mistaken. It struck me afterwards that he had simply forgotten, as we do.

To mark the events of 1989 BBC Radio Four ran a daily five-minute archive slot presented by one of those veteran reporters, Sir John Tusa. It was expertly enough done, with lots of music and atmosphere and vivid snatches of interviews and dispatches. But there was also something unreal, remote, almost puzzling about the palpable charges of excitement and optimism crackling in the air as the correspondents described the Wall coming down, the surging streets of Prague, the scenes as East Germans poured through the broken-down barriers into Hungary. Here was Havel in shirtsleeves, Dubček blinking, Wałęsa with moustache bristling, Gorbachev waving, the Ceauşescus cringing. Other players flitted on stage and off: the Berlin hardman Erich Honecker pushed out of the way; Jaruzelski in his curiously shaded glasses swept aside in Poland; Czechoslovakia's last Communist leader, Miloš Jakeš, sent packing by velvet revolutionaries. Where were they now, these shadows, and where were the world leaders who looked on and made their solemn pronouncements – Thatcher, George Bush the first, Gorbachev, Yeltsin, Kohl, Mitterrand? Dead, senile, retired, left behind in a past which they had helped to shape, but which soon moved on.

For a few weeks in the autumn and winter of 1989 Europe surrendered itself to elation and hope in a way that had not been seen since VE Day in 1945. But that kind of mass uplift occurs very rarely and by its nature quickly dies away, tending to leave those who were swept up in it a little perplexed as to what came over them. By the time I set off in my little red car at the beginning of May 1990, the dust had settled and other stories had intervened. Nelson Mandela was freed from prison in February. There were riots in London against Mrs Thatcher's poll tax. In Brussels, European Community leaders (it was still the EC then) wrestled with economic union. While I was away the BSE scandal unfolded, an earthquake killed tens of thousands in Iran, the unravelling of the Soviet Union accelerated, West Germany won the football World Cup. Within days of my return Saddam Hussein's forces invaded Kuwait and Brian Keenan was released after five years as a hostage in Lebanon. By the end of the year Germany had been reunited and both Thatcher and Gorbachev had been overthrown.

In the countries I had fished my way through, people were learning to face very uncomfortable realities. Factories and farms were closing as subsidies ran out. Wages stayed low, prices shot up, shops were empty, fuel was unobtainable, queues got longer. The gulf between them and us seemed as deep and wide as ever, even if they were now allowed to shout across it. Politics was a shrill shouting match, and no one believed the promises, least of all those who made them. The Stasi and the Securitate and the other forces of secret police had officially been disbanded, but were lurking on the sidelines. Hundreds of thousands of Soviet troops were still present and visible, threatening who knew what.

The Europe that has emerged since would have been regarded as a fantasy, an impossibility. Now a generation has come of age – like my Romanian fishing companion, Calin, for whom pre-1989 is another chapter of ancient history. No one pretends that this new Europe is anything other than deeply flawed. The infection of corruption runs deep. The law creaks and grinds with infinite slowness and considerable partiality. Bureaucracy stifles and strangles. Politicians caper and declaim and are found with their fingers in the till. The left may have been routed (only the Czech Republic still has a functioning Communist Party) but the far right keeps feeding hungrily on residual xenophobia and bubbling prejudice. In Hungary the virulently nationalist Jobbik (whose leader urged Jews critical of its attitude to Israel to 'go and play with their little circumcised tails') won fifteen per cent of the vote in last year's European elections. Slovakia's National Party – which artfully promotes hatred of gypsies and prejudice against the sizeable Hungarian minority – has been part of the ruling coalition since 2006.

In general the politics is rough, vindictive, tribal and volatile. Swings in public opinion are extreme, as leaders strive to reconcile the impossible expectations of their electorates with harsh economic facts and the stern admonitions of foreign lenders. On the other hand, the new democracies still function. People vote, and their votes are counted and count. The far right is a force in Hungary and Slovakia, but in Romania and Poland it has been in retreat. Nostalgia for the orderliness and full employment of the distant past may still be potent, but none of these countries has seriously flirted with the necessary concomitants: namely one-party rule and the command economy.

Two decades ago freedom was the word on every lip and the idea in every heart. Freedom has come, and it's proved itself a complicated and troubling reality. For some – the elderly, pensioners, workers in redundant industries, officials in bloated bureaucracies – it has been hard, often crushingly so. But for the majority, the advent of free markets, free exchange rates, free trade, free movement of labour and freedom from central control has brought a tremendous, astounding transformation in their lives. People are more prosperous, better fed, healthier, warmer, better able to enjoy themselves than their parents or grandparents would have dreamed possible. Within the obvious constraints they can go where they want, say what they like, vote for whom they please, spend their time and money as they see fit.

So what has been lost?

Before writing this final part of my book, I read William Blacker's *Along The Enchanted Way,* an account of living in Romania between 1996 and 2004. Blacker settled first in a village in Maramureş, in the remote north beyond the Carpathians, and subsequently in Transylvania, where he set up house with a gypsy girl. It is a story of love: for the gypsy girl Marishka and her sister, Natalia, for the country people of Maramureş, for the wild landscapes and customs and beliefs. It is saturated with an intense, nostalgic passion for the old, simple ways, and sadness at their passing. In the village the cherry trees are felled to pay for TVs and washing machines. The young put away their traditional smocks and leggings in favour of jeans and T-shirts, and leave to take jobs in the west. Blacker's friend Mihai, whose life has spanned the passing of ages, dies. Blacker and his gypsy girl go their separate ways.

His regret is the same as that expressed with piercing eloquence by Norman Lewis in *Voices of the Old Sea* and his other books of travel. It is the regret of the exile, fleeing from his own noisy land in search of remote, pristine places still beyond the confines of our modern world. It is for the loss of peace, beauty and particularity. The Spain Lewis discovered sixty years ago disappeared under concrete and beach parasols. William Blacker's Maramureş has surrendered its scythes and horse-drawn ploughs, and fashioned its country dances into visitor attractions.

But implicit in the passion of the exile is the disparity between him and the community that accepts him. He may dress as they do, work with them, learn to speak their language, but he can never be one of them. The reason the sanctuary is special is that its people are poor, cut off from the means that enabled him to find them. They toil with their hands in the fields, not because they choose to, but because they know no other way. Once they have a choice, they seize the conveniences and comforts that the exile has left behind.

I felt something of the same sadness as Blacker and Lewis when I went back almost twenty years on. I found myself wishing that the restorers had been less thorough in the ancient towns and cities, that the meadows beside the streams I fished had been kept clear of chalets and weekend cottages, that cars had never reached the valleys. Almost everywhere – even the Danube Delta of my imaginings – had been invaded. Almost nowhere was as quiet, as empty, as unspoilt as I remembered.

But, of course, the only way that could have been avoided would have been if the people who lived there had remained as poor and deprived as they were when I first came. I was able to travel there because I had the car, the time, the dollars. How could I wish to deny all that to them? And further, although I might sigh over the replacement of the rasping of the sharpstone against the scythe blade by the clatter of the mechanical grass-cutter, would I have wanted to embrace the peasant life, bent in the fields under the broiling sun, any more than I would have wanted to return to a medieval evening meal of pottage, and a life expectancy of forty-two?

In time I learned that others detected more than a whiff of double standards in my nostalgia for the past they had left behind. I learned to accept that the faraway places were no longer so faraway, that their distinctiveness, the 'otherness' that had made them so attractive, had gone and would not return. They were hard but necessary lessons.

I am in debt to a good many people for this book. I am grateful to my first wife, Linda, for making it possible for me to be away from home and children in 1990, to Michael Green, whose extraordinary generosity saved me from penury, to Clare Alexander, who encouraged me to write the book that never was, and to Max Wilkinson of the *Financial Times* for his support. Much later Mark Booth, then of Century, had the faith to commission me, Charlotte Haycock provided essential editorial scrutiny, and Katie Duce took up the reins and brought the lumbering beast to the finish. My incomparable agent, Caroline Dawnay, made it all happen. My dear friend, Stephen Taylor, was an unfailing source of cheer, support and sound advice. Jason Hawkes gave me essential help with the photographs. Friends and acquaintances in Poland, the Czech Republic, Slovakia, Hungary and Romania made the book what it is. I thank Leszek and Isa Trojanowski, Jurek Kowalski, Andrzej Fox, Józef and Dorothy

Jeleński, Marek Kowalski, Marek Kot, Tomáš Kroupa, Pavel Janicek, Peter Bienek, Gábor and Márta Hegedüs, and Grigore Lungu. I wish I was able to thank Dana Lungu and Janusz Wanicki.

Finally, I could not have done any of it without Helen.